THE
STOVEPIPE

A MEMOIR

Bonnie Jo. Virag

THE STOVEPIPE

A MEMOIR

BONNIE E. VIRAG

Langdon Street Press
212 3rd Avenue North, Suite 290
Minneapolis, MN 55401
612.455.2293
www.langdonstreetpress.com

ISBN-13: 978-1-936782-30-7
LCCN: 2011930064

Distributed by Itasca Books

Cover Design by Alan Pranke
Typeset by James Arneson

Printed in the United States of America

Dedication

I dedicate this book to my sisters three,
who walked the unknown road with me;
Whose endearing and cheerful company
kept my hopes high and my spirit free.

~ Betty, Jean and Joan ~

Author's Note

My purpose in writing this memoir is to tell about my life in foster care and not to slight or cause embarrassment to anyone. Many of the people in the story have passed on but have left children and grandchildren. And so I have changed family names and the names of locations to protect their privacy. I set forth each incident as I remember it, occasionally relying on my sisters to fill in some of the gaps—bearing in mind that each of us saw through a different set of eyes and may have perceived things differently. Some of the dialogue I remember clearly and recount verbatim. Where memory fails me, I created dialogue based on the way my sisters expressed themselves. The rest is as accurate as I can make it. It is the story of my life, and I have tried to be true to my thoughts and memories.

Acknowledgments

I give my wholehearted thanks and appreciation to the following courageous souls who stood by me and helped bring my book to fruition:

My dear husband, who read and reread every chapter as it ground from my printer. I thank him for his unflagging support and understanding.

Also, to my wonderful sisters, who shared the task of helping to jog my memory. Without their input, this book would be just that—only a memory.

And my kindhearted friends, Adele and Hank Gartner, who, along with Dee Vogrin, gave me their early support and whose gentle prodding helped keep the wheels rolling.

Countless kudos to my cohorts at the Deadwood Writer's Club of Northville, Michigan, who encouraged me, critiqued my work and helped me conquer my vulnerabilities.

I cannot give enough praise to my gracious, tireless, and understanding editor, Marsha Glenn, of First Class Writing Projects. Her professional editing and critiquing skills and her ability to guide me along the way were certainly over the top.

To my kind and good friend, Ken Bachand, a retired English teacher who tidied up my dangling participles, checked my punctuation, and gave me English lessons to boot.

And to Katherine Pickett of Langdon Street Press who did a fantastic job of pulling everything together and tidying up all the loose ends.

"Bless you all!"

Prologue

Children should have memories that can be displayed on a shelf in a china cabinet, not stored away in a cardboard box in a dank and dusty basement.

~ Author

Memories ... They can haunt us, trouble us, or bring us moments of joy and happiness. But what would we be without them, for they do, indeed, define and shape us. Some memories are fleeting, like pieces of chaff that get blown away bit by bit with every little breeze. Others are longer than time, hanging around forever like barnacles on a ship, refusing to let go. Then again, others pop up like a jack-in-the-box when you least expect, when something triggers them. Yet many will tumble to the forefront of our minds like ocean waves and then quickly recede and vanish forever.

We all have different ways of filing away memories, I suppose. I picture mine as being stored in a filing cabinet, deep in the recesses of my mind, to be retrieved at will. It is from these stored memories of my life upon which this book is based.

1

Seeking Answers

I sit upright in bed and cling to the blankets. The lights are out now. The room is cloaked in darkness. The noise from the other children in the home has subsided. They are asleep. I peer deep into the darkness. *Where am I? Why am I here? What did I do wrong? Why did they take us away from everyone we loved?* I wonder. *Will Mommy come to get us? Will she be able to find us?* The pain of being away from our home is unbearable.

Frightened and lonely, I burrow down in this strange new bed, close to my twin sister, and listen to the rhythmic sound of her thumb-sucking. As I lie quietly in the eerie darkness, my thoughts turn to my big sister Muggs, the one I love so much. The picture of her, axe in hand and chasing the car as it sped away with us, is fresh in my mind. I can still feel the warmth of her body as I nestle in her lap—smell the scent of her hair and hear the sound of the rocking chair as it creaks back and forth across the floorboards. I begin to cry. I bury my head deep in the pillow. Images of my wild brothers and playful sisters flit through my mind. I think of our happy, fun-filled days together — laughing, singing, rolling around on the warm grass, romping in the haymow, and swimming naked in the farm pond. Tightening the blankets around me and curling up in a tight ball, I try to sleep.

Maybe if we're good, they'll let us go home tomorrow.

• • •

During the early years of my marriage, I often wanted to write my autobiography. I would include the lives of *some* of my siblings as we were "warehoused" in one foster home after another. I would tell of the times some of us were together only to be torn apart again and again as we entered into one home after another. My head was full of these life struggles and events, and throughout the years I would jot them down lest they fade from memory. But it was not until my family had grown and left home, making me an "empty nester," that I began to give serious thought, as the saying goes, to putting pen to paper.

It was a nice fall day in September while visiting my sister-in-law in the little town of Simcoe, Ontario, Canada, that I asked her where the Children's Aid Society was located. I had finally mustered up the courage and fortitude to go to them and request any records they may have on my childhood. I wasn't certain whether Canada had the Freedom of Information Act that would allow me access to my records, and if so, would they be reluctant to release them — or worse yet, had the records been destroyed? There were so many questions pertaining to my young years for which I wanted to find answers. I knew that five of us — my brother Bobby, who was eight; my twin sisters Jean and Joan, who were six; and my twin sister Betty and I, who were just over four —

were put into the foster care system at the same time. But I never knew why.

Upon locating the address, I parked my car and peered through the side window at the large, formidable red-brick building with big, green double doors. THE CHILDREN'S AID SOCIETY was boldly printed in gold block letters across the window pane. *Well, this is it,* I thought. *It's now or never.*

Still harboring feelings of intimidation, I took a deep breath and braced myself as I walked up the steps and through the doors. There was a small waiting room to my left with green padded benches lining two adjacent walls and a table with books nearby. As the room was empty, I saw no need to wait, for I was in a hurry to get on with my mission before I lost my nerve. I approached a lady sitting at a desk behind the counter. *She looks pleasant enough,* I thought.

Apparently she had not heard me enter and seemed startled as she looked up. "Oh! May I help you?"

"Yes, I hope so. I'm in the process of writing my auto-biography and would like to gain access to my foster care records. Is this possible?"

"Oh, I see," she said, peering at me over her half-glasses in a seemingly questioning manner. This unnerved me a bit. "I'm not certain if it's our policy to release those records, but Mr. Parker, our branch manager, would be the one to make that decision," she stated flatly. "Please have a seat while I speak with him." I watched as she disappeared into his inner office.

I bit the side of my lip as I watched them through the window discussing my request. I observed their hand and facial gestures and sensed some negativity. *Oh, damn!* I thought, *I hope I don't have to go through a lot of red tape to get this stuff.*

Within a few minutes she summoned me into the manager's office.

I sat down across a mahogany desk from him, explained my reason for being there, and told him I had been taken into the shelter's care when I was four years old. That would have been in the early forties.

I told him this was not the building we were taken to. That building was a two-story, beige brick building, and I recall going up large steps to the second floor where huge windows overlooked the street below. I told him that the windows in particular stayed in my mind because I had never before seen such big windows. He was surprised by my remark and questioned my ability to recall this event from such a tender age. He then excused himself, saying he would go into the basement to check for my files, forewarning me that they might have been transferred to the main office or even discarded.

"God, please don't let that be the case," I muttered with my hand clasped over my mouth.

It seemed like an eternity, but he finally returned with a large manila folder, and I breathed a sigh of relief.

"I've located your files, and you're correct. The Children's Aid Society was located in the old Woolworth building, with large windows overlooking Norfolk Street, but we have been in this building for as long as I can remember."

During the course of our conversation, I described some of the events that took place on that frightening, unforgettable day when we were torn away from our home and family.

"It's wonderful you have such a good memory," he said. He paused and then added, "Or then again, maybe it isn't."

"Well," I said, "some events are so traumatic they can be permanently etched on a young mind."

"I'll have to agree with you there," he replied.

He then told me that my file would have to be sorted out from my sisters' files, and all the names of the foster families with whom we stayed would be blackened out for their protection. He added that when he had completed this task, he would consult with the head of the society before final release of the records. "You'll hear from me by post within a week or two," he assured me.

Before leaving, I thanked him for his help, and he shook my hand and wished me well on my book.

• • •

I stared at the large brown envelope, taunting me as it lay in the middle of the kitchen table. I had picked it up moments earlier from the mailbox and taken note of the address sticker in the corner, which read, "The Children's Aid Society." *Well, it finally arrived,* I thought. But in truth, I was surprised that it had arrived at all.

I put the kettle on to boil and stood at the kitchen counter, preparing myself a cup of instant coffee. I poured the cream into the coffee and stirred it in—and continued stirring— barely aware of the clinking sounds of the spoon hitting the cup. My thoughts were adrift as I eyed the envelope. *The chronicles of my young life are in that envelope,* I mused. *Am I really up to looking at it?* I thought about it for some time. My stomach tightened as I took another long sip of the coffee, set the cup down, and picked up the envelope. I flipped it over a few times—scrutinizing every aspect of it, reading the address label again, checking the amount of Canadian postage it required, and calculating the length of time it took to get to Michigan. At the same time, my thoughts were flitting back to my childhood—a past that seemed buried so deep in my mind and yet still so close to the surface. I was feeling uptight about opening the envelope, torn between wanting to know and not wanting to know. I scolded myself. "For Pete's sake, just open it!"

I grabbed a knife from the butcher block and nervously slit open the envelope. Then, tossing the knife on the table,

I made my way to the back bedroom. Seeking refuge in the farthest corner, I sat down on the floor, propping myself up against the corner walls as if they would render some emotional support. I slowly withdrew the stapled contents of the envelope and flipped through the pages, noticing that it also contained Betty's records. *Wow, this is great . . . two for the price of one! This will help me a lot.*

But true to his word, Mr. Parker had blackened out any reference to names of foster parents. I smiled. *Did they think I wouldn't remember?*

. . .

The report began by stating that I was one of several children who were abandoned by their mother.

"Abandoned!" The word jumped off the page at me. Abandoned? I certainly didn't expect this to be the reason we were taken away from our parents. I don't recall ever feeling abandoned while we lived at home. Abandonment? I thought again. That feeling certainly became a reality when we were torn away from our warm and happy home—away from our loving older siblings and shoved into uncaring foster homes.

Many homes often took children for the government money and the work they could get from them. In many of these homes no one read us stories, gave us a warm hug, prettied our hair, told us they loved us, kissed our boo-boos, or tucked us into bed and kissed us goodnight. Now, that's abandonment!

The report documented yearly accounts of our journey in and out of different foster homes and how we fared in them. Little did the social workers realize how fearful we were of some of those families. It was our love and emotional support of each other that had given us the strength to get through those frightening, turbulent years.

Reading through the report was a gut-wrenching experience. If I hadn't known it was about me, I certainly wouldn't
have recognized myself. Many lies had been told to the social
workers, and it pained me to read them. So much of the past
was coming into focus, and many questions were being answered. Judgment calls that were completely false had been
made about our behavior and emotional problems, and so
many clues of abuse and neglect had not been picked up by
the social workers when they came to check on us. A familiar
proverb flitted through my mind: *There are none so blind as
those who will not see.*

2

Recollections

*"One of the luckiest things that can happen to you
in life is, I think, a happy childhood."*
~ Agatha Christie

I grew up not knowing how many siblings were in my family. Someone would give me one count, and then someone yet another. It wasn't until my older sister Joan—during the writing of this book—sent me an official document she had received from our mother that I became aware of the real number.

My mother, Flossie Bell Mudford, gave birth to eighteen children, including two sets of twins. *My God*, I mused, *my poor mother was more horizontal than vertical, and she wasn't even Catholic!*

But then it came to mind that back in the early '30s, large families—a dozen kids or more—were the norm. After all, that was long before TV and BC (birth control), and the winters in the Canadian back country were long and cold.

"Guess what?" I called to my husband, who was reading nearby. "My mother, Flossie Bell, bore eighteen children. Isn't that amazing?"

"Wow, eighteen!" he repeated, glancing up from his book. "You weren't born," he teased; "you were spawned. That's a mess of kids. But with a name like Flossie Bell, what can you expect?"

"Oh, hush up. I said *Flossie*, not *Floozie*. Are you feeling cheated?"

"Nope, two kids are enough for me." He put down his book and came to my side to look at the document. "Goodness' sakes, it looks like she had her first three children out of wedlock."

"Yes, I know, and the first one at the tender age of fifteen."

"Look," he pointed out, "it appears she had three more children with her second husband. Did you know that?"

"No, I was long gone by then, but years later my sisters told me she had two sons and a daughter from this man, and I guess this confirms it."

"Who of your family do you remember?" he asked, continuing to look over the list.

"Well, let's see," I said, counting on my fingers. "I remember my oldest sister Margaret; brothers Jimmy, Henry, and Bobby, sisters Jean and Joan; and of course, my twin sister, Betty. Some of the children—Zella, Charles, Todd, William, Harry, and Albert—were older and had left home by the time I was born. My memories of them are vague and fragmented, to say the least."

"What about your parents and grandparents? Do you have any memories of them?"

"Yeah, I do," I said, a touch of melancholy in my voice, "some pleasant and others not so pleasant."

• • •

The earliest memories of my childhood begin about age four. My mom was a petite and pretty woman with dark brown eyes, curly brown hair, and an olive complexion. She loved to dance and sing. At times she would playfully grab my small hands and, holding tight, swing me around and around the living room until, dizzy and giggly, I would fall at her feet. Smiling, she would pick me up in her arms, give me a hug, and quickly turn to grab one of my sisters, who were eagerly waiting their turn. In the evenings she often left me, along with the rest of my sisters and brothers, in the care of our older sister Muggs, who was a teenager, while she went off to drink and dance at the local dance halls.

Perhaps it was her wild nights out that often angered her dad, who was known to us kids as Grandpa Pete. Grandpa Pete — Watts was his last name — was a big burly Englishman with a booming voice that matched his size. He sported a large, black, bushy handlebar moustache that curled up at the ends. He was the chief of police in a two-man police department in a nearby town. Whenever he came stomping into the house — his big, black, polished boots creaking the floorboards — all dressed up in his police uniform with billy club in hand, he'd strike fear in the hearts of his grandkids.

One hot summer night I remember we little kids huddled safely behind the wood-burning stove and watched in fear as our angry grandpa chased our poor mom through the house — wildly waving his billy club, calling her bad names, and swearing at her as she ran screaming and hollering in and out the doors, climbing in and out the windows, with him hot on her heels. I wondered what Mom had done to upset him so, and why she deserved such a beating.

Grandma Mamie, Grandpa Pete's wife, was, I believe, part Mohawk Indian. She was a stout, dark-skinned woman with dark hair that she wore coiled in a tight braid at the back of her head. She was rather severe-looking, so I mostly kept my distance from her. I would catch a glimpse of her now and then as I peeked around the porch and quietly watched as she rocked back and forth on her porch rocker, smoking a straight pipe. I had never before seen a woman smoking a pipe, and it held my attention. Other than that, I remember very little about her.

My father, Charles Mudford, was a tall, thin man with fair skin, close-set blue eyes, and sandy blond hair that he wore parted in the middle. I have one vague memory of being terrified of him. It was when he came home one night in a drunken rage and threatened to poison us kids and set the house on fire. I was frightened along with everyone else but was too young to realize what was going on. He was seldom around, and Mom told me that he was in jail, but I didn't understand what all this meant.

I do, however, have one fond and clear memory of him. It was on a cold and snowy Christmas Eve when the door to the house suddenly burst open and he walked in carrying a bushel basket heaped to the brim with toys. All of us kids, surprised and excited, ran to crowd around him.

"Daddy! Daddy!" we all cried, "Where have you been? Are you gonna stay for Christmas? What'd ya bring us?" We peppered him with questions.

I ran to him and clung to his cold pant leg. I didn't want to let go. His very presence filled the small room as he bent to place the basket of toys in the middle of the floor. He then scooped me up, and I felt so happy and secure as he cradled me in his strong arms. I didn't care that his coat was freezing cold against my bare skin. Everything, at the moment, felt so good.

"Here," he said, as he gently lowered me to the floor. "Merry Christmas! I brought toys for all of you. Now, don't go fighting over them, ya hear?" He didn't answer our many questions but gave us each a big hug before strolling into the kitchen to stoke the stove and find some "grub" to eat, as he'd call it.

We all dived into the basket, grabbing the toy that we each liked best. It was a great Christmas!

In the early morning of Christmas Day, Daddy had to leave us and woke us up to say good-bye. He mumbled some reason why he had to leave, but I didn't understand. It was then that he told us he'd lost his false teeth while stumbling over the plowed fields, lugging the basket of toys, and that in the dark of night he was unable to find them. Not knowing when we might see him again and wanting to spend every last minute with him, we begged to go outside to help hunt for his teeth. We quickly dressed and hurried outside to search the frozen furrows of the plowed field.

It was bitterly cold. The wind whistled and howled around the old farm sheds. I was chilled to the bone. We searched and searched for his teeth, and after a while one of my brothers finally found them. Daddy wiped them off on his shirttail and plopped them back into his mouth. He stooped and hugged us all good-bye.

"Will you come back agin', Daddy?" Bobby asked.

He shrugged. "Dunno," he muttered.

I watched as he stumbled across the frozen furrows and disappeared from sight across the fields, the glow of the early morning sun shining on his fair hair.

• • •

I lived with my family in an old, drafty tar-papered house that was two stories high and sat in the middle of a small farmyard. A few chickens were always scratching around the house and at times sneaking into the kitchen if the screen door was left open. An old, ratty couch sat kitty-corner in one corner of the living room with two worn sofa chairs nearby. A small crib, where my twin sister spent many long hours, sat just outside my parents' bedroom door. Close to the crib was my favorite chair—an old wooden rocker that was always kept busy.

In the kitchen, Mom kept a wood-burning stove fired up, which she used for both cooking and heating. More times than once one of us kids managed to burn ourselves on it. A long wooden table with many chairs scattered around it filled most of the kitchen.

I was big enough now to push a chair up to the table and climb onto it in search of food. Even though I was too short to see the tabletop, I knew Mom always kept the butter dish up there.

Whenever my brothers caught me shoveling the butter into my mouth with both hands, they would gently grab me and put me, kicking and screaming, back onto the floor.

It was in this house that I spent the first few years of my life along with some of my brothers and sisters.

There was my twin sister, Betty, but because I stammered so much, I called her Bubba. There were my sisters Jean and Joan and brothers Jim, Hank and Bobby. And then there was my sister Margaret, but we all called her Muggs.

Betty was tiny and thin with blonde hair, blue eyes, and fair skin. She was sick most of the time and spent long hours in the crib. Reaching my hands through the bars, I would play with her or gently pat her to stop her crying.

She didn't look at all like me. I was a healthy, robust "little butterball," as my brothers called me. I had an olive complexion, brown hair, and dark brown eyes.

Betty and I were the youngest girls in the family and hardly looked like sisters, let alone twins.

My sisters Jean and Joan were six-year-old identical twins, two years older than Betty and me. They had dark brown hair and brown eyes, and their faces were covered with freckles. They played with Betty and me all the time, keeping a watchful eye over us and tattling on us whenever we got into mischief.

Muggs, my fifteen-year-old sister, was the oldest of the bunch, and feeding and caring for us youngsters usually fell on her shoulders. I loved Muggs and always followed her around, trying to get her attention by grabbing and tugging at her clothes whenever she came near me. Scooping me up and heading for the rocking chair, she would cradle me in her arms. And as we both settled down, she would ask, "Shall I sing your favorite song, 'My Bonnie Lies over the Ocean'?"

"Yes, yes," I would cry, clapping my hands.

And then she would sing:

My Bonnie lies over the ocean,
My Bonnie lies over the sea,
My Bonnie lies over the ocean,
Oh bring back my Bonnie to me.

"Why do I hafta lie on the ocean?" I would ask when she finished.

She would try to tell me about the song, but I didn't understand. Soon, snug and secure in her arms, I would drift off to sleep with the sound of her voice and the words of the song still floating in my head.

• • •

We were very poor, and with so many mouths to feed, food was scarce. I cried often for food, and when my brothers couldn't stand to listen to me anymore, one of them would sprinkle a handful of white sugar along with some dry, uncooked oatmeal into a paper bag for me. Or sometimes they'd punch a couple of holes into a can of blackstrap molasses and give it to me to drink.

Clutching my food, I would immediately crawl back behind the couch to gobble it up, afraid that if I didn't hide, one of my siblings would snatch it away from me or, at the very least, expect me to share it.

My brothers—Bobby, Hank, and Jimmy—whose ages ranged from nine to eleven, were a wild, naughty, and mischievous bunch. They would often find excitement in tying a bunch of tin cans to a hound dog's tail and rubbing kerosene on his rear. Then, holding their stomachs and rolling around in the grass, they would laugh their fool heads off as the poor animal, yelping in pain, ran wildly down the dirt road with the tin cans rattling noisily behind. Other times they would grab a couple of stray cats, pin their tails to the clothesline, and then snicker and act silly as the poor things squalled and scratched, trying to free themselves.

Muggs, hearing the racket, would come tearing out of the house to free the animals. "One of these days I'm gonna pin your ears to the clothesline and see how you like it!" she would yell at my brothers. "I don't like your cruel pranks one bit. Now get your lazy bones out to the barn and do your chores. And make sure you milk old Daisy and bring up enough milk for supper, or you won't get anything to eat."

There was never much peace and quiet when my wild brothers were home from school. They were always getting into quarrels and fistfights that often ended up with them throwing stones at each other.

It was during one of their stone-throwing scraps when a large one missed the intended target and hit me squarely in the head. My brothers, realizing how badly I was hurt, quickly picked me up and took me beside the house. "She's hurt real bad! Go and fetch Mom!" Bobby yelled at Muggs.

"But Mom's not home. Quick, Hank, you run down the road to get the neighbor lady. I think she was a nurse at one time. Tell her to come quickly!"

Hank took off running, and the lady came right away. I was crying uncontrollably, blood streaming down my face, as she tended to my wound. She put some stuff on my head that stung so much I was sure it was the same stuff the boys put on the dog, for I too yelped in pain. I thought the whole top of my head was off and she was pouring it full of some horrible burning stuff. I still bear a large scar, which occasionally brings back memories of my mischievous brothers.

A torn screen on the kitchen door allowed a few hungry barn cats to come into the house in search of food. My brothers would run around wildly, trying in vain to catch or shoo them out while loudly singing this crazy little ditty:

Lissin' lissin', the cat's pissin',
Where, where? Under the chair.
Run, run, get the gun!
Never mind. He's all done!

My brothers got a kick out of teaching me these funny poems—not because I was able to memorize them so well but mostly because they enjoyed making fun of my stuttering when I tried to repeat them.

Muggs would be quite angry with them when she overheard them teaching me this poem:

A woodpecker pecked
On the schoolhouse door,
He pecked and pecked
'Til his pecker got sore.

I didn't understand what got her so upset, but she would pick up the kitchen broom and try her best to chase them out of the house, threatening to beat their brains out.

My brothers would stick their thumbs in their ears and wave their fingers or laugh hilariously while making fart sounds with their armpits and then run off in different directions.

My sisters and I knew her efforts were useless against our wild brothers, but we enjoyed the craziness of it all.

• • •

Muggs had a young boyfriend who always hung around our house, and I didn't like him being there and getting all her attention.

One day while playing with Betty as she lay sick in her crib, I knew that Muggs was in Mom's bedroom with her friend. Hearing lots of screaming and laughing, I hid behind the door and peered through the crack. They were naked and rolling around on the bed. *What's he doing to her? Is he hurting her?* I wondered. I was so afraid for her and wanted to help, but I was too little and could only watch.

I saw him hold a bottle of her nail polish over her naked body, dipped the brush into it, and then try to paint between her legs.

Muggs giggled and screamed as she tried to get the bottle away from him.

I stood quiet and scared behind the door, trying to understand what was going on.

At last Betty's cries got her attention, and she came out to tend to her. I was so happy that she was okay. Soon she spotted me behind the door. "Come out of there, you little rascal," she demanded. "Why aren't you outside playing with your sisters? What are you doing back there anyway?" She pulled me forward and peeked through the crack. "Oh, so you were peeking on me," she said, nodding as she picked up my chin and looked into my eyes. "You naughty little bum."

"B . . . B . . . But I d . . . d . . . didn't want him to h . . . h . . . hurt you," I blubbered, giving her a sad look and wrapping my arms tightly around her legs.

"He's *not* gonna hurt me. Now hurry outside and play with your sisters while I tend to Betty." She kissed my forehead, pulled my arms from around her legs, and, with a little slap to the backside, sent me scurrying outside. I was happy knowing she was safe, didn't mind that she had scolded me, and hurried off to find my sisters. *They're probably makin' mud pies out behind the barn,* I thought. So I headed that way.

My brothers started back to school in the fall, and things at home quieted down.

But during the start of the school year, there was an outbreak of head lice. Two nurses came to our house to check us all for lice, or those "little critters," as my brothers called them. And so Muggs called us together.

"Come on, you kids; stand in line here so the nurses can check your heads."

I watched one check my brother's head, peering at it through a big glass and then sending him on to the next lady who shaved off his hair.

"B . . . B . . . But I ain't g . . . g . . . got any cr . . . cr . . . critters," I cried out to Muggs as she pulled me hard toward the strange lady.

"If everyone has critters, then you have critters!" she snapped.

"They're gonna h . . . h . . . hurt my h . . . h . . . hair," I complained pitifully, curling out my bottom lip.

"Yeah, it's gonna hurt really baaad," Bobby teased as he held his bald head and danced and screamed around me as if he were in terrible pain.

"Stop your silliness right now, Bobby," Muggs said. "You're scaring your little sister." Grabbing a dish towel, she snapped it smartly at his backside as he tried to duck behind the kitchen door.

Muggs was right. We all had lice. The nurses quickly shaved all our heads and rubbed them down with some brown, stinky stuff. I sat and pouted as Muggs got the broom and swept up all the hair. None of us liked getting our heads shaved, but soon we were laughing and giggling as we poked fun at ourselves in the wall mirror and wrinkled our noses up at our stinky, funny-shaped bald heads.

3

Torn Asunder

When the warm days of summer rolled around, we young kids had barrels of fun playing in the backyard under Muggs's watchful eye. Jean, Joan, Betty, and I—clad only in our underwear—ran around barefoot, feeling the warm grass tickling our toes.

Sometimes Muggs would bring up bran sacks from the barn for us to play in. These empty, dusty burlap bags had held chopped oats for the farm animals. Climbing into them and pulling them up around our waist, we would jump and chase each other around the yard.

At the back of our house was an old root cellar with a large wooden door that sloped downward from the side of the house. This old door provided many hours of fun for us and had become worn and shiny from our use. In the winter when the door was covered with snow, we would gather pieces of scrap cardboard and use them as toboggans to slide down it and out into the yard. In the summer we would climb into the bran bags and, with some difficulty, climb to the top of the door and slide down. Muggs would always be watching over us, and we would all sing our favorite song:

I don't want to play in your yard,
I don't like you anymore,
You'll be sorry when you see me
Sliding down our cellar door.

You can't holler down our rain barrel,
You can't climb our apple tree,
I don't want to play in your yard,
If you won't be good to me.

We squealed and giggled as we landed up in a heap of crumpled bodies at the foot of the door and playfully rolled around in the soft grass. This was our favorite way of spending these long, hot summer days, and we loved every minute of it.

One day, without warning, our fun came to an abrupt halt when we saw a large, black automobile drive into our lane. It pulled slowly into the backyard and stopped beside the house where we were playing. We all stood frozen. In a poor rural area, it was rare to see an automobile on the road, let alone have one pull into our own yard. Muggs must have known it meant trouble, for she quickly opened the cellar door and herded us all inside. But it was too late, for she had been spotted. No sooner had the door been slammed shut than it was flung open, exposing my sisters and me as we huddled fearfully inside.

"Come out," a man said as he tugged on our arms, pulling us out one by one.

As we hurried to Muggs's side, the man said, "We'd like to speak with your mother."

Muggs shook her head. "I'm sorry, but she ain't home right now."

At that, without saying another word, he and a woman who had come with him grabbed my sisters and me and pushed us, kicking and screaming, into the backseat of the car.

They then rounded up Bobby and shoved him in beside us.

We were all scared, crying out for Muggs to help us; but they quickly slammed the doors, trapping us like wild animals. We watched Muggs through the window and saw a look of sheer panic on her face as she made her way to the woodpile. Grabbing the axe that was wedged in a nearby stump and waving it wildly above her head, she came running erratically toward the car. She seemed scarcely bigger than the axe.

But the driver immediately sped off, forcing us backward. Turning in our seats, we crammed our heads together to peer through the small back window. We watched in horror as Muggs, axe still in hand and screaming at the top of her lungs, chased the car as far as she could down the dirt road. We watched as she began to disappear in the swirling dust. She was almost out of sight when we saw her slump helplessly to the ground. And then she was gone.

• • •

As we rode in the backseat, sobbing, the woman turned to calm us by promising us some milk and cookies when we reached our destination. The promise of a treat settled us down somewhat, and we soon became fascinated by the car ride. Having never been in a car before, we found it a new and exciting adventure.

My sisters and I enjoyed looking out the windows, watching the trees and farms go by so fast. Bobby was busy looking around the inside of the car, checking out all the knobs and handles.

We were squeezed in the back like sardines in a can with Betty sitting beside me next to the door. She was restless and fidgety, and I was trying to quiet her down when she grabbed onto the door handle. Before I knew what was happening, the door flew open and she started to fall off the seat. I tried to hold her, but she slipped from my grasp and tumbled out of the car. I watched out the back window as she rolled head over heels down the dusty road like a tumbleweed in the wind.

We screamed for the driver to stop. "Betty fell out! Betty fell out!" we cried.

Realizing what had happened, the man brought the car to an abrupt stop. Quickly hopping out, he ran down the road to where Betty's crumpled body lay in the tall roadside grass. We then watched wide-eyed and anxious as he carried her limp and dirty body back to the car. *She looks like my rag doll,* I thought, as he handed her off to the woman.

Betty seemed to be stirring a bit as the woman spoke softly to her and tried to tidy her up. Turning to us in the backseat, she told us that although our sister was bruised and shaken up, she didn't seem too badly hurt.

We clapped our hands. We were so happy.

We finally arrived at a large brick building, which was the office of the Children's Aid Society. We entered and went up some wide steps to the second floor. Here my sisters and I were separated from Bobby as the man led him into a separate room.

Jean, Joan, Betty, and I were taken to a washroom where we were cleaned up and dressed in fresh, clean dresses.

The social workers seemed very nice and, as promised, sat us down at a table and served us milk and cookies. We had become less frightened by now, and after we had finished our treat, they led us into a large room where there were shelves stacked with toys. They turned to leave and told us we could play there for a while.

My eyes grew wide as I looked about the room.

"Ohh, look at all the toys!" Jean squealed. "I hope we can play for a long time."

I had never seen so many beautiful and colorful toys and ran wildly from one toy to another, playing with each one until another caught my eye.

We had all played for some time when the door opened and a pretty young lady walked in. She came to me and took my hand. "Come on, little girl. I want to visit with you."

I took one look back at my sisters as she led me from the room.

She took me into a small office stall and told me to wait there for her.

I was drawn at once to the big windows that went almost from the ceiling to the floor. I went over to touch them and looked down from the second floor to the street below. I was taken in by the big buildings across the street, the cars going back and forth, and all the people scurrying about.

Soon the lady came over and smiled down at me. She seemed to sense my fascination with the large window and all the activity down below. She stood watching with me for a while. Then, sitting down in a small armchair, she gently picked me up and put me on her lap.

I could smell the scent of her perfume and feel the silkiness of her blouse as I wiggled my way into her lap. I looked at the little pink pearl buttons that went down the front of her blouse and played with the silky sleeve between my fingers.

Noticing what I was doing, she smiled and asked, "Do you like my pretty blouse?"

I nodded.

She then picked up a book from a nearby shelf. "We're going to look at some pictures in this book, and I want you to study them very carefully."

As she opened the book, I noticed that the pages were all white with black outline drawings of people and animals. It looked like a coloring book that had not yet been colored.

We studied one of the pages carefully; it was a picture of a man attempting to mount a horse. "Can you tell me what's wrong with this picture?" she asked.

I looked and looked at every part of the picture but couldn't find anything wrong. "I can't find nuthin' wrong," I said, shaking my head.

"The man's mounting his horse from the wrong side. He should be mounting it from the left side."

She then flipped the page and pointed to a picture of a man dressed up in a suit and vest. "Look at the picture and tell me if you can find anything wrong with it."

I stared hard at this new picture and attempted a few guesses, but again they were all wrong.

"The buttons on the gentleman's vest are on the wrong side," she said, pointing to the vest.

"Ohh," I said, as I started to sniffle. I was feeling bad that I couldn't find the mistakes in the pictures, for I wanted to please her, hoping she would take me back home.

I was beginning to fuss a bit now and wanted to get back to my sisters.

"Don't feel bad," she said, squeezing my hand. "These are hard questions for one so young. Let's see if perhaps we can find an easier picture." Flipping through the book, she stopped at a picture of a rooster standing beside a nest. I thought of the chickens at home and was sure I could find the mistake here.

"I know that's a r . . . r . . . rooster," I stammered, pointing at his head.

"Yes, you're right," she said. "I'm proud of you. But the right answer is that roosters don't lay eggs and there should have been a chicken beside the nest. We'll put this book back on the shelf now. The questions are much too difficult." She smiled down at me as she lifted me off her lap, took my hand, and led me back to the playroom.

Jean and Joan were nowhere in sight, and Betty was sitting in the middle of the floor, clutching a doll in her arms.

"Where's Jean 'n Joan?" I asked, kneeling down beside her.

She shook her head, clutching the doll closer.

"I dunno. A lady came and took them away."

"Are they c . . . c . . . comin' b . . .b . . . back?" I stuttered anxiously, still wondering what had happened to Bobby.

She shrugged her shoulders and shook her head as tears began to fill her eyes. "I don't know."

"The lady didn't say nuthin' to you?"

"Uh-uh."

The door then opened, and a lady, holding two small brown paper bags, walked toward us. "Here," she said, handing us each a bag, "these are for you."

We looked puzzled as we took the bags.

Noticing the looks on our faces, she explained that it was new pajamas and clothes for us.

"Are we going home now?" I asked anxiously.

"We're going for a car ride now," she said, "and you're going to a brand-new home." She bent down to our eye level, put her arms around our shoulders, and said softly, "You'll be having a new mommy and daddy who'll take good care of you."

"But I don't want a new mommy and daddy," I sobbed. "I wanna go home to Muggs!"

"I'm sure you'll be quite happy at your new home," she said as she took a handkerchief from her purse and wiped our noses.

My heart sank as I grabbed onto Betty's hand and numbly followed the lady to the car.

"I feel bad. My tummy hurts," Betty whispered to me as she held her hands over her stomach.

I put my arm around her waist. "Oh no, please don't be sick!"

As we settled into the backseat, I pulled Betty close to me in the middle, fearful that she might fall out again. Then in a quavering voice, I asked the lady, "Will Jean, Joan, and Bobby be at our new home?"

"No," she replied as she started the car. "They have already been taken to their new homes."

My heart sank even further. My world was crashing down around me, and I could make little sense of it all. I scrunched as far down as I could into the backseat, wanting to disappear. I felt so sad, so lost, and so scared. I looked at Betty. Her face was pale, and she was shivering. I squeezed her hand, hoping to comfort her, but we were both so frightened. We rode in silence, clinging to each other, fearful that we, too, might be torn apart.

4

Total Despair

As the car sped down the gravel road, I closed my eyes and leaned my head against the seat, still clinging to Betty's hand and trying hard to understand why they were taking us away from our home. I felt so sad but was unable to cry. After what seemed like a long ride, I felt the car jerk to a stop. Opening my eyes wide, I peered through the dusty window.

My heart skipped a beat as I saw a bunch of kids playing around in the front yard. *Maybe the lady was wrong,* I thought. *Maybe Jean and Joan are here.*

I searched the group of kids to see if I could spot them. I wanted to ask the social worker again but was too afraid of what her answer might be.

As we got out of the car, Betty surprised me by speaking up and asking, "Are Jean and Joan here, too?"

"No, dear, I'm sorry," the lady replied, laying a comforting hand on her shoulder. "They aren't at this home, but hopefully you will see them again soon. Right now this will be your home until we can find you a more permanent one. Just remember to be on your best behavior, and everything will be fine. Mrs. Reeves is a lovely lady, and I know she'll take good care of you."

She hustled us toward the house where Mrs. Reeves met us at the door. She was very friendly, and it didn't take us long to warm up to her.

Once the social worker had left, Mrs. Reeves called the rest of the children to the porch and introduced them to Betty and me.

Looking over the group, I realized that Betty and I were the smallest of the bunch. This frightened me a bit, for I didn't like being the smallest, and Jean and Joan weren't here to look after us.

In the days following, Betty and I were able to get along with most of the kids, but there was one young boy who, whenever he got the chance, found fun in pinching us or twisting our arms behind our backs. So we did our best to keep away from him.

Sticking close to each other at all times, we often hid from him either under our bed or under the dining room table. The table was our favorite spot, since the big, white tablecloth fell almost to the floor, and we could listen to the sounds of Mrs. Reeves working in the kitchen. Being well concealed, we would pretend we were back home as we played with small toys or, in whispered voices, played the little game of patty-cake that Muggs had taught us:

Patty-cake, patty-cake, a baker's man,
Bake a cake as fast as you can,
Put it in the oven and mark it B and B,
That's a cake for Bubba and me.

Mrs. Reeves occasionally peeked under the tablecloth to coax us out. "Come on out of there, you little rascals, you should be out playing in the fresh air," she would say.

But we would shake our heads and cross our arms over our chests in stubborn refusal.

Realizing that we were not going to budge, she'd smile at us, drop the cloth, and leave us to our play. As she returned to the kitchen to make supper, Betty and I would grin at each other, happy that she was nice to us.

Shortly, she would return to set the table, and from where I was sitting, I would watch her feet as she moved around. Then I would smile at Betty as we dared each other to tickle her ankle. But neither of us could work up enough nerve.

After setting the table, Mrs. Reeves would ring the dinner bell, and we could hear the noisy footsteps as the other children came bursting into the house. Betty and I would then creep out from under the table and take our places around the crowded table.

Once we were served spaghetti. But neither Betty nor I had seen spaghetti before, and I found myself sitting and staring at it, thinking it was a plate of worms. I had no idea how to eat it or if I even should. I looked around the table at the other children, and some of them were shoveling it into their mouths with their hands. I looked at Betty and saw that she was doing the same thing.

"Eat it," she said to me, nudging my elbow. "It's pretty good."

I followed her lead and started shoveling it in with both hands. She was right: it tasted so good. We giggled at each other when we realized what a terrible mess we had made of ourselves.

"Do you think we can ask for some more, Bubba?" I asked. But before she could reply, a wet cloth was swiped across my face and the empty plate removed.

It seemed that we had been there for a short time, perhaps only a few months, when Mrs. Reeves sat us down and told us the bad news. "The lady from the shelter is coming today to pick you up, so we must get your belongings packed."

"Why do we hafta go? Are we going home?" I asked, looking hard into her eyes.

"I don't know, dear," she replied, then quickly moved to get our brown paper bags from the closet.

We wiped tears from our cheeks as we watched her pack our belongings into the bags. *I wonder if she feels sad to see us go.*

"Let's go and hide in our special place," Betty said, and so we quickly snuck under the table.

"I'm never coming out," I said. "I don't wanna leave."

"I wish they were coming for someone else. Why do they hafta take us?"

Soon we heard a knock on the door, and I knew it meant that the lady was coming to take us away again. I listened as Mrs. Reeves invited her in. "You must be the lady from the shelter, here to pick up the girls."

"Yes. Are they ready to go?"

"Well, I have to find them first, but I think I know precisely where they are."

We waited, remaining very still, but soon Mrs. Reeves picked up the tablecloth, and we knew our little game was over.

"I think they're a bit frightened at the thought of moving again," she said.

"Yes, I can understand their reluctance," the lady replied, as she stooped to pick up our bags. Looking at us she said, "You'll be going to a new, *permanent* home, where I'm sure you'll be happy and stay for a longer time."

We said our good-byes to Mrs. Reeves as she bent down to give us a hug. Then we waved good-bye to some of the other kids who'd gathered around, and we reluctantly climbed into the backseat of the car.

I could feel my stomach shaking as I sat down, wondering what the lady meant by "permanent." Was it possible that we might be going back to our own home? I hoped so. I missed Muggs so much and wanted to be back with her.

Betty and I wiggled close together in the backseat and held hands. I swallowed hard to fight back the tears as we drove away. My heart ached for home as I leaned back against the seat and listened to the stones hitting the bottom of the car.

5

Brotherly Love

Betty and I were a little over four and a half years old when we arrived at the Fred Sebold home just outside the town of Simcoe. As we drove up the narrow lane, I noticed an old barn with a couple of small sheds and what looked like a chicken coop with a small chimney stack sticking out of the roof. A few chickens were scratching and pecking about the yard, and one lonely cow was chewing her cud in a nearby pasture. I thought of my own home as a feeling of sadness swept over me.

The social worker helped us out of the car, and Betty and I grabbed our bags of clothes and followed her to the house. Before we reached the door, it swung wide open, and a tall, fat lady greeted us. Her large body completely filled the doorway. I stared at her. I had never before seen such a big lady. She had on a black print dress covered over with a full white apron, and her dark hair was knotted in a tight ball at the back of her head with a few wire hairpins sticking out of it.

"C'mon, c'mon in!" she barked, as she held the screen door open with one hand while trying to shoo the flies away with the other.

We stepped briskly inside, and she quickly closed the door.

I looked her over from head to toe, still surprised and frightened by her size. I felt so tiny beside her. *Like a little fly,* I thought. She had a very severe and mean look about her, and I knew right away I wasn't going to like her. I looked over at Betty, who was nervously twisting the belt ties on her dress as she always did when she was frightened. We were both afraid of being put into this new home.

"Girls, this is Mrs. Sebold," the social worker said, "and she'll be taking care of you. She's your new foster mother," she added as she tidied our hair a bit. Then, pulling a folder from her bag and laying it on the table, she continued, "We're going to be discussing some final arrangements."

Mrs. Sebold suggested that Betty and I go outside to play but remain close by until she called for us.

As we were busy looking about the yard, I noticed a young boy come out of the chicken coop. Startled, I grabbed Betty's hand and started towing her back closer to the house. Then I turned to look again at the boy, and my heart almost leaped from my chest. "It's Bobby! It's Bobby!" I screamed.

He turned to look at us, realized who we were, and waved his arms wildly.

We ran as fast as our little legs could carry us and flew breathlessly into his arms.

"What're you kids doin' here?" he asked, while practically squeezing the last bit of breath out of me.

"They brought us here to live," I said, bubbling over with excitement. "This is supposed to be our new home, but no one told us you'd be here."

"I've been here since the day they took us all away," he said.

"Oh, Bobby, we're so happy you're here!" Betty cried, still clinging tightly to his waist.

Bobby had grown a lot since I had seen him last. He was nine years old now and quite a strong young boy. His hair was all ratty, and there was a bit of wildness about him. But other than that, he looked like the same Bobby. "C'mon, Betty," he said. "Let's see if I'm still strong enough to give you an airplane ride."

Betty quickly lay face-down on the ground, and Bobby picked her up by one arm and one leg and swung her around and around through the air. He then did the same for me. Around and around he swung us, up and down in the air, until we all fell laughing and dizzy into the soft grass. We were so full of happiness for being together again.

"Do you know where Jean and Joan are?" I asked.

"No, I don't know where they are, but one of these days I'm gonna run away from this damn place and try to find them," he said, planting his feet apart and placing his hands firmly on his hips. "I miss all my brothers, too, and I have no one here to play with."

"And I miss Muggs," I quickly chimed in.

"Will we ever see everybody again?" Betty asked, her voice full of longing.

"I don't know," he said with a faraway look in his eyes, "but don't worry. I'll look after you while you're here."

We hugged each other for a moment. I was confused and homesick, but at the same time so tickled that at least the three of us were together again. And Betty and I were happy to have Bobby here to protect us.

"C'mon, let me show you around," he said, taking hold of our hands.

We walked around an old gray barn that was starting to tumble down, out behind the white clapboard house, and past a grove of pine trees to where a cliff overlooked a small ravine.

"I play out here a lot," he said, pointing down toward the ravine. "I have lots of good hiding places down there."

"What do you hide from?" I asked, curious about his remark.

"Well, Mrs. Sebold's son, Richard, and his stupid friend, Clayton, always want to beat up on me, so I come here to get away from them. They're about fourteen years old, and we go to the same school. They're really mean, and I want you both to keep away from them as much as possible. Will you promise me that?"

We nodded, and he went on, "C'mon now, I'll show you where I live."

We followed him back to the barnyard, past a garbage dump at the corner of the barn, around a few old sheds, a chicken coop, and then in the direction of the chicken coop with the chimney stack. *Why are we going in here?* I wondered, as he walked up the steps and opened the chicken coop door.

"C'mon in," he said, "but watch the steps; they're kinda rickety."

As Betty and I walked inside, the bare plank floor creaked beneath us. I looked around and noticed a small, potbellied cast-iron stove that was almost level with my nose. Beside it was a blue, army-like cot with a gray woolen blanket lying in a crumpled heap at the foot of it. The only bit of light was from one small, dirty window. In the far corner, opposite the door, were two straw-filled chicken-nest boxes nailed to the wall.

"Do you live in here?" Betty asked, wrinkling her brow.

"Yep, this is my house," he said, puffing out his chest and crossing his arms. "I'm happy here, and I'm away from everyone else."

I was upset that Bobby had to sleep out here alone and not in the house. And I was getting more frightened, wondering where Betty and I would sleep. *Surely we won't have to sleep in the barn*, I thought.

He pointed out the window at the woodpile to show us where he got his wood to keep his stove going during the cold nights. "It can get pretty damn cold in here at times, but thanks to my little friend here," he said, patting his stove, "I can get it pretty toasty in no time."

"What do you eat and where do you get it?" I asked, getting more upset.

"They bring me food from the house, but sometimes if I get hungry, I steal some eggs from that chicken coop over there." He pointed his head in the general direction of the coop. "And then I scramble them up." Kneeling down, he pulled an old iron frying pan from its hiding place beneath his cot. "See, this is what I use," he said with a sneaky grin.

"Do any of the chickens lay eggs in here?" Betty asked, pointing to the nests.

"Come here," he said, as he waved us over to the nests and lifted up the straw. "This is where I hide all my stuff."

His "stuff" was a couple of handmade slingshots, a handful of stones, some twine, an old knife blade, a pitchfork prong, and other "boy junk."

"This is just in case those two try to get in here," he said, referring to the boys he had warned us about. "But don't worry," he added, "if they ever bother you kids, I'll beat the crap out of them!"

"Where do you think we'll have to sleep?" I asked.

But before he could answer my question, Mrs. Sebold yelled for us to come into the house.

As we left Bobby and made our way toward the house, I noticed that the lady from the shelter was already driving onto the road. We were now alone with the big fat lady, and I felt afraid.

Mrs. Sebold opened the door and quickly hustled us both inside. "Hurry," she snapped, "before we let all the flies in. Grab your bags there, and I'll show you to your room." Pointing to a staircase, she added, "You two scurry up the stairs ahead of me, and I'll be right with you."

We waited at the top of the stairs as she made her way up, huffing and puffing with each step. "Here," she said, as she paused at the top step to catch her breath, "this will be your bedroom."

We walked inside and set our bags on the bed. It was a small attic room that felt cold and damp and had a strange smell. There was a double bed, one chair, some hooks to hang our clothes on, and one small window. Just outside our room, to the right of the stairs, I noticed a small black box with a lid on top and a hinged door in the front. I wondered what it was used for. Mrs. Sebold, noticing me eyeing the box, walked over to it. "Now, let me explain this to you. This is called a commode." She lifted the lid to reveal a single hole. "At nighttime when you have to go to the toilet, you may use this, but if you do number two, then you must sprinkle some of this white powder in it to stop the smell." She held up a small, round canister with holes in the top. "During the day you must use the outside toilet. Every morning you open this little door, remove the pot, and empty it in the outhouse. Do you think you can manage that?"

"Yes, Mrs. . . . Umm . . ." I stumbled, forgetting her last name.

"It's Mrs. Sebold, but you can call me Mom. That will be easier for all of us. Now, hurry, unpack your belongings. Supper will be ready soon." Gripping both handrails, she slowly made her way down the narrow stairs.

Betty and I were fascinated by the black box. We'd never seen an inside toilet, and as soon as Mrs. Sebold disappeared, we decided it was time to pee so we could try out the fancy commode.

Betty clambered up first. "It's high," she said. "My feet can't even touch the floor."

I helped her down, and then it was my turn. We giggled when we had finished and headed back to our bedroom.

I closed the door behind us, and we sat sadly on the bed. I could smell the odor from the toilet coming under the door and pinched my nose.

"I don't wanna call her Mom," Betty said, stubbornly shaking her head.

"Me neither. She's not our mom. Besides, I don't even like her! And why doesn't she let Bobby sleep in the house?"

We were trying to make sense of everything when Mrs. Sebold hollered up the stairway: "You can come down for supper, girls."

At the table we met Mr. Fred Sebold and their son, Richard. Bobby wasn't there, so I thought someone must have taken his food to him.Mr. Sebold was a thin, slightly built man. He smiled at us and nodded when Mrs. Sebold told him and Richard our names. *He seems nice enough,* I thought.

As for Richard, I had already decided not to like him, so I lowered my head and peered at him from beneath my bangs.

Over the days that followed, we saw very little of Mr. Sebold, for we were also sent to the chicken coop for most of our meals, and a small wooden table and bench were brought in for our use. We would catch a glimpse of him only now and then as he walked up and down the dirt road to and from his work, swinging his black lunch bucket in his hand. He seemed like a distant stranger. Were these the new mommy and daddy we were promised that would take good care of us? The social worker's words still stuck in my head.

• • •

Bobby was right. After only a few days in our new home, Betty and I would fall victim to one of Richard and Clayton's cruel pranks when they decided it would be fun to make us lie face-down on the ground so they could ride their bikes over our bodies. We were preparing to lie down in the grass when Bobby — realizing what they were about to do and knowing he was no match for them — sped to the house to get help. Mrs. Sebold came to the door and screeched at them for their behavior, warning them that they could hurt us. But Richard and Clayton had no intention of giving up their nasty plan. Later in the day when Bobby had been called away to do chores and Betty and I were having fun on the teeter-totter he had rigged up for us, the two boys sneaked up, pulled us off, grabbed us by the back of our necks, and hauled us off behind the old barn, out of sight from the house.

I saw their bikes leaning against a tree and knew exactly what they were about to do. I tried to squirm from Richard's grasp, but his fingers tore deeper and tighter into my neck. We were both crying uncontrollably. Terrified and too small to resist, we could do nothing but what they asked.

We lay facedown on the ground, huddling together as close as we could. I wriggled my body, trying to bury it as deep as possible into the thick grass. I then closed my eyes and prepared for the worst. As we cowered in fear, everything suddenly became very quiet. *Maybe they're gone. Maybe they're just trying to scare us,* I thought. Then I heard their voices coming from the direction of the barn. Opening my eyes, I peeked out from beneath my arm to see the boys dragging an old mattress toward us. They had pulled it off the garbage dump at the corner of the barn. I whispered to Betty, explaining what they were doing. As they dragged the mattress close to us, I heard one of them yell, "Pick it up!" I tried to cover Betty as much as possible with my body as I waited for the heavy mattress to hit us. "Maybe it won't hurt so much with the mattress on us," I whispered to Betty. I closed my eyes tightly, waiting for whatever was to come next.

A minute or so passed before we felt them riding their bikes over us, doing their jumps and wheelies — one thump after another. Some thuds were more solid than others. I squirmed from the pain and tried to protect my head as much as possible.

It seemed like forever before they tired of their fun and yanked off the mattress.

We remained motionless, frozen in the grass, too terrified to move a muscle.

It was then that I felt something warm and wet hitting and running down the back of my bare legs. They were peeing on us. I squeezed Betty's arm, trying to warn her not to move.

After they had finished, they pulled us up by the hair, took one look at our frightened faces, laughed at our help-lessness, and took off on their bikes.

We waited until we saw them ride off down the lane and onto the road, well out of sight, before we tried to move.

"Are you okay, Bubba? Are you hurt?" I asked.

"I'm sore all over!" she groaned, rubbing her side.

"Me too. Let's find some leaves to wipe our legs, and then we'll go find Bobby and tell him what they did to us."

When we got to Bobby's coop, we burst in the door and found him lying on his bed, reading a comic book.

"Where were you kids?" he asked. "I was lookin' for you. Were you in the house?"

"No," we both babbled at once. "Richard and Clayton got hold of us and rode their bikes over us!"

"They threw that dirty old mattress over us — the one at the barn," Betty sniffled.

"Those bastards!" he exclaimed, shaking his fist, "I'm gonna get them one of these days. Just wait and see. Are you hurt?"

We pulled up our tops so he could look us over.

"Just a few red marks," he said, shaking his head in disgust. "But I think you'll be okay."

"They peed on our legs!" I sputtered.

"That was damn nasty of them," he growled. "They're filthy pigs! Someday I'll show you my hiding places down in the ravine. Maybe you'll be safe there."

Grabbing an apple from the top of the chicken box, he broke it smartly over his knee and gave us each a half. "Here, this will make you feel better." He locked the door of the coop and put a shim under it for extra security. "You'll be safe in here for now," he assured us.

"I hope they never take you away from us," Betty said, as she climbed up on the cot and snuggled close beside him.

• • •

During the days when all the boys were in school, Betty and I spent most of our time roaming around the large yard, climbing trees, playing in a sandy area behind the house, or hanging out in Bobby's coop. We picked wild flowers that grew along the fences that separated the neighbors' properties, and put them in a rusty tin can to decorate our little table. Many times we'd come upon a patch of ripe, wild strawberries or a raspberry bush loaded with berries and picked them as a treat for Bobby.

I felt sorry for him and wondered why he wasn't treated as nicely as Richard.

The weekends and holidays when Richard was home from school were the worst times for Betty and me. We spent most of our time plotting how and where we could hide from him and Clayton.

We weren't allowed to play in the house where Mrs. Sebold could keep an eye on us, and she never came outside to make sure we were okay. Many times she would yell at us from the doorway if she thought we were getting into mischief.

Whenever we got yelled at, Bobby would chant, "Fatty, fatty, two-by-four, can't get through the toilet door," knowing he'd get a giggle out of us.

• • •

When we first arrived at the Sebolds, Bobby gave me an old cup that he had salvaged from the garbage. It was a bright yellow tin cup with a large handle and black shiny rim. On the front was a picture of Humpty Dumpty sitting on a wall, and even though the cup was dinged up a bit, it was my very favorite toy. It brought back memories of Muggs, who had often read me the nursery rhyme.

On warm sunny days I loved to play in the sand with my little cup. I'd make mud-pie molds and decorate them with flowers, leaves, and pebbles.

One day as I was busy at play, I didn't realize that Bobby and Betty had left and I was alone until someone snatched the cup from my hands. Startled, I looked up to see Richard grinning down at me.

"Gimme back my cup!" I cried.

But he ran off toward the outhouse and soon came back with my cup filled with poop that he'd scooped out of the toilet. "Here, eat it!" he said, forcing the cup toward me.

"No, I don't wanna! I don't wanna!" I wailed, waving my hands wildly to keep it away from my face. In doing so, I managed to knock the cup from his grasp, and it landed in the dirt. I started to cry and looked around for Bobby and Betty, but they were nowhere to be seen. *Where are they?*

I was really getting scared. Ignoring the cup, Richard grabbed me by the hair and dragged me shaking and sobbing toward the outhouse. I knew he was going to do something bad to me. "Lemme go! Lemme go!" I sobbed.

When we were inside, he pushed me down on my knees. I felt his fingers pressing hard into the back of my neck as he shoved my head down toward his knees. "Lemme go!" I whimpered. "You're hurtin' me!"

I was terrified. I had no idea what cruel thing he was about to do to me as I kept struggling to free myself.

I heard the sound of his zipper being undone. Then he pulled something out of his pants, and with one hand twisting and gripping the hair on the back of my head, he tried to force it into my mouth. I had no idea of what he was trying to do, but I knew it was wrong. I felt sick to my stomach and wanted to throw up. I struggled to pull away, but he was too strong. I bit my lips real tight and closed my eyes as he kept jabbing away at my mouth.

He twisted my hair tighter and tighter in an effort to get me to open my mouth, but I wouldn't do it, no matter how much he tried to hurt me. I opened my eyes for a moment to see what he was trying to make me do, and as I looked down, I saw a piece of dark blue thread from off his trousers that was shaped like an "S" on the thing he was trying to put in my mouth. The picture of this blue thread would stay with me.

While struggling to get away from Richard, I could hear Bobby off in the distance, calling for me. I knew Richard heard it, too.

Scared at being caught in this horrible act, he knocked me hard against the wall, quickly zipped his pants, and ran from the outhouse.

I huddled in the corner, bawling my eyes out, afraid to move until Bobby heard me crying and opened the door. "What's wrong, Bonnie? Did Richard get to you again?" He gently lifted me up from the corner.

I clung tightly to him as he wiped away my tears with his shirttail.

"What did that creep do to you this time?" he demanded.

I was trying hard to describe to Bobby what Richard had been doing, but I stuttered so bad that he couldn't make sense of it.

"Okay, okay, calm down. He's gone now and I'm here." He tightened his arms around me.

After he quieted me down, I took him over to the sand pile to show him my Humpty Dumpty cup and told him what Richard had done with it. This he seemed to understand. He picked the cup up from out of the dirt and heaved it as far as he could into the bushes.

"I loved that cup!" I blubbered.

"I know," he said, as he knelt down to look me in the eyes. "I promise I'll find you something just as nice to take its place."

"I hate it here, Bobby! Why can't we run away?" I cried.

"Maybe someday we'll get away," he consoled. "But for now we'll just have to tough it out."

• • •

Bobby wasn't around to protect us from Richard when Mrs. Sebold gave him chores to do around the house or Mr. Sebold needed him to help with the wood cutting. "You have to earn your keep," they told him. And it was during these times that Betty and I would fall victim again and again to any mean things that Richard could think of.

When Richard and Clayton tired of their mattress game, they would amuse themselves by grabbing us when we least expected it and dragging us out behind the pine grove where the cliff overlooked the ravine. It was here where they'd hidden their ropes ready for use.

I would try hard to fight back my tears and put on a brave front so as not to add to their fun. But it was impossible; I was too full of fear, knowing what they had planned for us.

As Betty and I stood perched on the top of the cliff, they would each grab a piece of rope and wrap it under our arms and around our chests, knotting it tightly at our backs. Leaving several feet of slack rope, they would tie the ends to a nearby tree before lowering us feet first over the edge of the cliff.

I would hold my breath as I waited for the last drop when I knew the rope would tighten and burn deep into my body. As we dangled dangerously over the cliff, we could hear the boys laughing above. We could feel the dirt they were kicking down at us hit our heads and hear their hateful calls.

"If the rope breaks, you'll probably die," they would yell. "Yeah, or the birds might peck your eyes out. You're gonna stay here till the cows come home or your precious brother comes to rescue you."

When they were gone, Betty would start to cry.

One time the boys hung us farther apart than usual, and I was unable to reach Betty to quiet her. I knew she was in a lot of pain. The ropes were cutting into our skin, making our bodies sore and raw. "Don't cry, Bubba. Don't be afraid. Try to pretend it doesn't hurt." I tried hard to cheer her, but I couldn't.

"Where is Bobby? Why doesn't he come to help us?" she whimpered.

"Don't worry, Bubba. I'm sure he'll find us soon."

At long last, the boys came back to haul us up. We cried, and writhed in pain as the cliff scraped against our sore bodies. Once we were at the top, they untied the ropes and let us go.

"Hey, wasn't that fun?" they snickered. They then sped away on their bikes and left us alone.

Betty and I sat down together in the grass and bawled. We hurt so much. And as soon as we finished crying, we hurried back to find Bobby and tell him what had happened to us again.

He tried his best to console us as he wiped away our tears.

"Do you think I should tell Mrs. Sebold what the boys did to us?" I asked him.

"No. If you squeal on them, they'll only find some more horrible way to get even. I've tattled on them before, and things only got worse. Besides, Mrs. Sebold always takes Richard's side. It's just best to keep away from them."

6

A Blessing in Disguise

The three of us ate most of our meals in the chicken coop. Only on a cold winter day would Betty and I be allowed to eat inside the house, but Bobby remained in his coop.

Richard always ate with his family, but it was his job to bring our food out to us. Sometimes I'd watch from the coop window as he lugged a big, black cast-iron pot with a wire handle out to the coop. It must have been quite heavy, as he struggled to carry it.

The pot was usually filled with porridge or a thick soup. He would plunk it down at the foot of the steps and call out to us. "Here's your grub, come and get it!"

Many times as Bobby leaned down to pick up the pot, Richard would quickly kick it over with his foot and laugh out loud as the food spilled out into the dirt. "Hope you like it. A little bit of dirt and chicken shit never hurt anyone!" he would yell back over his shoulder as he made his way to the house.

"Go to hell, you stupid ass!" Bobby would yell back.

Betty and I would stand crying on the steps as we watched the chickens flock around to peck away at our food as the thick mush oozed its way through the dirt.

Bobby would quickly grab the pot in an effort to save what was left. We went hungry many times because of Richard's meanness.

• • •

As Bobby was younger than Richard, he always came home from school an hour or so earlier. One day when he arrived at his coop, Betty and I were sitting on his cot, waiting for him. As soon as he entered the door, we jumped up to complain to him.

"We're hungry, Bobby. We haven't eaten all day," I cried.

It was then that Bobby decided to take matters into his own hands. "Okay," he said, "that's it! I'm gonna get you somethin' to eat." He picked us up and sat us back on the cot. "Listen to me. I've got a plan, but I'm gonna need your help. I'm gonna be the captain, you two are my sergeants, and we're gonna play a little game," he said with a grin. "I'm gonna break into the neighbor lady's cellar and get some stuff for us to eat, but I need you both to post guard for me."

"But what if we get caught? What'll happen to us?" I asked.

"Then we'll probably all go to jail, but it can't be any worse than livin' here, and we'd probably have somethin' to eat at least. Okay, here's what I want you to do. Follow me, be very quiet, and do exactly as I say."

We made our way out of the chicken coop, and the three of us, crouching low, sneaked through the bushes and tall weeds that lined the fence row, being careful not to step on any thistles with our bare feet. At last we made it safely to the side of the neighbor's house. Bobby told Betty to stand at one corner of the house and keep a sharp eye out for the kids coming home from school. She was supposed to call to me if she saw them.

Then he told me to stand at the cellar window and warn him if Betty saw anyone coming. "If I find some food, I'll hand it out the window to you, and then you and Betty run like blazes back to the chicken coop. But be careful no one sees you. I'll catch up with you later."

Betty and I were jumpy, but Bobby's confidence helped settle us down.

He worked fast, and within minutes he was able to pry out the cellar window with his small knife blade. I watched as he squeezed his thin, wiry body through the small opening and slowly lowered himself to the cellar floor. *He's so smart. Has he done this before?* I wondered.

"Be careful, Bobby," I whispered as he disappeared inside.

Very soon he came back to the window and held up a jar of golden yellow peaches. For a moment I stared wide-eyed at them—they looked so yummy. As I knelt down at the window to reach for them, Betty turned to warn me that the kids were coming down the road.

"The ki . . . ki . . . kids are c . . . c . . . coming, Bobby!" I stuttered.

"Quick, grab the peaches!"

I reached through the window to grab the peaches, but the jar was too big and heavy for my small hands, and it slipped from my grasp and crashed loudly on the cellar floor below.

"I'm s . . . s . . . sorry, Bobby!" I blubbered. "I'm s . . . s . . . sorry!"

"It's okay," he said. "I should've known it was too heavy for you to handle. Just help me out of here before someone catches us!"

But it was too late. The lady in the house heard the noise and caught Bobby red-handed as he was trying to climb out the window. She yanked him back into the cellar and then brought him outside, holding the back of his shirt firmly in her hand. "I'm going to report this to the police, young man!" she snapped, as she marched him toward the house to have a talk with Mrs. Sebold.

Betty and I followed numbly behind. My heart was so heavy. I knew everything was my fault because I was unable to hold onto the peaches.

As we neared the chicken coop, the lady let go of Bobby. "You three wait in there," she growled, pointing at the coop. "I want to speak to Mrs. Sebold alone without a bunch of little ears eavesdropping on us."

We sat in silence on Bobby's cot, wondering what would happen to us.

Suddenly Bobby broke the silence. "Boy oh boy! Those peaches looked damn good, didn't they, Bonnie?"

"Yeah, they sure did!"

He smacked and licked his lips. "I can almost taste them."

"Me too!" I replied, rubbing my empty tummy.

Some time passed before we heard the police officer's car crunch to a stop on the gravel lane. He made his way into the chicken coop, followed closely by Mrs. Sebold and the neighbor lady. As he stepped inside, he hunched a bit to keep from hitting his head on the ceiling. He was dressed all in blue with a shiny badge on his chest.

My eyes followed his shiny black boots, up along the stripe on his blue pant leg, all the way up to his head and to the top of his hat. He was so tall, and it seemed as if his whole body filled the small coop. *He's dressed just like Grandpa Pete*, I thought. For some reason I wasn't the least bit afraid of him but was worried about what he would do to Bobby.

Betty and I sat quietly while he asked some questions and took notes on a small pad, and I prayed that he wouldn't take Bobby away from us. After closing his pad, he scolded Bobby for stealing and made him promise that he wouldn't steal again. He then told Bobby that the punishment for his crime was confinement to his bed for two weeks or until he heard further from him. Bobby nodded. The officer then told Mrs. Sebold that he'd be filing a report of the incident.

After he left, Bobby had to endure a further scolding from Mrs. Sebold. "Well, this is a fine mess you got into, young man. I hope you're proud of yourself. You're old enough to know better than to pull such a stunt!"

Bobby sat slouched on the edge of his cot, quiet and motionless, and I could tell that her words were falling on deaf ears. He had a sad expression on his face and a faraway look in his eyes. I knew he was worried about us.

Mrs. Sebold, realizing he wasn't listening, reached out and firmly cuffed his head. Bobby didn't flinch. She then turned abruptly on her heel and left the coop.

"Do you think we'll go to jail?" Betty asked.

"No," Bobby said with a wry smile. "Besides, you're such a skinny little pipsqueak that you could squeeze between the bars and get out."

It felt good to have Bobby make us laugh when we were feeling so bad, but I asked, "What about you? Will they put you in jail?"

"I don't think so. If they wanted to put me in jail, the policeman would've taken me with him. But I'm worried about what the Children's Aid will do."

"I hope they don't take you away from us, or we'll have no one to look after us," Betty wailed, as she inched closer to his side. The very thought of them taking Bobby away scared the daylights out of us.

"They won't really do that, will they?" I moaned, as I searched his face for an answer.

"Well, whatever happens, you can bet your life that I'm gonna spill the beans and tell them everything that goes on here, and that's for damn sure!"

No sooner had Mrs. Sebold returned to the house than the coop door swung wide open and Richard came in to laugh in our faces. "So, I hear they're gonna send you all to jail for stealing," he smirked.

With Bobby close by, I finally found the courage to speak out against Richard. "He wouldn't hafta steal if you didn't dump our food out to the chickens!" I shouted at him.

"Aw shut up, you mouthy little brat!" he snarled. And before I could run to Bobby for protection, he grabbed me by the neck and smashed my face hard into the cast-iron stove. The pain shot through my head like a hot poker. I screamed, grabbed my nose, and got a handful of blood.

At the sight of my bloody face, Betty ran to help me, and Bobby grabbed his frying pan from beneath the bed and chased Richard out of the coop, cussing and swearing at him. "Get outta here, you stupid ass, and don't ever come back, or I'll kill you!" He then locked the door, kicked the wooden shim solidly under it, and came back to tend to me.

"Boy, he really hurt you bad," he soothed. "You're a mess!" Putting his arms around me, he led me to a basin of water. "Don't cry, Puddin' Head," he said, giving me a squeeze. "I'll wash you up, and then you'll feel much better. I promise."

• • •

Just a few days after the peach-stealing incident, Betty came down with pneumonia. She was deathly sick, and Dr. Archer, the family doctor, was called in to tend to her.

She lay in bed for what seemed like forever while Dr. Archer and I sat beside her.

She was so frail and weak, and he knew her chances of pulling through were slim. "You must take good care of your little sister while I'm away," he said. "Here's a cool cloth.

You must wipe off her forehead and face to bring down her fever."

"Will she get all better soon?"

"Well, she's very sick, so we'll have to say some prayers for her."

"How do I say a prayer?"

He smiled down at me. "Well, you must get down on your knees beside the bed and put your hands together like this," he said, pressing his palms together. "Then you pray for God to make her all better."

I listened carefully to what he was telling me, and after giving me a little pat on the head, he called from the top of the stairs for Mrs. Sebold, saying he had to leave to tend to his other patients but would be back later in the day. He then asked her if she could please make sure the commode was kept empty and clean at all times as the odors could nauseate Betty.

Later on that day she let me spray some lilac toilet water, as she called it, around the area.

After the doctor left, I decided to try out my prayers. I knelt down beside the bed, carefully putting my hands together like the doctor had. "Please, please, God, please make Bubba all better again so she can come out and play with me. Please don't let her die!"

My prayers were soon interrupted by her moaning, and she tossed and turned under the sheets, crying out to me that there were snakes and bugs all over her bed. "Make them go away! Make them go away!" she begged.

I crawled in, around, and under her bed several times during the day, pretending to chase them away. "They're all gone, Bubba. I've chased them all away and told them never to come back. You can go to sleep now." I brushed the hair away from her sweaty forehead and mopped it with the cool cloth.

At long last the fever broke, and she was getting better. I was so happy to be able to feed her, to brush her pretty blonde hair, and to have my playmate back again.

Dr. Archer made one more visit. "It looks like your sister's doing much better," he said, patting me on the head again. "You know what, little girl? I'm sure it was all the love you had for her that got her through this. I really didn't think she was going to make it."

He made me feel proud.

Before Betty was out of her sick bed, and much to our surprise, Mrs. Sebold allowed Bobby to come to our room for a visit.

"How'd you get here?" I asked. "Did they let you outta bed?"

"Well, yes," he said hesitantly, "but I really came to say good-bye. They're taking me to another home." He immediately saw the frightened and sad looks on our long faces and added, "Don't be afraid. I overheard that they'll be takin' you both away, too."

"Won't we see you again?" I asked, feeling my lips trembling as I fought back my tears.

"Perhaps someday is all I can promise for now. But I'll keep looking for you until I find you, and that's for darn sure!"

We hugged each other tightly, not wanting to let go.

But soon Mrs. Sebold called from the stair landing to let Bobby know the social worker was waiting for him. We peered out of our bedroom window, blew kisses, and waved wildly at Bobby as the car made its way slowly down the lane and disappeared among the trees. Once it was out of sight, we threw ourselves on the bed, broke down in tears, and sulked away the rest of the day.

Lost without Bobby, we played mostly in our room, too afraid to go outside.

Mrs. Sebold let us have our meals in the house now, and the chicken coop was locked.

Our stay at this home, or the "hell hole," as Bobby called it, had lasted eleven long months when, a few days after Bobby left, a lady from the Children's Aid Society came to get us. I was sure that Bobby had "spilled the beans" and the police officer's report was the reason for our removal from this awful home. Getting caught stealing the peaches had proved to be a blessing in disguise.

7

Mixed Emotions

It was only a short drive to the offices of the Children's Aid Society from the Sebold home on the outskirts of Simcoe. As the social worker pulled her car into the parking lot, she turned to us. "You two little girls are awfully quiet back there. Do you have any idea where we are?"

We shook our heads.

"We're back at the shelter, and we'll get a bite to eat before we go on to your next home. It's a bit of a drive."

As I made my way up the wide stairs to the second floor, events of the past came flooding back to me. I suddenly felt sad and chilled, and my arms were getting goose bumps. While walking down the long, narrow hallway, I glanced to my left at the room with the huge windows and took notice of the chair in the corner where the lady with the pretty silk blouse had sat and asked me questions from a coloring book. Then Betty and I walked down the hall to the toy room.

"Well, I see you didn't forget where the toy room is," the social worker said as she opened the door for us. "Play in here for a while until we can rustle up some lunch." She winked as she closed the door. A picture of Bobby flashed in my mind, for he had often winked at us. I was overcome with sadness and wondered about where he was and how he was doing.

As I looked around the familiar room, I could feel the walls closing in on me, my breathing getting tight. "I don't like the door closed, Bubba; it scares me. Do you think we can open it?"

"No, we'd better not. We might get into trouble. Look," she said, picking up a red fire engine with ladders on the sides, "this is the truck that Jean and Joan were playing with."

We handled it fondly for a while and then put it back on the shelf.

"I don't feel much like playin', Bubba," I said. "Let's go look out the window."

We crossed the room to look outside, but since there was nothing to see but the wall of another building, we plopped ourselves down on the wide window ledge to wait for the lady to call us for lunch.

Soon the door opened and a different lady came in. "Hello. My name's Mrs. Coldwell, and I think you're Bonnie and Betty. Now let's see. A little bird told me that Bonnie has brown eyes and Betty has blue eyes. So you must be Bonnie," she said, laying her hand lightly on my shoulder. "And you must be Betty," she continued, pulling her closer. "Am I right?"

We nodded and shyly dropped our gazes to the floor.

Sensing the uncertainty in our demeanor, she said, "Well, come on now. Lunch is ready, and I'm sure you must be hungry."

At the mention of the word "hungry," Betty's tummy gave a noisy growl, and we both giggled.

"I think that says yes," the lady said with a chuckle, "so let's go eat."

After a tasty lunch of egg sandwiches, cocoa, and cookies, Mrs. Coldwell excused herself and left the room. A few minutes later she returned, holding her hands behind her back. "I have something very special for each of you to take to your new home. Would you like to see what it is?"

We glanced uncertainly at each other, nervously fidgeted with our hands, and then looked back to her and nodded.

"Close your eyes, then," she said. "That'll make it a better surprise."

We did as she said, and when she told us to open our eyes, she was holding two beautiful dolls. "Here, the one with the brown hair is for Bonnie and the one with the blonde hair is for Betty."

Neither of us had ever had anything other than a rag doll, and we were so happy that we forgot to thank her. Bending down to face level, she gently reprimanded us for our lack of good manners. "When someone gives you a present, you must always remember to say 'thank you.'"

"Thank you," I said shyly, feeling ashamed. "This is my first dolly ever."

"Mine too," Betty said, hugging her doll close to her chest.

"Well, then," Mrs. Coldwell said, "let's pick up our things and get back on the road."

We followed her out to the parking area, and she helped us into the back of a little gray coupe. I was surprised that it had no back doors, and I leaned over to whisper in Betty's ear, "Look Bubba, you can't fall outta this car."

• • •

As the car moved along, we played quietly in the backseat with our dolls. Mine had a long, silky green dress with lace at the neckline and a bright pink sash tied in a bow around the waist. She had long, curly brown hair and dark brown eyes. Her arms and legs were stuffed with cotton, but I was drawn to her tiny, black patent-leather Mary Jane shoes that were removable. "Look, Bubba," I whispered. "We had shoes just like these. Remember? Muggs used to buckle them for us."

"I know," she sniffled. "They're the same color, too."

"What're you gonna name your dolly?" I asked.

But before she could reply, Mrs. Coldwell interrupted, glancing at us in the rearview mirror to tell us that we would be arriving at our new home in a few minutes.

I was feeling anxious about going to a new home and wished we could just keep riding in the car. Standing up, I peeked over at Mrs. Coldwell and stammered plaintively, "Will this be our p . . . p . . . permanent home?"

"Hopefully, yes," she replied with a soft chuckle.

"What does 'p . . . p . . . permanent' mean?"

"'Permanent' means a long time. Hopefully you will be at this new home for a nice long time. And in the fall you'll be starting school. Mr. and Mrs. Miller live in the little village of Woodsville. They're very nice. You should be able to find lots of new friends and playmates there, and I'm sure you'll be very happy."

Satisfied with her response, I sat back down. As soon as I did, Betty nudged me in the side with her elbow and said, "Ask her if there are any boys there."

I stood up and peeked over the seat again. "Are there any boys at our new home?"

I waited as she thought over my question. And then she said, "No, dear, no boys. The Millers have a grown son named Edmund who is away serving in the air force. He won't be home for some time."

Betty and I grinned happily and squeezed each other's hand. And then she asked hesitantly, "Will we . . . Uuum, wi . . . will we have to eat in a chicken coop?"

"My goodness, no!" Mrs. Coldwell said, turning to look back at her. "Whatever gave you that idea?"

Betty's unexpected question must have startled her, for before she turned back to watch the road, the car slid on the snow and went into a shallow ditch, throwing Betty and me off the seat.

"Oh goodness, what have I done now?" she exclaimed. "Are you girls all right back there?"

"We're okay," I said as we crawled back onto the seat.

"Well, it looks as if I've got to go and get some help," she said, as she got out to check on the car. "You two stay here and don't get out of the car. I'll be back soon."

She had gone only a short distance down the road when two men in a car came by and stopped to help. In no time at all they had pushed the car from the ditch and we were on our way again.

As we pulled into the lane of our new home, Mr. and Mrs. Miller hurried out to greet us. Then Mrs. Miller herded us into the house where she immediately busied herself preparing a pot of tea. "You simply must stay and have a spot of tea," she said to Mrs. Coldwell. "It's such a dreadfully cold day. Why, my heavens, you must be chilled nigh to the bone. I'll prepare some hot chocolate for the girls."

Turning to Betty and me, she asked, "Now, let's see, which one's Bonnie and which one's Betty?"

Before either of us could answer, Mrs. Coldwell said, "The one with brown eyes is Bonnie and the one with blue eyes is Betty."

"But I call her 'Bubba,'" I quickly added.

"Well," Mrs. Coldwell said, "her name is Betty, and you're much too big to be calling her Bubba. You must learn to call her by her right name. Will you promise to do that for me?"

I nodded, even though I wasn't too happy with the idea. "Bubba" was fine with me and much easier to say, I thought.

As Betty and I sat at the table drinking our cocoa, I glanced around the kitchen. It seemed so warm and cozy, much different from the Sebold home. And Mr. and Mrs. Miller seemed so nice.

When we'd finished our cocoa, Mr. Miller picked up our belongings and waved his hand at us. "Come on with me, little girls. While the *missus* is busy finalizing things, I'll show you to your room."

Missus? That tickled my tummy. *I wonder what we'll have to call her? Surely not missus!*

Our bedroom was a small room next to the kitchen, and the heat from the stove made it warm and comfy. The walls were covered in soft, patterned wallpaper. Lace curtains adorned the window, and a pretty, pink chenille bedspread covered the bed. At the foot of the bed was a small dresser with towels hanging at the side. A floral pitcher sat inside a matching washbowl, and a mirror hung on the wall above.

"It's so pretty, isn't it?" I said to Betty.

"Yes, it really is, and it isn't stinky like at the Sebolds."

"I wanna sleep next to the wall, just like at the Sebolds," I said with a snicker. "I feel safer with my back to the wall, and if the bogeyman comes, he'll grab you first!"

Betty giggled. "That's okay. I like to sleep in the front anyway. I won't have to climb over you if I have to get up to pee, and I'll be the first one to the breakfast table in the morning."

We were in high spirits as we laid our dolls down on the pillows for a nap. So taken up were we with our new surroundings that we scarcely heard Mrs. Coldwell say her good-byes.

After our first dinner with the Millers was over and the dishes cleared away, Mr. Miller bundled us up and took us down to the village grocery store to buy us some candy. He seemed to take pride in introducing us to the store-owner, Mrs. Emma Hoover. On the way home he joked with us. "You must both be respectful of Mrs. Emma. After all, she's the one who guards the candy counter — and with a very keen eye, I might add. So don't ever try snitching any, for she'll grab you, hang you by your toes on the clothesline, and shake the candy right out of your pockets."

Picturing the ridiculous scene in my mind, I broke out laughing. "You're teasing us. She wouldn't really do that!"

"Oh, one never knows what she's apt to do," he teased.

"Well, she'll have to catch me first," I chortled.

Holding tightly to his hands, Betty and I skipped and hopped our way back to the house.

That evening the Millers retired to the living room where they settled into their matching sofa chairs, one on each side of a large floor-model radio. After propping his stocking-covered feet on a footstool, Mr. Miller asked if one of us would bring him his slippers. As we both wanted to please him and gain his affection, Betty and I quarreled over who would get them. To settle the dispute, he told me to bring the right slipper and Betty to bring the left one.

"But I don't know which is the right or which is the left," I complained.

"Makes no mind, child," he said. "Just bring me the first slipper and the other one will always be left."

I glanced up at him from my kneeling position at his feet and saw a mischievous grin. I wrinkled my brow, at first puzzled by what he had said. When I smiled, he knew that I understood.

After his slippers were on and his feet comfortably propped on the footstool, Betty and I nestled on his lap while he read us a short bedtime story. We then hustled off to bed while they listened to the radio.

• • •

Because it had been such an event-filled first day at the Millers, Betty and I slept soundly and awoke refreshed in the morning. Not knowing what was expected of us, we waited quietly in our room until Mrs. Miller opened the door and called us out.

I was disappointed that Mr. Miller was nowhere around. *Is he going to be like Mr. Sebold and I'll catch a glimpse of him only now and then?* I wanted to know. Wiggling into my chair at the kitchen table, I asked, "Where is Mr. Miller?"

"Today's Monday, and he's off to work. He'll be home about five o'clock, and if you're good girls, I'll let you go and meet him at the Hoover store."

In the days following, we learned that the Millers were quite concerned about their son, Edmund, who was serving in World War II. It was a time of great emotional stress for them, and I often found them sitting around the radio, ears pressed close to the speakers, listening for the latest war news.

It was during this time that many food supplies and necessities—like sugar, butter, meat, and gasoline—were rationed. Families were given a certain number of ration coupons depending on the number of people in their households. However, there never seemed to be a shortage of headcheese, sardines, or Spam. Spam would always churn my stomach, and I absolutely hated it—especially because of the yucky taste of the clear gel that smothered it and the disgusting sucking sound it made when it plopped out of the can and jiggled briefly on the platter before settling down.

These were difficult times in Canada, and many families struggled to make ends meet. No food was allowed to be wasted, and Betty and I soon learned that we must always clean our plates. Any sign of rebellion got a stern reprimand from Mrs. Miller, who would remind us about "all the starving children around the world." But at times, if we were fortunate to have pockets in our dresses, some food, such as fat from meat, wound up there to be disposed of later in the outhouse. And so our time at the table would often be a game of cat and mouse with Mrs. Miller.

• • •

Adjusting to this new home took its toll on both of us. Betty was constantly scolded for twisting her belt ties and chewing on her hair, and I for biting my nails down to the quick. Added to this, my stuttering was becoming worse. Mrs. Miller proved to be very strict with us, and since we had no concept of good manners, we were constantly being corrected about everything from posture to table manners.

"Keep your back straight, no slouching, and keep those elbows off the table!" she would bark. She kept a teacher's pointer stick at the ready, and if our elbows appeared on the table, they got a quick whack.

Betty and I kept a keen eye on that stick as it lay menacingly across the table, for we were never sure when she was going to wield it. We often plotted to get rid of it.

For some unknown reason, Mrs. Miller favored me over Betty and was often unrelenting in her criticism of her. Sometimes she was downright mean, and I felt sorry for Betty. Then, there were times when I took advantage of my sister, knowing I was the more privileged one. "Please bring me my shoes, Betty," I might ask.

"Get 'em yourself," she would reply tartly. "I ain't your servant!"

Mrs. Miller would quickly command, "She asked nicely, so go and get her shoes for her! And 'ain't' isn't a proper word, so mind you don't use it again!"

Poking out her bottom lip, Betty would reluctantly obey, setting my shoes down with a thud at my feet and giving me a scornful look.

And I would usually feel sorry that I had caused her to get yelled at.

At breakfast one day we were served eggs prepared sunny-side up. This was a new experience for us, as we'd never had eggs like this before. The whites were semi-transparent and runny, and the yolks barely held their own. We sat dumbfounded, staring at them. They looked disgusting and unappetizing — *worse than Spam,* I thought. Finally I poked at my egg with my fork, and it wriggled on my plate. I leaned over to Betty and joked, "I think it's alive!"

She gave me a sickening look and whispered, "I can't eat this."

"Just try your best," I whispered back. "She won't let us waste any food, and we can't put *this* in our pockets."

I managed to choke down most of my egg by following each forkful with a bite of toast, but Betty continued to poke at hers.

"Eat it, Betty, it won't kill you," I whispered again.

Mrs. Miller, hearing us whisper — which was not allowed — turned to reach for her pointer. Betty quickly took her first forkful of egg and stuck it in her mouth. No sooner had she done so than she threw up all over her plate. At that, Mrs. Miller angrily cracked the stick on the table. Startled, we jumped in our chairs.

Raising her voice, Mrs. Miller snapped, "You're going to clean up your plate, young lady, if you have to sit there all day!" She then turned to me. "You're excused from the table."

I flew from the table to sit in the chair beside the stove and looked at Betty as she sat staring at her plate. The color had drained from her face. I felt pity for her and wondered why Mrs. Miller was so mean to her. *She doesn't deserve to be treated like this*, I thought.

Betty made several attempts to eat the eggs all covered with vomit, but she only kept gagging and gagging until Mrs. Miller finally relented and sent her to our room.

We were happy that she didn't serve us eggs like that again.

• • •

Each new day brought new problems for Betty and me and more challenges for Mrs. Miller. My stuttering got worse and the more I stuttered the more Mrs. Miller made me stop and repeat myself.

As for my nail biting, she painted foul-tasting stuff on my nails, but nothing seemed to help break this bad habit. As a last resort, Mrs. Miller even jokingly threatened to tie my hands behind my back.

On the other hand, Betty was continually being scolded for one thing or another, and her punishment was usually more severe than mine. She was starting to develop a bedwetting problem. The first time she had a mishap, Mrs. Miller left the room, returned with Mr. Miller, and pointed to the wet spot on the mattress.

"Why did you wet the bed?" he barked at Betty.

"I didn't know I did it," she whimpered, her voice shaking.

"It was an accident," I piped in. "She didn't mean to do it!"

"You best be quiet, little girl!" he commanded, wagging his finger at me. "I'm not talking to you!" He turned his attention back to Betty.

"We'll have no more of this, do you hear? You do this one more time, young miss, and I'll rub your nose in it! There's a chamber pot under the bed, and you had best make sure to use it!" he snapped. He turned and walked out of the room.

It isn't like him to speak so mean to us. She put him up to it, I thought.

The following night Betty worried about going to sleep, afraid of having another accident. "What if I wet the bed again? I'm so afraid to go to sleep."

"You'll be okay," I said, trying to comfort her.

"Mrs. Miller doesn't like me at all," Betty sniffled. "She just likes you. What if I wet the bed again and they take me away like they did Bobby?"

The thought of something like that happening frightened us to death. "I won't let them do that. I just won't let them!" I cried, trying to convince myself as well as her.

Wrapping our arms around each other and snuggling down deep into the center of the bed, we fell fitfully to sleep.

Several days later, Betty shook me from my sleep. "Bonnie, Bonnie, wake up!"

The panic in her voice told me immediately what had happened. I sprang up in bed and saw her feeling the wet area with fear in her eyes. "I've done it again! I've wet the bed again! I'm sooo afraid! What are we gonna do? I wish I were dead!"

"I'll tell her I did it," I tried to console her. "Maybe she won't do anything to me. It's worth a try."

Betty and I sat on the edge of the bed, dreading the time when Mrs. Miller would open the door to tell us breakfast was ready. When she finally entered the room, she sensed something was wrong. "What's the matter?" she asked. "You look like a couple of frightened jackrabbits."

"I w . . . w . . . wet the b . . . b . . . bed," I stuttered.

But she saw through my lie at once. "Oh, I don't think so," she said, reaching her arm around me to feel the back of my nightie and then feeling Betty's.

"George, come in here at once!" she said, calling from the door. "She's wet the bed again," she told him as he appeared at the doorway.

"I'm sorry! I'm sorry! I won't do it again!" Betty sobbed, backing up against the wall.

Mr. Miller grabbed her by the back of the neck, forced her to her knees, then shoved her face into the mattress, and rubbed it back and forth in her pee. "Now, I hope you've learned your lesson, young lady, as I'll have no more of this. Is that understood?"

With a pained expression on her face, and eyes casting downward, Betty nodded.

"Now, both of you get cleaned up and ready for breakfast," Mrs. Miller said, leaving the room and closing the door firmly behind her.

"I know you couldn't help it, and it was mean of him to do that," I said to Betty, trying to console her and wipe her face with a damp cloth at the same time.

"I feel so ashamed of myself," she said.

I felt her pain and my heart ached. Believing a prayer worked before when she was sick, I decided to pray again and maybe she wouldn't have any more accidents.

8

Fitting In

Christmas was fast approaching, and Mrs. Miller got us involved in the holiday preparations. We were beginning to fit in now and felt more at ease with Mr. and Mrs. Miller. And fortunately, after only a few more incidents, Betty had no more nighttime accidents.

A few days before Christmas, Mr. Miller took Betty and me into the wooded lot behind the house to pick out a small pine tree to decorate for the holidays. That evening we helped pop the popcorn on the wood-burning stove, and Mrs. Miller taught us how to string and hang it on the trees. After that she carefully hung a few delicate glass bulbs around the tree, and we held the stepladder while Mr. Miller put a gold-painted wooden star at the top.

Betty and I stood back, clapping our hands as we admired the finished results.

I was bubbling over with excitement on Christmas Day like a balloon ready to burst. It was a new experience, and I didn't know what to expect or how to behave. So I held back, waiting for some clue from Mrs. Miller.

"Come on, girls, let's sit around the tree," she said, patting our place on the sofa, "and we'll open our presents."

I looked at the first present she handed to me. It was nicely wrapped in white tissue paper with the folds held together by a small gold star. I was hesitant about how to open it and looked to her again for instructions.

"Oh, just open it, my dear," she said. "It doesn't matter if you tear the paper. We won't be using it again except perhaps to light the fire in the stove."

Wanting the thrill of anticipation to last as long as possible, I took my time unwrapping it. And when the box was opened, I found inside a large coloring book, crayons, a small blackboard with a wooden frame, and a few sticks of white chalk.

Mrs. Miller knew how I loved to draw and color, and now I had all my own stuff. Jumping up and down with gleeful excitement, I ran to give them both a big hug.

"Now let's not get carried away, little girl," Mr. Miller teased. "I expect to see some nice work in those books, and starting in the New Year, the missus will be teaching you your ABCs to prepare you both for school in the fall. She used to teach school, so you'll have a tough master, mind you."

I'm very sure of that, I thought.

Betty and I happily opened the rest of our gifts: Shirley Temple cutout paper dolls and storybooks about Princess Elizabeth and Princess Margaret Rose. It was a wonderful Christmas for both of us, and the rest of the day was spent playing with our presents.

After a nice Christmas dinner of roast beef with Yorkshire pudding, mashed potatoes, and plum pudding, Mrs. Miller surprised us by bringing out some new winter coats from the closet. "Here," she said. "Your old winter coats are quite worn and threadbare, so I got permission from the shelter to buy new ones. These are the ones I picked from the Sears catalog. The burgundy one's for Bonnie and the blue one's for Betty. Try them on and let's see how they fit."

I slipped my bare arms into the cool, silk-lined sleeves and shrugged the coat onto my shoulders. Then I held the sleeve to my nose and breathed in the smell of the newness. "Ooh, it's soo pretty!" I said, circling about in the middle of the room. "I feel like Shirley Temple!"

"Hold still and let me button it up," Mrs. Miller said. "It looks like it's just a tad big. But with a sweater underneath, it'll be fine, and you'll be able to get two winters' worth out of it."

I was overjoyed with my new coat. It had brass buttons down the front with a fur collar and side pockets, a brimmed bonnet with velvet-corded chin ties, and a fur pom-pom attached to the end of each tie. It even came with a fur muff to keep my hands warm. There was a pair of funny-looking pants that fastened near the bottom with tiny buttons. "What are *these* things?" I asked, holding up the pants.

"They're called leggings. They'll keep your legs warm on very cold days," she replied, noticing my puzzled look.

Betty was just as thrilled with her new blue coat and hurried off to admire herself in the hall mirror as Mrs. Miller watched.

"Hmm, it looks like we're going to have to fatten you up a bit over the winter to get you to fit in this coat," she said.

After we'd repeatedly admired our new coats, Mrs. Miller said, "All right, girls, you can put your coats away now. You'll be wearing them to church and Sunday school."

"Oh, I don't ever wanna take it off. It makes me feel so *special!*" I said as I made one more twirl around the room before removing it.

• • •

Betty and I whiled away the winter months, playing in the snow and occasionally taking our sleigh down to meet Mr. Miller where his ride dropped him off. He often pulled us home on the sleigh, and when we arrived, supper would be on the table.

Most days I did what I loved best—coloring and drawing in my books while Mrs. Miller taught Betty how to knit. True to Mr. Miller's word, Mrs. Miller taught us the alphabet and how to read and write, and so we were well prepared for school. However, conquering my stuttering problem was her biggest challenge.

"We simply must get that stuttering taken care of before you start school," she said. "I don't want the other children poking fun at you."

Sunday mornings we hustled about getting ready to go to church and Sunday school with the Millers. The old Baptist church was a couple of blocks from our house and diagonally across from Woodsville school where we would start first grade in the fall. Betty and I would skip down the road ahead of the Millers and then stop and wait for them to catch up.

When we got home from church, we would eat a light lunch. Then Betty and I would remain at the table to memorize our assigned Bible verses. I was good at memory work and could remember the verses after the first reading, but Betty struggled with them. As soon as I recited mine to Mrs. Miller, she would give me a big red apple and send me outside to play.

"Can't I stay in and wait for Betty? I need someone to play with," I would ask. I felt uneasy about leaving my sister, for I knew Mrs. Miller wasn't as patient with her as she was with me.

"No," she would usually say curtly. "She has to memorize her verse first without any distraction. If you can do it, so can she."

I would then run off to the swing in the backyard. I would wind and unwind myself in it until I was dizzy but still clutching my apple so I could eat it with Betty.

What's taking her so long? I would wonder. *I hope Mrs. Miller isn't scolding her.*

At last she would come bounding around the house, apple in hand. "Are you okay? What took you so long?" I would ask.

"I'm okay, but I just don't understand those silly Bible verses. They're so hard to learn."

"Look, I saved my apple so I could eat it with you."

We would smile at each other as we bit into our apples and sat down under a shade tree to eat them.

• • •

It was difficult at first to call the Millers Mum and Dad, but it became easier as time went by. And we were treated much nicer here than at the Sebold house.

More than four months had passed since our arrival, and although Mrs. Miller was very strict, she made sure that we had nice clothes and were warm and well fed. Mr. Miller was always caring, amusing, and good-hearted, and there was never any shortage of hugs or praises from them.

Betty and I were happy and carefree during the spring and summer months and looked forward to the weekends with Mr. Miller. We enjoyed following him around the yard as he puttered about, cutting his grass and trimming the bushes.

In the early spring he tilled a small plot of land for a vegetable garden, and Betty and I begged to help him with it. He dug the holes, and we sprinkled in the carrot, lettuce, and radish seeds. When it came time to plant the seedling potatoes, Mr. Miller preferred to plant them, for they had to be placed sliced-side down. But Betty and I dug the holes.

"Let's play a trick on him," I once whispered to Betty. "We'll get far ahead, dig a really big hole, and then push his feet into it."

After we finished digging a sizeable hole, we waited for him to catch up to us.

"My goodness, that's a pretty big hole you've dug. Are you going to bury me in there?" he joked.

"Yes," we said, laughing and grabbing his pant legs and ankles, trying to force him into the hole.

Playing along with our little game, he fell easily into the hole, then picked up the small spade and chased us. "You little rascals, I'm going to get you for this," he hollered as we scampered away.

We laughed and ran off in different directions but soon came back to finish the planting.

He always kept some hard candy called "humbugs" in his pockets. If we worked well, he treated us to some. They were small, striped candies that resembled tiny little pillows and came in different flavors. I chose the licorice or root beer, my favorite flavors.

Betty and I enjoyed a great summer with our new dad, and as he towed us into the house at the end of each day, he would often remark, "Why, I do declare, you're both as brown as the missus' Sunday biscuits."

• • •

The warm summer days were soon pushed aside by the crisp, cool days of September, and preparations were being made for our first school year. It was an exciting and scary time for us.

Mrs. Miller escorted us to school the first day. She returned to get us for lunch and again at the end of the school day until we got the hang of things.

The school was a one-room, red-brick building with a large furnace in the back. It had an entrance hallway with coat hooks along both sides. Shelves lined the back of the room where children put their lunch buckets. The school stood on a slight hill at the edge of the village where two dirt roads intersected. There was a wooded lot behind the school that led down to an old millpond. To the left of the school was a large playground and one small brick building that housed the boys' and girls' toilets.

Mrs. Patrick was my first teacher. She was slender and stiff and walked like a board. But she was a pleasant lady with short, curly, brown hair. Large-framed glasses perched at the top of her small, up-turned nose. She had a soft voice, and her smile seemed pasted to her face. I liked her at once.

My grade one class had the first row beside the left wall. The next row was grade two, and the others rows went on up to the eighth grade to the far right wall. Each day, Mrs. Patrick began by teaching the first grade, then worked her way up to the eighth grade, assigning work to each class as she moved along. There were forty students in all.

My stuttering became more pronounced during the early weeks of school, prompting Mrs. Miller to seek permission from the Children's Aid Society to have me homeschooled. Her request was denied, and I remained at the mercy of some of my classmates who enjoyed mimicking me. Within a couple of months, however, as I became more self-assured and excelled at my studies, my stuttering lessened and became troublesome only when I became nervous or overly excited.

I enjoyed my days at school. And as I was good at memorizing, spelling and reading were easy for me.

Art class was my favorite time of the day, but I struggled with arithmetic and hated it with a passion. Betty was quite good with numbers, so she helped me with my arithmetic, and I helped her with our spelling assignments.

In the evenings, under Mrs. Miller's ever-watchful eye, Betty and I sat at the kitchen table and worked on our homework. I drilled Betty over and over again on the twelve words we had to spell, and eventually she'd learn them perfectly — only to get several wrong on the next day's test. It upset me that she couldn't remember them. "How come you got some of your words wrong?" I would ask. "You got them all right last night."

"I just forgot how to spell them," she would whine.

"But how can you forget? They're right up in your head. You just look at them." I would shake my head, unable to understand her problem.

"Well, I'm better at arithmetic than you are," she would counter.

Mrs. Miller would then cut in. "Quit your quibbling this minute and get on with your homework!"

Just as Betty had trouble with memorization, I had difficulty writing the number 8, even though she showed me over and over again how to do it. I made two circles, one on top of the other, and fudged an "X" in between in an attempt to cheat, but she always caught me. I also hesitated over printing the letter "S," as it brought back memories of the time Richard Sebold dragged me into the outhouse.

Thursday was my favorite day of the week. Mrs. Henderson, a music teacher who traveled around to various schools in the county, stopped by for the weekly music lesson. At this time we were allowed to join in with the rest of the grades to learn about music.

She gave us each a song sheet and played the piano while we sang along. It was fun singing with the older kids, and she taught us many little songs, or "ditties," as she called them.

Betty and I enjoyed our school days and found many new playmates. I even had my first crush on a handsome boy named Walter McLean. One day, while spending the weekend with his grandparents down the road, Walter came over with another boy to play tag with Betty and me. He was chasing me around the trees, trying to tag me, and yelled, "I'm gonna fuck you when I catch you!"

That strange new word troubled me, for I didn't know what it meant he wanted to do to me, and so I bolted in the front door to tell Mr. and Mrs. Miller what he had threatened to do. I was surprised and unprepared for the commotion I caused.

The Millers stormed outdoors and ordered Betty and me inside to be dealt with later.

Mr. Miller grabbed Walter firmly by the ear and marched him down the road to have it out with his grandparents while Mrs. Miller waited on the front lawn. Betty and I sat inside, dreading Mrs. Miller's return. I knew we were in for a severe reprimand. Washing our mouths out with soap when we said something naughty or putting pepper on our tongues when we told fibs was her way of disciplining us.

"What did Walter say to you that made Mr. Miller so angry?" Betty asked.

"It's that *word* that's scrawled across the front of the road sign by Mrs. Tillman's house. Remember? I don't know what it means and he probably doesn't either, but it must be really bad."

Mrs. Miller returned to the house and admonished, "That young boy said a very naughty word, and I don't ever want to hear either of you saying it. It's a good thing you came and told us. That boy deserves a good dose of punishment."

Betty and I were relieved that we got off so easy this time.

On Monday, when I met up with Walter on the way to school, he was angry and called me a tattletale. "You got me into a whole mess of trouble," he said. "I got a big lickin' and had to sleep in the haymow in the barn all night with the stinky animals. I ain't ever gonna play with you again!"

"Well, I got my mouth washed out with soap," I lied. "And I don't ever wanna play with you either. So there!" I ran off to catch up with the rest of my friends.

• • •

It was a hot and sunny Sunday in mid-September when Mrs. Miller let us put on our favorite sun suits and sent us outside to play. My suit was a tan-and-white-striped seersucker with short pants, a front bib, and straps that crisscrossed in the back and buttoned to the bib in front. Betty's was identical but with blue and white stripes. We liked these little suits and felt so fresh and pretty in them.

Mrs. Miller often took a nap on Sunday afternoons when dinner was over and the dishes were cleaned and put away, leaving us in the care of Mr. Miller.

That day, Mr. Miller was out checking on his garden, but since it was Sunday, it was his "day of rest."

He walked over to where we were playing on the swing and said, "It's terribly hot." Wiping his brow with his red farmer's handkerchief, he added, "I'm going in to check on the missus and will bring you each a glass of cool lemonade."

He soon returned and handed us each a lemonade. We thanked him, and he smiled as we took a few quick sips. We were delighted when he took our hands and led us to a small park bench in the backyard. It was a wooden bench with wrought-iron sides, and it sat some distance from the house, just past the clothesline and under a cherry tree. The back of the bench faced the house and the front looked out over the garden.

"Come; let's set a spell," he said, "while we cool off a tad."

We snuggled up on either side of him, sipping our

lemonade and chatting on and on about school, telling him about some of the little ditties that Mrs. Henderson had taught us. I started to sing one of the songs to him, but stopped at once when I noticed him slowly unbuttoning the front of his trousers. *What's he doing?* I wondered.

I glanced over at Betty and she had a blank look on her face. We were both surprised as he pulled out his private parts for us to see. "Touch it," he said softly. "It won't bite you."

Betty shied away, but I was more obedient and trusting, and with some hesitancy, I reached over to touch it. "It's soft and warm," I said. "What's it for? What do you do with it?"

"Oh, I poke it in the missus at night."

"Doesn't it hurt her?" I asked, surprised at his strange answer.

"Naw, she's usually asleep. I'm gonna put it away now, but not a word of this to anyone. This must be our own little secret. Do you understand?"

"Yes," we both said, delighted to have a little secret to share with him.

After he finished buttoning up, he turned to me and said, "Now, let's hear that song about the little pig that your teacher taught you."

So I began to sing:
Betty Pringle, she had a pig,
Not too little, and not too big,
When it lived, it lived in clover,
Now he's dead, and that's all over!

"Now, I dare say, that's quite a nice little jingle," he said.

"But I feel sorry for the pig because it died," I pouted. "Do you think it died because it ate too much clover?"

"No, he was probably just old, and when we get old, we die."

"Do you think he'll ever come back?"

"No, he probably went to pig heaven and is very happy there. As for you, little girl, you ask far too many questions. I'm going to leave you both now to check on your mum and listen to the world news."

That night as we were getting into our nighties, we started talking about our little secret.

"Where do you think he pokes it in her?" Betty asked.

"I don't know," I said. "Maybe her bellybutton."

We both giggled and checked our bellybuttons.

"That's probably the place, all right," we agreed as we climbed into bed feeling smug about our little secret.

The Children's Aid Report reveals:

An uncle of ours had met with Mr. Miller in town and asked permission to bring our father to visit us. Mrs. Miller sought the advice of the Children's Aid, who left the decision to her. She refused to let us see our father, believing that it might unsettle us.

9

A Stranger Arrives

One day in the early fall, a knock on the front door caused much excitement. Mr. and Mrs. Miller's son, Edmund, returned home from the air force. The news spread throughout the small town, and soon the little house was filled with friends.

Mrs. Miller put the tea kettle on to boil, and some of the neighbors brought over cookies and pies. The aroma of the freshly baked goodies filled the kitchen. It was an exciting day for everyone.

Edmund arrived dressed in his blue air force suit and cap and was quite a dashing figure—his tall, thin frame filling the doorway.

I was fascinated by the shiny silver buttons so evenly spaced down the front of his jacket and the silver wings and decorations adorning his left shoulder. Betty and I couldn't take our eyes off this new stranger, and he finally turned to Mrs. Miller and remarked tartly, "For Pete's sake, can't you tell those little girls to stop staring at me?"

She responded by shooing us outside to play.

When things calmed down the next day, Edmund surprised Betty and me with two toy soldier dolls—an air force doll all dressed in blue for Betty and an army doll dressed in a brown uniform for me. "The air force doll is me," he said, "and the army doll is my buddy, Jim."

We named them Edmund and Jim, and though we were fascinated and thrilled with the new boy dolls, we didn't know just how to play with them. We finally set them up on our dresser and continued to play with the worn dolls we'd gotten at the shelter.

• • •

A few days following his homecoming, Edmund surprised his parents by telling them that he had taken an English bride while stationed in England. He told them her name was Elizabeth and that she would be arriving in a few days to meet them.

"I've secured a job in Toronto, and we'll be living in the suburb of Scarborough, close to my work," he said to Mrs. Miller. "Our house will be ready for us to move into in November. I'd like very much for Dad and you to consider moving in with us. There's plenty of room, and the house is near stores and medical facilities."

"Goodness," Mrs. Miller said, "I've never even thought of something like that. Your dad and I will have to discuss it at some length. But what will I do with the girls? They've just settled into their new school and are feeling quite at home here now."

"Can't you return them to the Children's Aid?" he asked.

I was sitting at the kitchen table, coloring in my books, and eavesdropping on their conversation in the living room. My ears perked up at the mention of the Children's Aid, and as I strained to listen, I heard Mrs. Miller say, "Well, I've grown very fond of Bonnie and have asked the Children's Aid on several occasions for permission to adopt her. The two of them are too much for me to handle. However, they have steadfastly refused to separate them. Their decision has upset me to no end."

I didn't understand the meaning of "adopt," but an uneasy feeling in the pit of my stomach told me something bad was about to happen. *They're gonna take us away again*, I thought. Panic began to grip me, and my hand froze to the coloring book as my fingers squeezed hard on the crayon. *"Please, please, don't let them take us away,"* I prayed as I felt the tears catching in my throat. I shoved myself away from the table and ran outside to get some fresh air and find Betty. *Should I tell her what I overheard – that we might be taken away again? Or should I wait? I don't want to upset her.* I was tossing it over in my mind, wanting so much to share this news with her but afraid to do it.

I found Betty in the backyard, swinging high on the swing, her blonde hair flying behind her as she flew forward and then partially covering her face as she came back. I heard her singing our favorite swing song:

Oh, how I love to go up in the swing,
Up in the air so blue,
Oh, I do think it's the most pleasantest thing,
Ever a child can do.
Up in the air and over the wall,
'Til I can see so wide . . . .

"Look, Bonnie, I can go so high that my toes are even with the rooftop," she shouted gleefully down to me.

"I just hope the rope doesn't break, or you'll fly through the air like a bird and land like a dead duck," I called back. She was having so much fun that I decided not to tell her.

Edmund's wife arrived late on a Sunday evening to meet the family.

Betty and I sat on the living room carpet and listened as she chatted away about her life in England, about the war, and about how she had met Edmund. I was taken in by her — the way she neatly crossed her nylon-covered legs; the black, open-toed, high-heeled shoes adorning her tiny feet; the dark curly locks tumbling over her shoulders onto her beautiful red suit; the scent of her floral perfume filling the room; and the sound of her English accent.

"Isn't she pretty?" Betty asked as we readied ourselves for bed. "I wanna be pretty like her when I grow up."

A few days later they said their good-byes and left for Toronto. I was sad to see them leave so soon, and I was left wondering what was planned for us. I never did mention anything to Betty about the conversation I had overheard. *Maybe they changed their minds about sending us away,* I hoped and prayed.

• • •

It was hard to believe how fast the year had flown by, and our second Christmas with the Millers was upon us. Betty and I, feeling right at home now, trudged through the snow with Mr. Miller to the woods to pick out our Christmas tree. We had fun decorating it, and in addition to the popcorn strings, we learned at school how to make decorations with colored construction paper. We pasted rings of green and red circles together to make long garlands to go all around the tree. We were proud of the job we had done.

"This is the prettiest tree ever, isn't it, Bonnie?" Betty said proudly, her eyes sparkling with excitement.

"It is! It is!" I agreed exuberantly while checking it one more time to make sure everything was perfect.

"Look, Mrs. Miller, isn't it beautiful?" she said, grabbing her hand and pulling her away from her kitchen chores.

"You've done a fine job," she said, gathering us close, giving us big hugs, and planting kisses on our foreheads. "Come on, now; we'll have some cocoa and cookies and then it's off to bed for the both of you."

It seemed that I had barely dozed off when I awoke to the sound of the doorknob being turned. "Merry Christmas!" Mrs. Miller said cheerfully as she opened our bedroom door. "Hurry and get dressed. Santa has been here, and you can come out and open your presents."

We threw on our clothes and ran out to the tree.

"There are lots of presents — many more than last year," I whispered to Betty as we sat down on opposite sides of the tree.

"Here," Mrs. Miller said, "you can open these first." She handed us each a large, identically wrapped present.

We tore off the paper and opened our boxes. "Ooh, it's a beautiful red cardigan," I said. Betty and I lifted the cardigans out of the boxes and held them against our bodies.

"They're sooo pretty," Betty said as she hurried to try hers on.

"Yes, they're very nice. I requested the shelter to send you both a sweater for Christmas, so after dinner you must write them thank-you notes."

My other gifts were a pencil box, more coloring books, storybooks, crayons, and a big box of colored pencils. I was thrilled. I got everything I wished for and more.

Mr. Miller handed us our last gifts. "Here, this is something special," he said.

We tore into the boxes and found brand-new, shiny pairs of CCM bob skates. They had double runner blades attached to a metal base that fit on the bottom of our shoes. Two straps went over the top of our feet and latched, while another one latched around our ankles.

Betty and I were eager to try them out, but we weren't sure how to put them on.

"Here," Mr. Miller said, kneeling down beside us. "I'll show you how they work. Pay close attention now; I'm going to show you only once. After breakfast you can get bundled up and go outside to try them out. There are some icy patches in the garden."

Betty and I spent the biggest part of the day playing outside on our new skates and were cold and hungry by the time Mrs. Miller had Christmas dinner on the table. Taking our places at the table, we bowed our heads as Mrs. Miller said the blessing. She then served a tasty holiday dinner, complete with plum pudding with brandy sauce for dessert.

Betty and I were so wound up over all the excitement of the day that we had a hard time settling down to sleep. It was late at night before we ended our chatter and dozed off.

A few days after Christmas, the Millers called us into the living room and asked us to be seated. "We have some news to share with you," Mrs. Miller said.

I sensed what was coming and wanted to plug my ears and run from the room.

"We have to tell you that Dad Miller and I will be moving to Toronto to live with Edmund and his wife. The Children's Aid won't let us take you out of Norfolk County, so they'll be coming early in January to take you to another home."

I barely heard her voice. It seemed so far away.

Betty and I were too stunned to utter a word, and we stared down at our laps.

"We're very sorry. We've grown very fond of you," Mr. Miller said. "But your mum's eyesight is beginning to fail her, and I fear she'll need some help soon."

"But I don't wanna go! Can't we help her?" I begged.

Betty and I started crying and clung to each other.

"There, there, now," Mrs. Miller said as she put her arms around us. "Things are never as bad as they seem. I'm sure they'll find a nice, new home for you. I'll make you both a cup of hot chocolate, and after a good night's sleep, you'll feel much better."

"I'm never gonna feel better!" I blubbered. "I don't wanna leave!"

It was a terrible night for us, and after hearing our cries, Mrs. Miller came and sat on the side of the bed. "There, there," she said, putting her arms around us. "You must try to get some sleep. The Sandman will be coming soon."

"But he's only gonna bring me a bad dream," I wailed.

She patted me one more time and planted a kiss on my cheek. "Things will be okay," she said, as she quietly left the room, leaving the door ajar for us.

• • •

It was a cold, blustery day in early January when the social worker arrived to pick us up. Betty and I spent the morning packing our belongings in paper bags. We were sad that we didn't get a chance to return to school to say good-bye to our friends, but nothing equaled the pain and sorrow we felt at leaving the Millers.

Soon it was time to go. Mrs. Miller held my beautiful burgundy coat for me as I reluctantly slipped my arms into the sleeves. She watched as I fumbled nervously to button it. *It fits me perfectly now,* I thought, *but I don't feel very special in it.*

Once we were both bundled up, Mrs. Miller took our hands and walked with us out to the waiting car. The lawn was covered with freshly fallen snow. It looked so beautiful, sparkling in the morning sun that I hated to disturb it and hesitated to step off the bottom step of the porch. I was lost in my thoughts when I felt Mrs. Miller gently tug my hand.

The social worker patiently held open the back door of the car as we kissed Mrs. Miller good-bye. Wiping the tears from my eyes with the hem of her apron, she gave me one last big hug, pried my arms from around her waist, and helped me into the car. The door slammed shut with a solid thud as if closing off our happiness.

Mrs. Miller brushed a light dusting of snow off the side window so she could see our faces, and we waved at her through tear-filled eyes as the car backed out of the driveway. As we turned out onto the road, I looked back briefly at my one-way tracks in the snow and saw Mrs. Miller still standing in place. *Will I ever see her again? Will she miss us?* I wondered, sniffling and wiping my wet nose on my sleeve.

10

First Impressions

Betty and I spoke not a word on the way to our next destination. We were both sad. Empty of all feeling and emotions, I felt as hollow inside as a chocolate Easter bunny.

As we sped away, the social services woman explained to us that because of our hurried removal from the Millers, we were going to live in a temporary home until something else could be arranged. "The lady here will make arrangements for you to see a dentist and a doctor. Then I'm sure we'll be able to find you a nice new home."

Betty gave me a weak smile, and I said, "Wouldn't it be nice if we went back to the house where we hid under the tablecloth? Remember? Where all the kids were?"

She nodded, her eyes laughing at the thought of it.

A week passed before we were taken back to the shelter to be readied for pickup by our new foster parents. The social worker who was brushing my hair noticed me nibbling away at my fingernails and chatted amicably in an attempt to cheer me. "Did you know that you're going to a small farm where there are chickens, cows, and pigs?" she asked with a lilt in her voice. "Isn't that exciting?"

"There are chickens?" My thoughts raced back to the Sebold farm as I pictured chickens pecking at our food. *I hope they aren't taking us back there,* I thought. "Are we going back to the Sebolds?" I held my breath waiting for her reply.

"Oh no. You're going to a brand-new home. You're going to live with a Mr. and Mrs. Bender."

Relaxing, I smiled at Betty, and, hoping for more good news, she asked, "Will Bobby be there?"

I searched the lady's face, expecting an answer. But she ignored the question. "Come, Betty, let's get your hair brushed now so you'll look pretty for the Bender family. They'll be here soon."

We watched from the large second-story windows as a black car pulled up in front of the building. "Oh, that's them now. You girls scurry on ahead. We don't want to keep them waiting," the social services lady said, obviously excited.

But I wasn't excited. I was nervous and afraid, reluctant to leave. I plodded down the stairs, sliding my hand slowly along the stair railing. I wanted to go back to the Millers where I felt safe. I didn't want a *new* home.

"Come on, let's not be poky," the lady said as she pushed gently on my back. And as we came out onto the sidewalk, the Benders got out of their car to meet us. After greeting us warmly, Mrs. Bender turned to the social worker and asked, "Now, how old did you say the girls are?"

"They'll be seven years old in April, I believe, and they'll be finishing the last part of the first grade. All their documents are in here," she said, handing Mrs. Bender a large white envelope.

Mr. Bender helped Betty and me into the car where I sat, muddled and confused, squirming around to get comfortable. Watching trees pass by and feeling every bump in the road, I was lost in my thoughts, thinking about this new home and wondering what it would be like. *Will these people be as nice to us as Mom and Dad Miller? Where will we go to school?*

Betty reached over to touch my hand as if she knew what I was thinking. The Benders hadn't spoken a word to us, and we were feeling awkward and ignored.

"Should I say something to them?" Betty whispered, leaning close to my ear.

"Like what?"

"I dunno. Maybe ask how much farther we have to go?"

I shook my head and leaned back against the seat.

The long, narrow lane that led to the Bender farm was lined with trees on both sides. The barn and sheds were on the opposite side of the main road. The house was a white, two-story frame structure with black shutters. It sat high on a bluff, nestled among tall pines and overlooking a large lake.

What immediately caught my eye as we rolled to a stop was a huge old tree. From the lowest limb hung a fat rope with an old tire tied to it. Nudging Betty and pointing to the swing, I whispered, "Look at the funny swing."

Her eyes widened, and I pointed to the lake, "And look at all the water out there."

We pressed our noses close to the windows to get a better view of our new surroundings and, lost in a moment of excitement, grabbed each other's hand.

As we got out of the car, Mr. Bender pointed to the lake and said, "That's Lake Erie out there. When springtime comes, I'll be setting my traps down there to catch muskrats, and you can come along and watch."

Betty and I smiled and shrugged; we didn't know anything about muskrats.

In the days following, we learned that the huge tree on the lawn was an old mulberry tree and that we were living on an apple-orchard farm. Betty and I could hardly wait for warmer weather so we could go down the cliff and play along the lakeshore.

As we trailed Mr. Bender into the house, the porch door slammed loudly behind me. "Hang on to the door! Don't let it slam like that!" Mr. Bender snapped, giving me an angry look.

"I'm sorry," I choked, feeling hurt at being scolded already.

• • •

Once we were inside, Mrs. Bender pointed to a cot by the kitchen wall. "There, you can both sit over there until we get things squared away."

We promptly did as we were told and watched as they unloaded some groceries and Mr. Bender lugged in our brown bags, setting them near our feet.

"Well, I got chores to do," he said abruptly. "Mary will tend to you now." With a quick nod, he headed out of the house.

As he walked away, I noticed that he was a tall, lanky man. He was nice-looking, with blue eyes and dark, wavy hair that was graying a bit at the temples. A pair of striped suspenders, worn over a dark flannel shirt, held up his trousers and made him appear taller yet. Comparing him with Mr. Miller, who was short and stocky, I felt a bit frightened by his height. I was sure there would be no playful snapping of *those* striped suspenders the way I had snapped Mr. Miller's as I sat on his lap while he read a book.

Would he even read me a book? I wondered. I was missing the Millers even more.

Mrs. Bender was a short, chubby lady with curly black hair; flashing green eyes; a clear, porcelain complexion; and a full, round face. And although she was pleasant and had an easy smile, she could turn stern at a moment's notice. Her laugh was high pitched and cackling. She always seemed absorbed in her work and had little to say to Betty and me.

Feeling awkward and shy as I watched her prepare the table for supper, I hoped to start a conversation by pointing to a picture on a small stand and asking, "Who are these people?"

She stopped her work and picked up the picture. "These are my children. This is May, our oldest daughter. This is Charles, or Chuck, as we call him. And these are Jack, Margaret, and Doug," she said, pointing to each of them. "They all work in town except Doug. They come to visit on occasion when they have some time off. Doug is the youngest and is at school now. He'll be home soon."

Not another boy! I thought. I glanced at Betty and frowned, seeing the fear in her eyes.

Mrs. Bender set the picture down and was going back to her work when she looked out the kitchen window and said, "Oh, here comes Doug now."

The door swung open, and Doug came in, setting his lunch bucket on a chair and tossing his heavy coat onto the kitchen cot. Taking a few steps backward, he removed his peaked cap and twirled it swiftly through the air, landing it precisely on top of his coat.

Show-off, I thought. He was sweating, and the musky stench of his body odor was overwhelming. His presence seemed to fill up the only open area of the small kitchen.

I looked him over from head to toe, wondering what to make of him. I wasn't sure of his age but thought he might be at least fifteen. He was a round-faced, heavyset, muscular fellow with beady green eyes that were set so close together there was hardly room for his beaklike nose—a nose that went well with his sneering, lopsided grin. He wore a green plaid shirt, blue trousers, and a pair of black farm boots with an orange rim circling the top edge. "Who are those little twerps?" he asked, jutting his chin in our direction. "And how old are they?"

"That's Bonnie, and that's Betty," she replied, pointing to us as if we were just a pair of fence posts. "They'll be seven in a few months and will be starting school next week."

"You mean I gotta walk to school with them?" he sneered.

I gritted my teeth. I wasn't happy with him and inched myself back against the wall. I was getting sharp hunger pangs now, and the smell of the food took my mind off him.

Ignoring his rude remarks, his mother simply said, "Oh, Doug, behave yourself. Grab a chair and let's have supper."

• • •

Betty and I soon found that there was lots of work for us to do on this farm. At the Millers' we had only a few light household chores, like polishing the furniture and tidying our room, but here there were pigs to slop, pens to clean, eggs to gather, plus a few chores in the house. But we tried not to complain as we hoped to fit into this family and wanted so much for them to like us. We already knew that even though Mr. Bender was usually easygoing, he was also quick to anger. Betty and I felt uneasy around him, and if we sensed he was in a bad mood, we would try to mind our p's and q's, as Mrs. Miller always said, and be on our best behavior.

A few days after our arrival, Mr. Bender handed me a six-quart, wooden basket and led me into the chicken coop to teach me how to gather eggs. There were about fifteen chicken-nest boxes nailed to each side of the hen house, about a foot off the floor. I noticed that some of them had chickens in them and others were empty.

"Here," he said, as he walked over to a nest with a chicken on it, "watch carefully, for this will be your job from now on. Gently slip your hand under her side near the back of the hen and remove the egg from beneath. Be slow and careful, or she might peck you." He explained that a *good* hen lays an egg a day but will sit on it for a while before jumping off the nest. Then she'll cackle to the rest of the hens to let them know she's done her work for the day.

"Some nests may already have an egg in them," he continued, "so collect all the eggs, put them in the basket, and try not to break any. Do you think you can handle all this?"

I nodded, excited about my new job.

The next day, I set about to collect the eggs. I wanted Betty to come with me, as I was feeling a bit nervous. But she had her own chores to do. I was doing quite well, until I reached under one nasty chicken and she pecked my hand. Surprised, I jerked my hand away, and she flew off her nest onto the floor. I looked for her egg, but the nest was empty. Feeling certain I had frightened her before she had had a chance to lay her egg, I watched as she stood confused beneath her nest, her feathers all ruffled. I grabbed and straddled her, hoping to somehow squeeze her egg out. I didn't want Mr. Bender to be angry with me or to lose the job he had trusted to me.

On his way to slop the pigs, he peeked into the coop to see how I was doing and caught me sitting astride the hen. "What on earth are you doing, child? Get off that chicken before you hurt it!"

"She didn't lay her egg. I must've scared her. I was only trying to help her get it out," I wailed as I eased myself off her back.

"They'll lay an egg when they're darn good and ready," he said, shaking his head at my useless antics.

I was happy he didn't seem too upset with me, but as he watched the chicken hobble away, he turned to scold me. "You see, you silly little girl, you've probably broken her back!"

My heart sank. "I didn't mean to hurt it, honestly I didn't," I whimpered.

"Well, I just hope you've learned your lesson. If she doesn't come around soon, she just might be our Sunday dinner."

I felt terrible about hurting the chicken but consoled myself by thinking that maybe it wasn't a *good* hen anyway.

• • •

Betty and I didn't mind helping out in the barn, but we didn't like being in there alone with Doug. Knowing we were afraid of the farm animals, he found countless ways to scare us. He enjoyed grabbing us and dangling us up over the top board of the pigsty while the pigs squealed and nudged at our bare legs. We were terrified, certain the pigs would bite us.

Other times he would throw us on the back of a horse while it was tied in the stall and laugh as the horse tried to shake us off. Clutching the horse's mane and hanging on for dear life, we would scream at him to get us off.

Mr. Bender, hearing the ruckus from the hayloft, would shout down at him. "Behave yourself, Doug. Quit scaring the hell outta those girls."

This stopped him for a while, but sooner or later he'd be back to his mean tricks.

"He's a big bully," I said to Betty. "Let's just keep away from him."

Doug was going rabbit hunting one day and coaxed us into a shed to see his white ferret. Removing the animal from its cage, he tried his best to frighten us by shoving it toward our faces. We instinctively backed away, and the ferret turned and sank its teeth into Doug's forefinger and wouldn't let go.

"Help! Get it off of me! Get it off of me!" he yelled at us as he squirmed in pain.

We scurried off, hid behind some bushes to giggle, and watched as he struggled to get the animal off his finger.

"Serves him right," I said. "He deserves what he gets."

"Yeah. Hope it bites his stupid finger off," Betty agreed.

When Betty and I arrived back at the house, Doug's mother was dressing his bloody finger. He was whining, and complaining to her about how we had run off, refusing to help him. When Mrs. Bender had finished dressing his wound, she scolded us and sent us to our room.

We were upset for the scolding but happy that we had gotten even with Doug.

• • •

One day the Benders had some errands to do in town and would be gone most of the day. They left us with Doug to make some stew for supper and had written instructions on how to prepare it.

Betty and I peeled the vegetables while Doug cooked the meat in a large, black cast-iron kettle on the wood-burning stove. Even though Betty and I were wary of being alone with Doug, we had fun cooking and tasting the stew until we were sure it was just right for supper.

When the Benders returned, I opened the door for Mrs. Bender as she carried in some grocery bags. "The stew's all ready to eat!" I said excitedly, feeling proud that she had trusted us with such a task and that we had accomplished it. I could hardly wait to eat.

Betty and I got the bowls from the cupboard while Mrs. Bender prepared to wipe off the red-and-white-checkered oil tablecloth.

"Hmm," she wondered aloud. "Where in the world did I put my dishrag?"

"Doug used it last," I said.

"Did not. You did," he countered.

"Did not."

"Did so."

"Oh, for Pete's sake, quit your bickering. I'll just get another one. It's bound to turn up sooner or later."

After she'd finished wiping the table, Betty and I put around the dishes and spoons while Doug lifted the big pot of stew and set it in the center of the table. Mrs. Bender reached in, took a spoonful of the hot stew, blew briefly on it, and with some noticeable apprehension, sampled it. We held our breath as we waited for her response.

"Mmm, seems like you did a pretty good job on the stew," she said with an approving smile as she meted out a generous scoop for each of us.

She tipped the kettle slightly, dipped out the last scoop of stew, and noticed something dangling from the ladle. "What in the world is *that* hanging there, Mary?" Mr. Bender asked.

"Well, for heaven's sake, I don't believe it!" she exclaimed, examining it up close. "It's my dish rag. How in the world did it ever get in the stew?" She looked around the table at us. We all laughed, shaking our heads.

"You said it was bound to turn up sooner or later," Betty said.

"Yes, I know, but I certainly *never* expected it to turn up in the stew!"

I made a funny face and giggled. "I guess we'll all have Dish-Rag Stew."

"You're right, because that's all there is to eat," Mrs. Bender said.

I was so happy she wasn't upset with us but seemed to enjoy the whole incident.

Enjoyable moments were rare with the Benders, but we still hoped to fit in and be part of a happy family.

11

A Bad Feeling in My Bones

I hated the first winter months on the farm. It seemed so cold and lonely compared to the small village we had left. There were no lights twinkling across the street, few cars driving along the country road, and no visitors ever stopping by. The winter days seemed colder than I could remember, and as there was no electricity in this rural area, darkness fell much too soon.

Betty and I were allowed an hour or so after supper to sit at the table and draw or read by the dim light of a kerosene lamp, but we were hustled off to bed long before we were sleepy.

Sitting in our beds in the darkness, we talked about the Millers, reliving the fun we had in the evenings as we lay on our bellies at their feet, playing Snakes and Ladders or Chinese Checkers while Mrs. Miller knitted and Mr. Miller puffed on his pipe and read the newspaper. The radio was always playing in the background, and we would often stop what we were doing when Mr. Miller tuned in to a favorite mystery story or comedy program.

"Wouldn't it be nice if she'd come up and tuck us in after we said our prayers?" I said, looking toward the stairs.

"I asked her once, but she said we were too old for that kinda nonsense," Betty said.

"But we forgot to say our prayers," I reminded her. We both jumped out of bed and kneeled to say our prayers as Mrs. Miller had taught us.

"Wouldn't it be nice if the Millers lived nearby so we could at least visit with them?" I asked. But there was no answer. Betty had fallen asleep.

I lay awake, listening to the wind howling, and thought about Mrs. Bender. She was usually friendly toward Betty and me but never gave us any hugs, kisses, or words of praise, even though we tried our hardest to do as we were told. She often scolded us for little things but never for lack of good manners. Mrs. Miller had taught us well.

At the table one day, I was brave enough to say to Doug, "You're not supposed to talk with your mouth full, and your elbows aren't supposed to be on the table either."

Mrs. Bender turned to me with a scowl. "Well, will you look at who's trying to be Little Miss Uppity? You'd think she was the Queen of England or something. If there's any correcting to do here, young lady, believe me, I'll do it!"

"I guess that puts you in *your* place," Doug smirked.

I stuck my tongue out at him, but he was right. I was put in my place and kept my mouth shut after that.

• • •

In January Betty and I started back to a new school to finish up our first grade. Because of our move, we had fallen behind and had some catching up to do. The school was a couple of miles from our home, and rather than take the dirt side road, Doug showed us a shortcut through the fields, down farmers' lanes with battery-powered electric fences, and out to the plowed main road. This was hard during the winter months when the snow was deep. Betty and I had short farm boots that came up only a few inches above our ankles, and the snow got over the tops and into them, soaking our stockings. And the hard edges of the boots chafed our legs. But if we complained or lagged behind, Doug took pleasure in giving us a quick cuff to the back of our heads.

By the time we arrived at school, we were both so cold and my cheeks would freeze and become white and bumpy. But Mrs. Keller, our teacher, was nice enough to let us sit near the furnace until we thawed out.

During warmer months, the walk through the fields on our way home from school was more fun. Betty and I searched for morels and wild strawberries or picked wildflowers for Mrs. Bender. Other times we removed our shoes and socks and waded barefoot in the small stream, trying to catch polliwogs and enjoying the tickle of the soft mud as it squished between our toes.

Betty and I were finishing first grade, while Doug was repeating his final year of grade eight and had perhaps failed some earlier grades, for he was nearly sixteen and the biggest kid in school. He walked to school with us, but since Betty and I were in the lower grades, we were let out of school an hour earlier than Doug.

We would walk along the main road with our schoolmates until it was time to take the shortcut through the pastures, and then we would enjoy our little adventures without Doug being around to annoy us.

It was a beautiful, warm day in late spring when Betty and I said good-bye to our schoolmates and carefully climbed through the two strands of barbed-wire fencing separating the road from the farmer's field to make our way home. The little creek was flooded by spring rains, so we stopped to play in it, looking for frogs and turtles.

Time was slipping away. "We better get a move on before Doug catches up to us," I said to Betty, grabbing her hand to hurry her along.

We headed toward the gray, dilapidated barn that stood in the middle of a farmer's field. We passed it every day but never dared to go inside for fear of getting punished. But because of our childhood curiosity, we often peeked through the wide cracks between the boards. We saw that it was mainly used for storing straw and hay for farm animals, but sometimes we'd spot some stray cats lurking around inside.

As we neared the barn that day, we heard Doug call out and turned to see him hurrying up the knoll toward us.

"Hey, wait up, you two," he called out.

"Pretend you don't hear him," I said to Betty. I clutched her hand again, and we quickened our pace.

"Hey, wait up! Wait up! There's somethin' in the barn I wanna show you!"

"What do you think he wants to show us?" Betty asked.

"I don't know, but I don't trust him one little bit. Let's just keep on going." I was upset because we had dawdled at the creek.

"Ask him what he wants to show us," Betty pleaded, curiosity getting the best of her.

"What do you wanna show us?" I yelled back over my shoulder, not slowing my steps.

"There's some baby kittens in the barn. I found their nest this morning," he shouted back.

"Wow, baby kittens! Let's wait and see them!" Betty begged, pulling me to a stop.

I hesitated, but soon her excitement rubbed off on me, and I forgot about being wary of Doug.

He was still huffing and puffing as we neared the barn, and suddenly I started to feel uneasy. I looked at his face and saw a sly, twisted grin. *He's up to no good,* I thought. I could feel it in my bones.

"Are you sure there are baby kittens in there?" I asked, looking him straight in the eye.

"Sure," he said, hunching his shoulders. "Would I lie to you?"

"Yeah," I shot back.

He swung to swat me, but I ducked.

When we came to the barn door, Doug kicked it open, grabbed Betty's arm, and dragged her inside before I realized what was happening.

She struggled to pull away from his grasp, but she was no match for his strength.

I tried to grab her, but Doug pushed her to the floor inside, then turned, shoved me backward, and slammed the door in my face. I heard the sound of metal against metal as the latch slid into place, locking me out. I heard Betty's frightened voice calling out for me, "Bonnie! Bonnie! Help me!"

"What are you doing?" I yelled at Doug through a crack in the door.

"I'm showing Betty the kittens. You g'won and fetch the cows up!" he hollered back.

"No. I wanna see them too!" I cried, pounding hard on the door. "Lemme in! Lemme in!"

He didn't answer, and so I slammed my shoulder against the door, hoping the latch would give way. But it held tight. *He's lying about the kittens. I know he is! He's up to somethin' bad.*

Really scared now, I ran hard to the far side of the barn. Groping my way through waist-tall weeds and stumbling over rocks, I searched frantically for a wide enough space between the boards, one where I might get a good look at what was going on inside.

At last I found one—a good, one-inch gap—and peered hard through the crack. The horrible sight I saw sent shivers up my spine. I felt sick. My little sister lay motionless in the straw; her left arm flopped out to one side. Her face was milk white, her blonde hair mingled with the golden straw. Doug was thrashing around on top of her, and I cried hysterically, "He's killed her! He's killed her!" My head felt like it was going to explode as I pounded and pounded on the boards, screaming at the top of my lungs at him. My knees weakened, buckled beneath me, and I fell to the ground sobbing. I was completely helpless, feeling guilty for not being able to protect my sister. I looked at my knuckles. They were raw and bloody.

I forced myself to peer through the crack again. Doug was kneeling now and appeared to be shaking Betty by the shoulders. I stared hard through the opening, straining my eyes in an effort to see them. I was sure she was starting to stir. I felt my heart pounding against the boards. *She's alive! She's alive! Oh God, she's alive!*

I watched him pull her up from the straw pile, and feeling an overpowering sense of relief, my feet barely touched the ground as I bounded toward the barn door to wait for her.

Betty was dazed and crying, unaware of her surroundings as Doug let her out of the barn. I glared at him as I threw my arms around her and tried my best to comfort her as she heaved and sobbed uncontrollably. I tried to straighten her hair and comb out the straw with my fingers. Then I bent down to brush the straw off her little brown-wool skirt. It was then that I saw it—bright red blood flowing heavily between her trembling legs. My stomach churned. "What did you do to her?!" I yelled at Doug, who was moving on away from us. "She's bleeding all down her legs! You big bully! What did you do to her?!"

He stopped, turned briefly, and saw the blood.

"I'm gonna tell on you! You hurt her! You hurt her really bad!" I screamed.

He seemed upset and frightened now. "You shut your big fat mouth and don't say anything. If Mom asks what happened, you tell her that she cut herself when she was crawling through the barbed-wire fence. You got that!"

"I'm gonna tell the truth. You aren't gonna get away with it!" I screamed defiantly.

"You do, and you'll get a taste of the same medicine!" he threatened, jabbing his finger hard into my shoulder.

"Bloody bugger," I muttered under my breath. "I hate your guts."

As we continued through the fields and down the cow path with Betty still sobbing in my arms, I noticed Doug had quickened his pace and was now quite a distance ahead of us. It was obvious that he wanted to get home first to tell his side of the story, knowing that his mother would believe him instead of us.

When Betty's sobbing quieted a bit, I asked softly, "Can you tell me what he did to you?"

"I don't know," she sobbed. "I was so scared, really scared! He hurt me somehow; then everything went black. I just don't remember!"

"How do you feel now?"

"I feel sore down here," she mumbled, cradling her hands below her stomach.

"I just hate him," I said, leading her by the hand through the pasture gate and latching it after us. The blood was still flowing down her legs and pooling on top of her blue canvas shoes.

We walked in silence the rest of the way home, my arm still wrapped around her trembling shoulders.

By the time we entered the kitchen door, Doug had already told Mrs. Bender his story, and she was waiting for us. She didn't question us as to what had happened. In a way, I was glad she didn't ask me, because I would have lied. I was too afraid of Doug's threat.

Mrs. Bender lifted Betty's skirt, carefully removed her bloody panties, and sat her down on a small stool next to the stove.

I tiptoed over to the stairs that led to our bedroom and sat down on the third step from the bottom. *Why did we listen to him? I should have known better. How could I have been so stupid?* I thought.

Mrs. Bender took a red-rimmed, white enamel basin from the sink and put it between Betty's feet. I sat silent and transfixed, hugging my legs, resting my chin on my knees, still wondering what horrible thing Doug had done to her. Everything seemed to be moving in slow motion as I watched the goings-on in the kitchen from the dark staircase.

My eyes were drawn to the blood as it trickled slowly down the side of the white pan. I noticed how it stood out, stark against the white enamel, and how the color of the blood matched the red rim.

Soon the silence was broken and I was shaken from my trance by Mrs. Bender's shriek. She turned to look at Doug, who was sitting like a statue in the farthest corner of the room. "Tell me again," she demanded, "what happened!"

Before Doug could reply, Mrs. Bender noticed me sitting on the stairs and yelled, "You! Get to your room at once and don't come down until you're told!"

I took one last glance at Betty, bolted upright, and flew up the steps. I hated leaving my sister, so I kept the door slightly opened to feel closer to her.

I waited and waited for Betty to come to our room. I listened at the door, but all was strangely quiet downstairs. I then went over to the window, looked down onto the driveway, and saw that the car was gone. *Maybe they took her to the doctor,* I thought.

Then it hit me. I was alone in the house with Doug. Terrified, I grabbed a wooden chair and pushed it firmly against the door, hoping it would keep him from getting in.

Night came, and the room grew dark. I climbed into bed, wrapped the blankets tightly around my arms, and covered my head. *No one's gonna get me*, I told myself. As I lay awake listening for any sounds from below, I thought over everything that had happened. I was worried about Betty and prayed that she would be okay. At last, I drifted off to sleep.

Later in the night I awoke with a start as I heard the scraping of the chair against the floor, but then relaxed, as I soon felt Betty snuggling in beside me. Crawling out from beneath the blankets, I peered through the darkness at her face. "Where were you? Are you okay?"

"They took me to see a doctor, but I'm sooo tired, I just wanna sleep now," she said.

"Okay. We'll talk in the morning."

I covered up my head again and wiggled my back up against her. Happy that she was home, I fell back to sleep.

When morning came, Betty tugged at the blankets around my head. "Bonnie, wake up," she said. "What's the matter with your silly head? Why do you have it all covered up?"

"I was alone last night, and I was scared. I didn't know where Doug was. I wanted to make sure he wasn't gonna get me. I'm gonna sleep with my head covered up forever and ever."

"Doug stayed at home. Mr. Bender told him to stay in his room or there'd be hell to pay. Mr. Bender waited in the car while Mrs. Bender took me in to see Dr. Archer."

"What did she tell the doctor? Are you gonna be okay? I was so worried about you."

"She told him I caught and tore myself while climbing through a barbed-wire fence. The doctor asked her to wait in the waiting room. Then he took me into another room and asked me to lie down on a table so he could look at me."

"What did he say? I wanna hear everything."

"He checked me all over and asked me to tell him exactly what happened and said he didn't want to hear any 'barbed-wire fence' story. So I told him that Doug pulled me into the barn, shoved me down in the straw, and pulled off my panties. And I told him I heard you yelling and banging on the barn. Then Doug really hurt me somehow. When I screamed, he covered my mouth and nose with his hand and everything went black. That was all I remember.

"Dr. Archer went out and talked to Mrs. Bender for a while, and then he came back to get me. Then we came home. I still don't know what Doug did to me, and the doctor didn't tell me anything, and nothing was said on the way home. He just put his arms around my shoulders, told me not to worry, and said it won't happen again."

Betty and I finished out the last month of first grade. Doug was not permitted to walk to school with us. Instead, he rode his bike down the dirt road. Betty failed school that year, but I moved on to the second grade.

12

Staring in Disbelief

To bring in some extra money, Mr. Bender trapped muskrats along the marshy shores of Lake Erie. If invited, Betty and I went with him to watch as he checked his traps. We either followed a few steps behind him or kept at a much safer distance, depending on his mood that day. We enjoyed these little adventures, running down the steep cliff to the water's edge, gathering stones and shells, or removing our running shoes and squealing as the frigid waters lapped the shoreline and chilled our naked toes.

Mr. Bender was happy and considered it a good day if he was able to bag "three big ones," as he referred to the muskrats. After removing the dead animals from the powerful teeth of the steel traps, he would stuff their limp bodies into a brown burlap bag and reset his traps for the next day. Tossing the heavy bag over his shoulder, he would head home to skin them on the back porch. When we arrived back at the house, Betty and I would dart off to play.

After he'd removed the skins from the animals, he would put them fur-side-down over a wooden, A-shaped board and then hang them on the backyard clothesline to dry and cure in the sun. When the pelts were cured, he would sell them locally for the best price he could get and keep the meat for meals. The meat was dark, tender, and stringy, with a slightly sweet taste. Betty and I didn't like it but managed to choke it down.

It was after one of these muskrat adventures when I was pushing Betty in the tire swing that I brought her to an abrupt stop. I had an idea to share with her. "Hey, let's go watch him skin the muskrats. It should be fun!" I said excitedly, as I steadied the tire for her.

"Do you think we should?" she asked, sounding fearful and reluctant.

"Well, he'll chase us away if he doesn't want us around. We'll have to be as quiet as mice, though."

She jumped quickly out of the tire, and we tiptoed silently around the house to the back porch where we spotted Mr. Bender kneeling down, intent upon preparing the muskrats for skinning. As he sharpened his long steel knife back and forth across the whetstone, we quietly took a position at the far end of the porch about six feet away from him. He gave us a quick don't-piss-me-off look and went back to his work.

Betty fidgeted and shuffled from one foot to the other. She was always a bit high-strung, and I had difficulty keeping her still so she wouldn't anger Mr. Bender. I took hold of her arm and whispered firmly, "Shuuush. Don't get too close, and be still." I tightened my hold on her arm to let her know I was serious. We had only been with this family for a few months and had not quite warmed to them. And Mr. Bender had already nicknamed Betty "Ditty" because, as he said, "She's always prancing around like some damn nervous cat."

We watched wide-eyed as Mr. Bender maneuvered the first big rat into the right position for skinning. I felt Betty's body tighten as he positioned the knife to make the first stab, but she remained still and silent. Soon, with one quick thrust of the razor-sharp knife, he split the rat's belly from throat to tail, and the bloody guts came spilling out.

Betty could contain herself no longer. "Oh, yuck!" she shrieked, immediately clamping her hand over her mouth to silence herself. But that was all it took to set Mr. Bender off. Quick as a flash he grabbed a handful of the disgusting guts and hurled them into her face.

"Oh no!" I cried out as my hands flew up to cover my mouth in utter disbelief of what I'd seen. *What a mean and disgusting thing to do,* I thought. Stunned, I watched as the sickening mess splattered on her face and tumbled down the front of her dress.

Her body jerked and stiffened, seeming not to know what had hit her.

"Now get the hell out of here!" he barked.

"Come on, Betty," I said as I yanked her away, trying at the same time to brush the stringy guts off her and keep myself from throwing up. I pulled her, crying and gagging, over to the rusty old pump at the far side of the house. Grabbing the tin cup off its hook, I quickly scooped water from the priming bucket to prime the pump. I was relieved that it took only one prime. As the first gush of water came out, I scooped it up in my hands. "Here, bend over."

I gently splashed the water over her face, cleaned her up as much as possible, and got her calmed down a bit. "You shouldn't have done that," I scolded. "You know how mean he can be."

"I'm sorry. I couldn't help it," she apologized.

"That's okay. I'm sorry I even suggested going to watch him skin the stupid rats. Let's go and play way back in the orchard, far away from him."

"I don't think I can ever get far enough away from him," she sniffled. "Why does he have to be so nasty, anyway?"

Once Mr. Bender was out of sight, we turned and thumbed our noses in his direction before running off to the safety of the orchard. We were still so angry with him. "We'll have to be more careful around him, and we *certainly* won't go and watch him skin those stupid rats again!"

13

A Dream Come True

What began as a routine midsummer morning breakfast turned into a thrilling day for Betty and me as we sat at the table with Mrs. Bender. Jumping up quickly from her chair, she hurried to open the door wide for Mr. Bender and Doug, who were struggling to haul an old mattress and spring set from the outside shed through the kitchen. As they were making their way up the stairs to the bedroom that Betty and I shared, I turned to Mrs. Bender and asked what they were doing.

"Well, a lady from the Children's Aid paid me a visit last week and told me that your sisters, Jean and Joan, need a new home. They thought it would be nice if you girls could all be together, so I agreed to let them come here for a vacation."

Betty and I looked at each other, eyes wide with excitement, hardly believing our ears and searching her face for more assurance. *This is just too good to be true,* I thought. We hadn't seen our sisters since we were taken from our parents three years ago and wondered many times what had happened to them. We were bubbling over with happiness as we squirmed excitedly in our seats and grinned at each other across the table. "For a vacation? How long is a vacation?" I asked, holding my breath, waiting for her reply. Mrs. Bender was usually tight-lipped about sharing information, and I knew better than to pry. But curiosity got the best of me. I had to find out.

"They're coming on a trial basis for the rest of the summer, perhaps until school starts," she said.

I nudged Betty. "That's almost two whole months!"

"I know," she said, clapping her hands. "Then will they have to leave again?"

"That remains to be seen. If you can all get along without too much quarreling and bickering, then I might keep them for a longer stay. But . . . if you misbehave, then I warn you, I'll have the Children's Aid come pick them up and take them away at once." Her stern look left little doubt in our minds that she meant what she said.

My heart sank. *Take them away again, just like that?* It seemed so cruel. I remembered that Mr. Bender would take the barn kittens away from their mother, throw them in a bran sack, knot it, and drown them in the horse trough. "Quickest way to get rid of them," he would say, brushing his hands together after he tossed the bag on top of the manure pile. I cringed at the thought of it.

"We'll be *really good*, won't we, Bonnie?" Betty promised.

"Yes, yes, yes!" I answered, nodding fervently. "When are they coming?"

"They'll be here tomorrow. So make sure you tidy your room in the morning."

"Tomorrow?" we squealed. "They're coming tomorrow?"

It wasn't until Jean and Joan's bed was fully set up next to ours that the thought of us being together again seemed like a real possibility. At bedtime Betty and I sat in the middle of our bed, eyeing what was to be our sisters' bed and chatting for hours in the darkness. We were so wound up that we couldn't think about settling down to sleep.

"Just think, Jean and Joan will be sleeping here at this time tomorrow night. Can you believe it?" Betty said, pointing at the bed.

"No, pinch me. I think I'm dreaming."

"I wonder how old they are and what they look like?"

"Bobby told me when we were at the Sebolds that Jean and Joan were two years older than you and me. So they must be around nine. Won't it be fun having our big sisters around?"

"Yeah, it will. And guess what. We can all beat up on Doug if he bothers us again. But let's get to sleep now so tomorrow will come faster," she said.

Pulling the sheets over my head and nestling down close to Betty, I lay awake, thinking about tomorrow. Everything seemed so hard to believe.

• • •

I woke early in the morning, as the first bit of daylight came through the window, and wanted to bolt downstairs and run straight away to the road to wait for my sisters. I knew, however, that I must wait in my room until called for breakfast or Mr. Bender would accuse me of "kicking over the traces" again. This was one of his favorite expressions whenever Betty and I misbehaved—referring to when he would hook the horse's harness traces to the equipment it had to pull and the horse would rebel and kick over the traces, forcing him to unhook it, thread it back around the horse's leg, and hook it back onto the whippletree. He would then give the horse a good smack to the hindquarter for being unruly.

It seemed like hours passed before Betty and I, already dressed and sitting on the edge of our bed, heard the latch click on the door below. "You girls can come down now. Breakfast is ready," Mrs. Bender called.

We raced downstairs and made short work of our breakfast. Jumping up from our chairs, we pushed open the screen door excitedly, letting it bang noisily behind us.

"Get back here and close that door properly!" Mrs. Bender yelled. "You'd think you were born in a barn, or somethin'!"

Annoyed, I turned back and gently closed the door, making sure it snapped into the roller lock.

"That's better," she quipped.

It was a beautiful, sunny Saturday, a perfect day for our sisters' arrival. After rushing through our barn chores, we hurried over to the old mulberry tree and planted ourselves side by side on the lower limb to wait for our sisters.

"Look," I said, pointing down the road. "There's dust flyin'!"

We knew this meant only one thing: a car was coming down the road. We watched and waited — our hearts in our throats — to see if it would turn into the driveway.

"It's turning in! It's turning in! I'm sure of it!" I squealed, shielding my eyes from the bright sun.

"They're here! They're here!" we shouted, jumping down out of the tree, clapping our hands, and bouncing up and down as if we were spring-loaded.

Betty started to run to meet the car, but I caught her arm and pulled her back. "Let's just stay here at the swing until we see what happens."

"Okay," she pouted, annoyed with me for hauling her back.

As the car pulled into the yard, Mrs. Bender came out of the house. Looking over at us, she beckoned with a wave of her hand. "C'mon, girls, and meet your sisters."

We watched as Jean and Joan climbed out of the car, each clutching a curly-haired doll.

The social worker led them over to Betty and me. Then, turning to one of them, she said, "Now, let's see. I think this is Jean. Am I right? No? Oh my goodness! Then you must be Joan." Looking bewildered, she went on, "You see, they look so much alike that I can't tell them apart. I'm completely baffled. Why, my goodness, Mrs. Bender will have to hang signs around your necks so she'll know who's who!

The thought of hanging signs around their necks like old cow bells made me giggle.

At that, Jean threw out her chest like a crowing rooster, pointed to each of us, and proudly announced, "And *you're* Bonnie, and *you're* Betty. See, I remembered them!"

Then the social worker asked Jean and Joan to tell us the names of their dolls.

"Mine's named Bonnie," Joan said.

"And mine's named Betty," Jean followed with a giggle.

"And my name is Mrs. Coldwell," she smiled. "I'm going to leave you girls to get acquainted while Mrs. Bender and I wrap up some final details."

Betty and I—feeling a bit shy and awkward at seeing our sisters again—dashed away to hide behind the mulberry tree. We peeked out at them and they stared back at us. Soon their persistent coaxing and teasing brought us out from behind the tree.

"You still have those silly spots all over your faces," I said, pointing at them and screwing up my nose.

"They're freckles, you know. Haven't you seen freckles before?" said Joan.

"Yes, but not *that* many," I replied, shaking my head.

"Did'ya think a brown cow sneezed on us?" Jean chuckled. We all giggled at that silly notion.

"Look," she went on, hiking her dress up above her knees, "we've got 'em all over, even on our arms and legs. See?"

"How are we supposed to tell you apart?" I asked.

"Jean has more freckles than I do," laughed Joan.

They're funny, I thought. *I like them already.*

Betty and I were about to take Jean and Joan down to the lake when Mrs. Coldwell came out of the house and walked over to say good-bye. "Now, if you girls get along and do what Mrs. Bender tells you, everything should go fine. I'm sure you'll enjoy each other's company." She gave each of us a pat on the head and told us to be good little girls. The four of us stood quietly together, watching as she entered her car and drove slowly out of sight.

With Mrs. Bender's permission, Betty and I took our sisters down to the lake to while away the rest of the day playing at the water's edge. They were thrilled to be near the lake and could hardly wait for the following day to go swimming.

When we tired of the water, we sat on the edge of the embankment, dangling our legs over the edge and talking about our experiences in different foster homes. Jean and Joan told us that before coming here, they were living with a family named Stevens in the little town of Waterford. "We liked living with Mr. and Mrs. Stevens," Joan said. "They were really good to us, and we bawled our eyes out when they told us we'd be moving. We had no idea we were coming here to be with you until they came to take us away."

Jean went on to tell us about Mr. Stevens's wooden leg and how he would take it off and show it to them. She laughed. "Sometimes we even helped him get it on and off, and he'd scream, pretending we were hurting him. One day I fell off the wagon and broke my leg, and Mr. Stevens told me that I'd be getting a wooden leg just like his. At first I thought he was serious but then realized he was just joking. He loved to tease us. Can't you just see me with a wooden leg? I'd have to paint freckles on it," she chuckled, "just to make it match."

Betty and I found Jean funny, and her silly stories amused us. She reminded me of our sister Muggs, and that brought back fond memories.

Joan sat quietly by, happy to let Jean do most of the talking.

"Do you know where Bobby is?" I asked. "We haven't seen him since they took him away from the Sebold home."

"No, we haven't heard from or seen any of our family. We've got no idea where Bobby, Muggs, Hank, Bill, Jim, Albert, or even our mom and dad are," Joan replied.

"Do you think we'll ever see them again? I miss everyone so much."

"I don't know," Joan replied, hunching her shoulders, her voice trailing off. "But at least we're together now."

In spite of so much that was sad to recall, we prattled on, warming up to each other and trying to piece together our tattered lives as if it were a giant jigsaw puzzle. But there were too many missing pieces and too many questions that didn't have answers. Finally we gave up trying to sort things out and just contented ourselves with being happy that we were together again.

"Do you know how long we can visit before they take us away again?" Joan asked.

"Mom Bender says that as long as we get along without fighting, you can stay until school starts—maybe even longer. But if we squabble too much, she'll send you back to the Children's Aid," I said, grimacing at the horrible thought.

"Then we'll just have to get along," she replied, giving me a playful nudge.

"I heard you call her Mom. Do you call her that all the time?" Jean asked.

"Yeah," I said, looking down at the ground and feeling ashamed, knowing she wasn't our real mom. "That's what she expects. But I try hard not to say it. One day I said, 'Hey, can Betty and I go down to the lake?' She snapped at me that her name is not *hey* and that only horses eat *hay*. We were to call her Mom."

"Hmm," Jean said, shrugging her shoulders and cocking her head to the side. "Well, I'll call her Mom—but only if I darn well feel like it!"

I liked Jean's spunk but hoped it wouldn't get us into trouble.

• • •

Mrs. Bender made us sandwiches for lunch, and we sat on the back porch steps to eat. That evening we sat around the kitchen table for our first real meal together in more than three years. It seemed unbelievable, and still giddy with excitement, we giggled our way through our supper.

This made Mr. Bender angry, and we were soon on the receiving end of a harsh scolding. "That's enough of your damn silliness," he barked. "The table is a place to eat, not to chatter. Now zip your lips and clean up your plates, or you'll be off to bed without your supper!"

Surprised, Jean and Joan looked across the table at each other. Their shocked looks told me they weren't used to being talked to like that.

After we'd finished eating, I broke the uneasy quiet by complaining to Mrs. Bender about my loose tooth, and she came to take a look at it. Turning to Mr. Bender, she said, "Jim, I think you had better get the pliers and pull this child's tooth."

"Naw, it's too dark now to go out to the shed. Come on over here," he said, while fumbling around in the cupboard drawer for some string. "Let's take a look at that tooth."

I opened my mouth, and he wiggled the tooth around a bit. "Well, it certainly has to come out." Taking one end of the long string, he tied it snugly around my tooth while I stood open-mouthed in the middle of the kitchen, whimpering.

He then opened the stairway door partway and tied the other end of the string to the knob while I watched, having no idea what he was going to do but afraid to say anything lest I get a quick clip to the head. He wasn't one to mess with, and he didn't like answering a lot of questions.

I looked over at my sisters and saw them sitting stiffly on the cot, closely watching the action with puzzled expressions.

"Hey, girls," Mr. Bender exclaimed, pointing toward the window, "look at that bear peeking in the window!"

We all turned to look. As we did, he kicked the door shut and out flew my tooth.

"Ooow!" I screamed. My hand flew up to cup my mouth as my tooth dangled on the end of the string, swinging back and forth from the doorknob like a pendulum.

I took it off the string, examined it briefly, and then ran to check the painful results in the wall mirror. "Uuuugh, I look so ugly!" I groaned, making a face at myself in the mirror. "Can I keep my tooth?" I asked, wiping the slobber off on my trousers.

"Yes," he replied. "Now get to bed, the whole lot of you — and no goofing around up there. Understand?"

Slipping my treasure into my pocket, I headed upstairs with my sisters.

"He's not gonna pull any of my teeth like that," Jean announced after the door was closed.

"Then what'll you do?" I asked.

"Mom and Dad Stevens let us wiggle our own teeth out when they got loose. We'd put them under our pillows at night, and while we were sleeping, the tooth fairy would come, take them away, and leave us some money."

"Should I put mine under my pillow? Do you really think a tooth fairy will come for me?"

"Sure. That's what a good tooth fairy does," she assured me.

It was really nice to have big sisters around who knew so much more than we did, so I tucked my tooth under my pillow, said goodnight to my sisters, and crawled into bed.

The next morning I checked under my pillow, expecting to find some money, but my tooth was still lying right where I'd put it. I was so disappointed. "Jean! Jean! Wake up!" I cried, shaking her. "You fibbed to me. There aren't any tooth fairies. My tooth is still here! See!" I held it up to catch the morning light streaming through the window.

Jean and Joan sat upright in bed, rubbing the sleep from their eyes.

"I didn't get any money like you said I would!" I wailed.

"I don't understand," Joan said, coming to Jean's defense. "When we lived with Mom and Dad Stevens, there was always a shiny new nickel under the pillow."

"Yeah," Jean cut in. "Maybe the tooth fairies here are cheapskates."

I didn't understand her remark, having no idea what a cheapskate was. But I didn't want to appear dumb, so I pretended I did and said nothing more.

• • •

New neighbors moved onto a small farm next door that summer, and we overheard Mr. and Mrs. Bender referring to them as a "bunch of Hunkies." There were daily conversations about how all the foreigners were coming to Canada from Europe and buying up all the land, especially the good tobacco-growing land. This was all very new and strange to us, for we hadn't the slightest idea what a Hunkie or a foreigner was, much less what they might look like. And so one day we decided to sneak through the orchard to their fence line to get a peek at them. We peered through the underbrush hoping to catch a glimpse, but we had no luck.

"What do you think a Hunkie looks like?" I asked Jean, since she always had the answers to my questions.

"Darned if I know," she quipped. "I probably couldn't tell a Hunkie from a scarecrow."

"Oh, they probably look somethin' like us," Joan said. "I don't think they have three eyes."

We laughed at the absurdity, and then I asked, "Mrs. Bender says they talk gibberish, too. What does she mean by that?"

"Beats me," Jean shrugged.

A few days after our spying trip through the orchard, a slender lady with a girl about our age came up the driveway. They saw us playing, waved to us, and continued toward the house. Mrs. Bender answered the knock, and they talked for a few minutes. As we stood in the shade of the mulberry tree, we watched as Mrs. Bender brought them toward us.

Mrs. Bender told us the little girl's name was Helen and that she was our new neighbor. "She has no one to play with and wants to play with you, so you're to treat her nicely. Her mother will be back for her shortly."

We stared at her, believing she was the little Hunkie girl. Then Joan stuck her nose in the air and whispered, "See, I told you so. They're just like us."

"Would you like to play hide-and-seek with us?" I asked.

"Yeah, that . . .sounds like . . .fun!"

We were surprised again. She didn't sound like a Hunkie. She spoke just like us, only more slowly, as if picking her words one by one out of a basket.

After tiring of hide-and-seek, we decided to play a game of tag. Soon we were all tired, thirsty, and out of breath. We stopped at the yard pump to get a cold drink of water, and as we gulped down the water, Joan asked Helen how old she was.

"I'm nine," she said. "I'll be in grade three at my new school."

"We're nine, too," Jean and Joan said excitedly, tickled that our new playmate was their age.

Then Jean wiped water off her chin with the hem of her dress and popped the question the rest of us were curious about but too afraid to ask. "Are you a Hunkie?"

Helen stared at us for a long moment without speaking. And then a painful look crossed her face as her mouth turned down at the corners and she blinked back tears. Without answering, she turned away and ran down the driveway toward home.

We looked at each other and hunched our shoulders, wondering why she ran off so fast. Then Joan asked, "Do you s'pose she didn't liked being called a Hunkie?"

"I dunno," Jean replied. "I just asked. I didn't mean to make her mad."

It wasn't long before Helen's mother came back over, had a short talk with Mrs. Bender, and left almost as quickly as she'd come. Mrs. Bender called us into the house immediately, and we knew by the tone of her voice that we were in trouble. "Who called the little girl a Hunkie?" she demanded.

We remained silent, not wanting to tattle on one another.

"Well, speak up. Don't all talk at once!" she snapped.

About that time Mr. Bender came in for lunch, overheard the questioning, and asked, "What's goin' on here, Mary?"

"Oh, the little foreign girl came over to play and one of the girls called her a Hunkie. She went home in tears. Her mom came back and told me off royally!"

Upon hearing this, Mr. Bender grabbed us, one by one, threw us over his knees like rag dolls, and gave us a spanking. "Don't you ever let me hear you use that word again," he scolded, "or next time you'll get the belt! Now, get to your room. And I don't want to hear another peep out of you!"

Burning with resentment, I stomped hard on each step as I followed my sisters up the stairs. Before reaching the top, I overheard Mrs. Bender say, "We must be very careful what we say around those girls, Jim. Little pigs have big ears, you know."

I gritted my teeth as we sat in our beds and sulked, furious about getting a spanking we didn't deserve and being called pigs.

"How were we to know we shouldn't have asked if she was a Hunkie?" Betty said.

"Who knew it would hurt her feelings?" I joined in.

"Yeah," Jean agreed, "how were we supposed to know? That's what they called them."

Soon after this, the Benders began distancing themselves from us. We were allowed briefer stays downstairs with the family and weren't allowed to talk at the table. "You'll speak only when you're spoken to," Mrs. Bender announced. "Children should be seen and not heard." After a few cuffs to the back of our heads, we got the message.

With each passing day, my sisters and I grew closer together and more distant from the Benders, taking it upon ourselves to solve our own problems and caring for each other if we were hurt. We became more fearful and worried constantly that if we were not careful, Jean and Joan would be taken away.

14

Mischief and Mayhem

Despite our fears, we enjoyed those summer months on the farm. Except for occasionally helping with the barn chores, we were free to roam, explore, and have fun together. We spent most of the hot summer days at the lake, playing on an old pier or splashing in the cool water. Many times a black water moccasin swam nearby, and we would make a mad dash for the shore. The lake was teeming with bloodsuckers, and we hated those soft, slimy gray leeches that stuck to our naked bodies. One day I looked down and noticed my groin was covered with these disgusting slugs. Panicked, I ran to the shore, jumping up and down, waving my arms wildly, and screaming for help.

My sisters scrambled out of the lake and rushed to my side. Joan looked at me and, seeing my predicament, doubled over with laughter. "Boy, you've got a bumper crop there!" she giggled.

"Get them off me! Get them off me!" I wailed.

"Hold still! Hold still! For Pete's sake, hold still!" they said as they pulled and tugged at the leeches.

"Yeah, we gotta get them off before they suck out all her precious blood," Jean kidded as Betty and Joan snickered at my dilemma.

"It's not funny!" I snapped.

Finally those horrible things were all removed, but it would be some time before I worked up enough nerve to go into the lake again.

• • •

We spent other days wandering in the apple orchard, picking flowers and braiding them into our hair or climbing the apple trees. As we were roving around in the orchard one day, we noticed an older girl playing in an adjoining yard. From a distance she appeared to be a few years older than Jean and Joan, possibly about thirteen. When she saw us, she waved us over to the fence. Fascinated and curious as to what she wanted, we ran to talk with her.

She was tall and slender with fair skin and blonde hair that was pulled tightly to the back of her head and braided into a large, single braid that dangled halfway down her back. Except for her large green eyes, which seemed to run off the side of her face, she was quite pretty. She asked our names and told us she was Sharon Ferris.

She wanted to talk to us, so we sat on the ground beside the fence and listened as she filled our heads with fairy tales and mystical lore.

She was quite entertaining, and as we got up to leave, we told her how much we had enjoyed her stories. And as we started to go, she said, "Come back tomorrow, and I'll have a surprise for you."

"What is it? What is it?" I pleaded, as I clung to the wire fence, eager to know what the surprise might be.

She smiled secretively and pressed a finger to her lips as if to say she would tell us no more. "Oh, you'll just have to wait until you come back to see me."

Our excitement was so great that we could hardly wait to wend our way back through the orchard the next day.

"What do you think her surprise is?" Betty asked.

"Who knows," Jean said. "If you want my opinion, I think she's a bit dippy."

"And did you notice her big eyes?" Joan chimed in. "Betcha she can see around a corner!"

I nodded agreement. "Yeah, and I thought she was looking right through me."

"Well, it doesn't take much to see through you," Jean quipped sarcastically.

"I don't care," I said, jutting out my chin defiantly. "I like her anyway!"

"So do I," Jean said, "but it still doesn't mean she's got all her marbles."

"Well, we've got to be nice to her. We don't want her to run away, too," I said.

"Gosh, no," Jean agreed. "We'll have our heads on the chopping block for sure if Mrs. Bender got wind of it."

Early the next morning, after finishing our barn chores, we made our way back through the apple orchard. The grass and weeds, still covered with dew, wet and chilled our bare legs. Arriving at the fence, we called out for Sharon. Seeming to appear out of nowhere, she hurried to the fence to greet us. Since she knew we were waiting for our surprise, she was fumbling to remove something from her dress pocket as she came toward us.

"Here," she said, poking her hand through the square opening in the wire fence and putting a small cellophane packet of white powder into Joan's hand. "This is your surprise."

We stared at the packet, puzzled over the contents and wondering what the white powder might be.

"What is it?" I asked, as Joan held it on her outstretched palm and Jean bent down to smell it.

"It's dream dust," Sharon replied. "You put a little bit of this on your tongue before you go to sleep, and you'll have the most beautiful dreams. And best of all, your dreams will come true!"

"Are you sure?" Jean asked doubtfully.

I jabbed Jean sharply in the ribs to shut her up. I was afraid Sharon might take back her dream dust, and I wanted so much to try it.

"You'll see," Sharon smiled as she backed away from the fence and turned to leave.

Excited about having something magical, we thanked her, said good-bye, and hopped and skipped our way back through the orchard, eager to get home with our mysterious gift.

We put Joan in charge of our precious packet, agreeing not to say a word about it to the Benders.

We were sneaking our way through the kitchen, past the watchful eye of Mrs. Bender, when she sensed we were up to something and stopped us cold. "What have you kids been up to? And what are you hiding behind your back, Joan?"

Reluctantly, Joan showed her the packet.

"I'll just take that," Mrs. Bender said, snatching up the packet of powder.

My stomach tightened as she opened the packet, sniffed the contents, and demanded, "What in the world is this stuff?"

"It's nothing. Just some dream dust," I said nonchalantly, not wanting her to take it from us.

"Where did you get this?" she demanded.

Jean, taking over, told Mrs. Bender all about our new friend on the far side of the orchard.

"Such a cockamamie story," she harrumphed. "She's filled your heads with a bunch of nonsense. For all you silly kids know, this stuff could be poison. I won't let you have it. Now, get out of here and stay away from that crazy girl."

My heart sank. I already had my dream picked out. I was going to be just like Cinderella. A handsome prince would rescue me and take me far away in a beautiful golden chariot, and then I would live happily ever after. *Mean old hag,* I thought. *Why does she have to rob us of all our fun?* I ran out of the kitchen and went to sit under the mulberry tree to pout. "I hate her! I hate her!" I grumbled aloud.

As we lay in bed that night, Betty asked, "Why does she always have to spoil everything for us?"

"Be quiet and get to sleep," Jean piped up from her bed. "Who knows? Maybe it really is poison."

"It's probably just plain old flour," Betty said.

"Maybe it's icing sugar. I bet that's what it is!" I said angrily, still upset over what Mrs. Bender had done.

"Well, we'll never know now," Joan said.

"Do you think Sharon will give us some more if we asked nicely?" I asked, unwilling to let go of my dream.

"Shut up, Bonnie, and go to sleep!" Jean snapped.

• • •

We were all excited a week or so later when Mrs. Bender had us move stuff from the kitchen, telling us that her daughter, Margaret, was coming home to help her wallpaper it.

Marge, as she was called, was an attractive, vivacious girl about nineteen years old. Soft, light brown curls adorned her pretty, oval face. She had nice blue eyes and a winsome smile, and even the brown mole just above her upper lip did not mar her beauty. She worked in town as a waitress and occasionally came home for a weekend. And though my sisters and I tried hard to get into her good graces, she paid little attention to us.

Watching Marge and her mother putting up wallpaper and being careful to keep out of the way, we waited for them to knock the end seams off the rolls. As soon as they hit the floor, my sisters and I scrambled to pick them up. We then shook them loose, pinned them in our hair, and raced outside to play with the beautiful paper ringlets bouncing up and down around our heads. We felt so pretty. *How wonderful it must be to have beautiful curly hair, I mused. It would be so much nicer than our straight, bobbed hair and too-short bangs, the way Mr. Bender always cuts it.*

Soon we heard Marge calling. "C'mon in, girls. I've made some tapioca pudding for you."

"Wow! That sounds too good to be true!" I exclaimed. "Marge actually made us pudding?"

"Yeah, I'll believe it when I see it," Joan added sarcastically.

Seldom were we ever on the receiving end of special treats, so we hurried inside and saw the four, clear glass bowls of pudding with a sprinkling of cinnamon on top, neatly arranged on the bare wooden table. With our taste buds primed for a treat, we hurriedly dragged some chairs to the table, settled into them, and waited.

Marge handed us each a spoon and announced, "Okay, I'll count to three and say go, and then you can all dig in."

Spoons raised, we impatiently played along with her game.

"One . . . two . . . three . . . GO!"

We plunged our spoons deep into the bowls, scooped up heaping spoonfuls of pudding, eagerly stuffed it into our mouths, and gagged on the awful stuff. We realized immediately what she had done. She had filled our bowls with wallpaper paste.

"Yuuuck!" we screeched, gagging, spitting the vile-tasting mush back into the bowls, and wiping our mouths with the backs of our hands.

Marge just stood there gloating and laughing at our predicament—satisfied that she had managed to put one over on us.

"Now, that was a cruel trick, Marge," Mrs. Bender said, trying to stifle the smile on her face. It was obvious that she had also enjoyed the prank.

Hurt and angry that we'd been the victims of such thoughtlessness, we shoved back our chairs and ran from the house. I was the last out and deliberately slammed the screen door as hard as I could.

We ran directly to the well pump to rinse the horrible taste out of our mouths. "She's so mean," I sputtered. "I hope she never comes home again!"

• • •

The month of July always brought forth an abundance of ripe, juicy berries on the old mulberry tree. Except for Joan, who was afraid of heights, we climbed to the topmost branches to stuff ourselves full of the delicious fruit.

"Hey, I've got a great idea," I called to my sisters as I sat straddling a sturdy limb in the middle of the tree. "Let's make some mulberry jam."

We scoured the backyard for a suitable container. Jean found an old salmon can that looked pretty good, and after rinsing it out at the pump, we filled it with berries. Joan, smashing and stirring them with a fat wooden stick, brought them to a thick, gooey spread.

We had just gathered around the base of the tree to enjoy our jam when Doug spotted us. "Whatcha got there?" he asked.

"We made some mulberry jam. Why? What business is it of yours?" I sassed, mad at him for nosing in on our fun. With my older sisters near for protection, I had no fear of sassing him, but at times I pushed my luck too far.

"Give it to me, you little snip!" he said, trying to snatch it out of Jean's hands.

"It's ours! It's not yours!" she blurted out, holding tightly to the can. "We made it!"

Doug threw a quick smack toward the side of her head, and as she ducked, he snatched the can from her grasp. "Not anymore it ain't!" he taunted with a nasty smirk.

We all watched, full of anger, as he wolfed down our jam. "Tasted pretty good," he grunted, wiping the stain off his mouth on his shirtsleeve, then tossing the empty can down in the dirt at our feet before sauntering off toward the house.

"You big meanie!" Joan hollered after him.

"Don't you just hate his guts?" I said.

"Haven't liked him since the first day I laid eyes on him," she said.

We'd barely finished crabbing about Doug and made our way up the tree again when Mrs. Bender angrily called us into the house. "What the hell did you do to Doug? What did you give him?"

Doug was vomiting into a basin. His face was all puffy, his lips, still blue from the berries, were swollen, and only rasping sounds were coming from his throat.

Jean scurried outside to fetch the can, handed it to Mrs. Bender, and tried to explain what had happened.

Mrs. Bender snatched the can from her hand, held it to her nose, and then turned on Jean. "You ought to have your heads examined. Whaddya use for brains? You should know better than to mix stuff in a dirty old can. For God's sake, you could kill someone! He has food poisoning, and we'll have to take him to the doctor — thanks to your foolishness! Now, all of you get out and don't set foot inside this house until you're called."

"Serves him right for stealing our jam," I said, as soon as we were out of earshot.

"Yeah," Betty said. "It's a good thing he ate it and not us."

"Oh God, what if it had killed him?" Joan said, muffling her words with her hand.

"Wouldn't feel the least bit sorry for him. Nope, not one little bit!" Jean said out loud, not caring if anyone heard her. "He deserves everything he gets . . . and then some!"

"Oh, sure," Joan said, "but what if they take us away because of this? You know the rules."

"Hey, it ain't our fault," Jean said. "He swiped our jam!"

We were glad that Doug had recovered by suppertime, but we got another round of scolding from Mrs. Bender as she told Mr. Bender what we had done.

"One more stupid prank like that from you kids and there'll be some big changes made around here," he threatened angrily, casting us a you-know-what-I-mean look.

• • •

Our otherwise carefree summer came to an end as the fall apple harvest brought us our first introduction to hard work. The apples were ripe and ready for picking.

Because they were taller than Betty and me, Jean and Joan climbed ladders along with Mr. Bender to do the picking while Betty and I gathered the fallen apples. After putting them into bushel baskets, we hauled them up to the grading table. At first the bushels were too heavy for us, but soon we built up enough strength to handle them more easily.

The grading table was a long, narrow wooden-framed table about three feet high. The center was made from bran bags formed in the shape of a hammock so as not to bruise the apples. Along the side of the table, cut into the wood frame, were various round openings used for grading the apples by their size. A bin stood nearby for the bruised, wormy, and scabby rejects.

Mr. Bender would dump the apples onto the table while workers did the grading and sorting. The apples were then bagged, ticketed by grade, and loaded onto a truck to be sent to the factory.

The harvest season lasted about one month. I was happy when it was over, for it was hard work, and I was eager to start back to school.

My sisters and I were all going to the same school now, and Betty and I took pleasure in showing Jean and Joan the shortcut through the fields, woods, and cow pastures. It was good that Doug had finished the eighth grade and had quit school, for we wouldn't have to put up with his nastiness.

We also passed by the old barn with wild Queen Anne's lace blooming around it, sitting alone in the open field. It cut into my thoughts every time I came near, but Betty and I had not told our sisters about the horrible thing that had happened there.

Enjoying our walks to and from school, we would have fun scaring the cows in the pasture, but if the bull was present, we were more cautious. Whenever he came charging toward us, we ran like wild fire, praying the electric fence would stop him. We scared the wits out of ourselves many times, but we also had loads of fun.

Other times we would dare each other to touch the electric fence. Once one of us worked up the nerve to touch it, we would form a chain, and the one at the tail end of the line would get the biggest shock. When the grass and fence were wet with rain or dew, we'd get some pretty good jolts. We enjoyed playing this silly game of "chicken" many times.

Betty, who was seven, started first grade over, and I moved into second grade along with Jean and Joan, who were nine but had been held back a year because of their having moved from one foster home to another.

Within the first few months of the new school year, the "needle doctor," as we called him, arrived at our school to give the kids the dreaded tuberculosis shots, otherwise known as the scratch.

To get out of going to school, Betty faked a stomachache on the morning of the day he was to visit. But Mrs. Bender would have none of her play-acting and sent her off with the rest of us.

On this scary day, I sat with my arms folded on my desk, watching closely as the white-smocked doctor, whom the teacher addressed as Dr. Reid, threw a white cloth over a small table and carefully set out his equipment. He looked like a reed, I thought as I giggled. He was a tall, skinny man with a long, thin neck and a huge, protruding Adam's apple. He had a narrow, straight nose; bulging, bright blue eyes; and a thatch of white hair that looked like a picket fence circling his bald head. It looked to me that if one pushed hard enough on his Adam's apple, his eyes would pop out of their sockets. He looked strange enough to scare the bejeebers out of anyone, to say nothing about getting a needle from him.

The teacher lined us up several at a time to be vaccinated. I turned to look at Betty sitting in the desk behind me. She was clutching herself with her arms, rocking slowly back and forth while staring at the cold, silver instruments on the table, her face as white as the cloth that covered it. "Don't worry," I said, touching her arm, "I'll go first to show you it doesn't hurt."

When my turn came, I walked bravely to the front and confidently pulled up my sleeve to the top of my shoulder. In spite of his odd looks, the doctor was kind and soft-spoken and gave the shot gently. It hurt a bit, but I tried hard not to flinch.

"Look," I said to Betty with a fake smile while still holding my rolled-up sleeve on the top of my shoulder, "I told you it wouldn't hurt."

As she noticed the small trickle of blood running down my arm, she and the girl behind her fainted dead away.

With the help of our teacher, Mrs. Kiley, and some older students, they were soon revived and comforted as the doctor gave them their shots.

• • •

The school was small and did double duty by serving as a church on Sundays. The Benders, who always kept to themselves and rarely had visitors except for family, didn't go to church. But as it was a requirement of the Children's Aid Society that we attend, Mrs. Bender usually followed the rule and let us go on our own.

There had been a heavy snowfall one night, and my sisters and I decided to take the side road to church rather than cut through the fields, for our boots were much too short to keep the snow from getting into them. This way we were able to walk in the tracks of a car or tractor that may have gone down the road earlier.

Thinking we had plenty of time, we poked along, throwing snowballs at each other. Since the snow was good for packing, we decided to build a snowman right in the middle of the road, hoping a car would hit it and knock it down before we returned from church.

"Let's put it right here," I said, stomping my feet at what appeared to be a good location. "This looks like a good spot."

We all agreed and began rolling some big snowballs to build it. We got quite carried away with our mischief, running here and there to find stones for the eyes and buttons and large twigs for the arms. After we finished, we stood back to admire our handiwork.

"I wish we had a hat for him," Joan remarked. "His poor head's gonna get cold."

We giggled as we started slowly down the road, hoping a car would come by soon so we could catch the fun.

"We forgot to give him a name," Betty said. "What do you think we should call him?"

"Let's call him Chet," I said, thinking about the big, fat man who had come to the farm the day before to get some straw for his pigs. We had snickered in our hands as he bent over to pick up a bale of straw, revealing a large, V-shaped, pumpkin-colored patch that had been put in back of his pants to make them bigger.

"Wait," Jean said, "I've got a better name. Let's call him Doug and pray that a car hits him!"

"Speaking of prayers, we'd better get a move on, or we'll be late for Sunday school," Joan reminded us.

We trudged on through the snow, picking up speed a bit but not knowing how much time we had lost.

As we neared the school, we couldn't see anyone around and wondered if perhaps church services had been canceled because of the snowstorm. Then, pointing toward the yard, I said, "Look, there are car tracks and footprints all around."

"Holy Baldy! Do you think they've come and gone?" Jean asked.

"Let's peek in that window," Joan suggested, pointing her finger at the window nearest the blackboard.

"But it's way too high," I said.

"Here, Betty's the lightest; let's lift her onto Jean's shoulders so she can see if there's anyone in there."

It was a bit of a struggle, but we finally managed to get Betty safely straddled over Jean's shoulders. Carefully straightening them up, we held onto them as they wobbled their way up to the window.

Betty cleared the snow off the window with her mitten hand and peered inside.

"Do you see anyone?" I asked.

"Uh-uh. There's no one inside, and there's no hymn numbers on the blackboard. They've all been erased."

"Well, that settles it," Joan said, as she struggled to pull Betty off Jean's neck. "They've come and gone. We'd better hightail it home."

"But we won't get our angel attendance stickers in our books, and what if Mrs. Bender checks them?" I whined, fearful that we might get a whipping. Anyway, I felt sad about missing my angel sticker. They were pretty, dark curly-haired little girls with white floral dresses and transparent wings. And I always gave them a name. Now one was missing and all because of a stupid snowman.

"Oh, don't worry. She doesn't give a toot about your silly angel stickers. She ain't gonna check them," Jean reassured me.

"Nothing ever ruffles Jean's feathers," Joan said. "She's like an old hen."

We were disappointed when we spotted our snowman still standing in the middle of the road. No car had come by to knock him down. "Let's beat him up and knock him down," Betty suggested.

"Good idea," Jean agreed.

"Take that, and that, and that!" we squealed as we pummeled and kicked him to the ground.

"Poor Doug," I said, as we took one last look at the sorry snowman lying scattered in chunks all over the road before hurrying on home.

Jean was right. Mrs. Bender made no attempt to check our attendance books, and I was happy about it, for none of us had come up with a good enough fib to tell her.

15

Plans Go Awry

It was the late winter of 1944. Betty and I were eight years old and our sisters were ten when the Benders told us that they had purchased a small tobacco farm near the town of Williamston, Ontario. We weren't sure what this meant, and no mention was made of what would happen to us when they moved. Moreover, we didn't have the faintest notion of what a tobacco farm was and could only make wild guesses as to what we would have to do there. We talked among ourselves, trying to figure it all out.

Mr. Bender smoked, and he always carried a packet of tobacco in his shirt pocket. We often watched as he pinched off some of the brown stuff from the packet and put it along a narrow sheet of thin, white paper. He then moistened the glue-side edge of the paper with his tongue, rolled the whole thing up with his fingers until it resembled a piece of chalk, and made himself a cigarette. We were always amazed at the way he lit his cigarette by jerking his knee up and whipping the head of a match across the seat of his pants. *Whoosh*, it caught on fire with the first quick rip.

Occasionally, Jean would swipe a few matches, and we'd hide far away from the house to try to light them the way he did, but we never got the hang of it.

"Maybe we need rough overalls like he has," Jean said.

"And dirty, too," I added.

Sitting on the floor in our room one night with our backs propped against the side of the bed, we talked about the tobacco farm and our futures.

"If we go to that tobacco farm, what do you think we'll have to do?" Betty asked.

"I don't know," I replied. "Maybe we'll have to roll cigarettes like Mr. Bender does."

"And do what with them?"

"I have no idea. Maybe he'll sell them somewhere like he did the muskrat skins."

"I wish they'd let us know what's going on and if we're moving with them," Joan grumbled. "They never tell us anything. They always keep us in the dark."

"Will the Children's Aid let them take us there?" Jean asked.

"Oh shit!" Joan blurted out, quickly putting her hand over her mouth as if to shove the bad word back in. "What if they split us up again!"

We all groaned, knowing this was a real possibility.

"Surely they won't tear us apart again. Will they?" I cried.

By then we had really worked ourselves into a dither, and Jean was so angry that she stood up, pounded her fist on the bed, and exploded, "Well, by God, I'm sure as heck gonna ask tomorrow! It's our lives. The least they can do is darn well let us know what's gonna happen to us!" The look on her face left no doubt about her intentions.

I buried my face in my hands. "I'm not so sure I wanna know. And besides, they'll just tell you to mind your own business."

"Either way, we'd better get to bed now," Jean said. "We'll just see what happens after I ask them."

I lay in bed that night thinking about Jean's decision. She was so gutsy. Even though her prying questions often brought a quick smack to the head, nothing seemed to stop her once she had her mind set. It had gotten to the point where as soon as she asked a question and someone moved a muscle, she would quickly throw her arm up to ward off the blow. She looked like a brave knight raising his shield, and I giggled under my breath whenever she did it.

Sure enough, while prancing alongside Mr. Bender as we made our way to the barn for the morning chores, Jean popped the question. "Are we goin' to the tobacco farm, too, or will we be sent back to the Children's Aid?" she asked, without any fear in her voice and leaving little doubt that she expected an answer. I felt proud that she was my sister.

But he neither broke step nor turned to look at her when he replied. "Nope. You'll all be goin' with us. There'll be lots of work to do that should keep the bunch of you out of mischief." With that said, he put his thumb and forefinger aside his nose and, with a quick flick of his wrist, blew his nose on the ground—a disgusting thing we often saw him do. We quickly dropped back behind him—side-stepping the snotty stuff while clutching hands and grinning from ear to ear, thrilled to learn that we would all be staying together.

• • •

As soon as the farmhouse was sold, we busied ourselves with packing for the move. But from the loud and angry conversations we overheard from our bedroom door, we knew that things were not going as planned. The tobacco farm was not ready for the Benders to make the move, and they had no place to go.

A kind neighbor, by the name of Steadman, who had a small hired-hand house that wasn't yet finished, heard of their dilemma and said they could use it until the house on their tobacco farm was ready.

Early the next morning, after loading all the boxes onto the hay wagon, Mr. Bender hooked up the horses and, with a quick snap of the reins and a loud "Giddyup," was off down the road to the little house. My sisters and I, running as fast as we could behind the wagon, tried hard to keep up but soon lagged behind.

From a distance, the small, white frame house that sat all by itself in the middle of a snow-covered field with hardly any trees around it looked lost and lonely. And when we got there, my sisters and I hurried inside to check it out.

It was only half finished. The white plasterboard walls were still uncovered, but it seemed from a few scattered items lying around that someone had lived there before. Except for a large, wooden rectangular table in the kitchen, the rest of the house was unfurnished. There were only two small bedrooms, a tiny pantry, and a door that opened off the kitchen to a narrow staircase that led to a dark and spooky attic. None of us cared to go up there, so we quickly closed the door.

"Well, it's not much of a house," Mr. Bender said as soon as the last box had been brought in, "but at least we got a roof over our heads for the time being."

Marge came home to help with the move and fill in for Doug, who had moved out of the old house and found work elsewhere. I wasn't happy to see her and wished that May had come instead. She was the older of the two Bender daughters, about twenty-one, and looked a lot like her mother—the same dark, curly hair, full round face, sparkling blue eyes, and thin, tight smile. Although not nearly as attractive or nicely shaped as Marge, May was always thoughtful and kind to us, often bringing each of us a candy bar when she came home. We all adored her. As for Marge, we were still mad at her for the pudding prank she had pulled on us.

As we were setting up the beds, my sisters and I wondered aloud where we were going to sleep. "You girls will be sleeping in the attic for the night," Mr. Bender said.

It's only a large, spooky crawl space, I thought. I wrinkled my brow and gave him a questioning look, hoping he was joking. But the set of his jaw told me he was serious.

Later in the day he lugged in a small mattress and, with much difficulty, we helped him shove it up the narrow staircase and lay it across the uncovered attic two-by-fours. We had to hunch over, since there wasn't enough room to stand without bumping our heads on the rafters. We weren't too happy about this idea and griped among ourselves. "I wouldn't put an old flea-bitten dog up here. I don't know why they couldn't put the mattress on the kitchen floor," Jean complained as we made our way back to the kitchen.

"And it's so dark up there," I added. "How are we gonna see?"

As Betty and I were helping to bring in the chairs and put them around the table, I noticed some red paintlike spots on the ceiling and wall. "What's that red stuff?" I asked Marge.

"Oh, that's just some old dried blood. Some woman was murdered by her husband on the table here, and that's her blood splattered around up there. The house is still haunted by her ghost. You might even see her in the attic tonight."

As if we weren't frightened enough about spending the night in the attic, Marge had now managed to scare the living daylights out of Betty and me.

At bedtime, Mr. Bender gave Joan a flashlight so we could see our way to the attic. We had just started up the dark stairway when he closed the door behind us and hooked the latch. "He's locked us in!" Betty whimpered. We were locked up like prisoners, and we were terrified.

Joan turned on the flashlight and pointed the beam toward the black hole at the end of the stairway. We immediately stopped, afraid to go any farther.

"I'm not going up another step," I said. "Marge said there's a ghost in this house, and it might be up there!"

"Oh, don't be silly, Bonnie. She was just pulling your leg and trying to scare you," Joan said. "I'm more scared of rats and bats. I already saw a mouse run across the kitchen floor."

"That settles it. I'm sleeping right here!" Betty said, crossing her arms and plunking herself down on the step. "I hate mice!"

"Well, you'd better get used to them. There's probably more around here than you can shake a stick at. Besides, they're probably more scared of you than you are of them," Jean said.

We didn't get past the third step. Instead, we huddled there together, shivering and angry, dozing on and off until morning.

Joan kept the flashlight on, and by morning it was no longer working.

Mr. Bender scolded us for burning out the batteries. "Can't trust you kids with a damn thing," he said, tossing the flashlight into an empty box.

We were happy the next day when Marge left to go back to town, for we could then sleep in her room. But that was little satisfaction, since settling into such a small house was causing a lot of tension between Mr. and Mrs. Bender. And though we tried hard to be on our best behavior, there seemed to be no pleasing them, and we often got on their nerves.

Although we were now farther from school and the weather was bitterly cold, we were happy when the weekends were over so we could get back to our classes and away from the problems at home.

Our walk to school took about forty-five minutes, and during these bitterly cold winter days, we thought we would freeze before we got there. Our clothes never seemed warm enough to keep out the chill, so we would wrap our arms around each other for warmth. With teeth chattering and fingers and toes turning numb, we stumbled our way over the snow-covered roads. We were so miserably cold that Betty and I wanted to cry, but Jean and Joan always did their best to cheer us up. "You'd better not cry," they would say, "or your tears will turn to icicles and hang from your eyelids." The thought of this would make us smile, though we weren't altogether certain that it wouldn't happen.

As there were no farm chores or much else to keep us occupied in the evenings after the supper dishes were cleared away, the Benders, not wanting us to hear their squabbles, would shoo us off to bed while it was still light outside. Lying in bed with light still streaming through the uncovered window, we could see that the wall plasterboard, facing the foot of our bed and running the length of the room, did not meet the ceiling, leaving a two-inch space. As the room grew darker, we could see mice running along the top edge of the plasterboard. Their antics amused us, and we giggled every time they stopped in the middle of their run to peer down on us as if we were some strange creatures invading their home. Wrinkling their noses and twitching their whiskers, they would scamper back and forth across the wall.

Sitting up in bed one night, each of us decided to pick out our own mouse and give it a name to see if we could recognize it when it reappeared. Later we started quibbling over which mouse belonged to whom because they pretty much all looked alike.

Our playful noise soon brought Mr. Bender bursting through the door, wielding the kitchen broom. We quickly ducked under the blankets and covered our heads up tight.

"What the hell is going on in here?" he bellowed as he banged the broom across our bodies—WHUUUMP, WHUUUMP, WHUUUMP! Scrunching down in bed, we tried to make ourselves as small as possible, protecting our heads with our arms.

"Now, shut the hell up and get to sleep," he barked, "or you'll get more of this!" He then left the room, slamming the door behind him.

As soon as he was gone, we popped out from under the covers. "Are you okay? Are you okay?" we all asked at the same time.

"Damn, that hurt!" Jean groaned, rubbing her elbow.

"Yeah," Joan agreed, "especially when the darn handle gets you!"

"He's a horrible old fart," I said.

Jean snickered. "Yep, and you can bet that's somethin' he ain't gonna outgrow."

"Do you think the mice might get into our bed and bite us?" Betty whispered to me.

"No, they only eat cheese, and you don't look like cheese," I replied.

"And you sure don't smell like it, either," Jean chuckled as she sniffed beneath the covers.

"Shuuush. Shut up and get to sleep," Joan warned, "or the old grouch will be coming in here again."

We were bored. It was hard for us to settle down and behave ourselves going to bed so early, and we got the broom treatment many times while huddling tightly together to keep from rolling off the small bed.

16

New Rules Are Set

We stayed at this house for a few months while we waited for the tobacco farm to be readied. Then one day, with my sisters and I all buttoned up, boots on, and set to go out the door for school, Mrs. Bender stopped us. "Listen up," she said. "You're not to come home today. You're to wait at the school until your dad comes to get you. He might be a few minutes late, but you're to wait for him. Is that understood?"

We nodded and were walking out the door when she picked up an envelope from the table. "Oh, I almost forgot. Give this note to your teacher." She handed it to Joan. "Now off with you." She held open the door, shooing us out into the frosty air before it chilled her.

"Why didn't you ask what was in the note?" I kidded Jean. "Did you lose your nerve this time, huh?"

"No, darn it. I was all set to ask until you poked me in the ribs," she replied, giving me a playful shove.

"Why do you think he's comin' to pick us up?" Betty asked. "He's never done that before. Do you think we're goin' to the tobacco farm?"

"Beats me," Jean said, "but that's as good a guess as any. Let's see the envelope."

As she reached to grab it, Joan quickly held it behind her back.

"Oh, for Pete's sake," Jean huffed, "I just wanna look at it."

"No, she trusted it to me, and besides, it's sealed." She then flipped the envelope over and poked it into Jean's face. "See?"

"Oh, la-di-da! You'd think you were carrying the crown jewels or somethin'. The only reason she gave it to you was because you were the last one out the door. You're always the pokiest."

"Am not."

"You are too."

I smiled as I listened to their bickering. Jean was right. Joan was our poky sister. She was the last one to get dressed, the last one downstairs, and the last one away from the table. It took her forever to eat, and she was often sent away from the table before she'd finished her meal.

"Let's hold it up to the sun," I suggested. "Maybe we can see through it and read what it says."

"Good idea," Joan agreed, as she held the envelope up against the bright sun.

We gathered around and tried to peer through it but were unable to make out a single word. "Naw, it's no use. It's all folded up inside," Joan said.

"Shucks," I grumbled, kicking at the snow, "I really want to know what it says."

Joan shoved the letter back into her pocket, and we continued on to school.

Mrs. Kiley took the note, read it, and set it aside. But I was antsy all day, wondering what Mrs. Bender had written.

Finally, around midday, just before our last recess, Mrs. Kiley picked up the letter and called for our attention. "The Mudford twins are moving away and will be attending a new school."

"The Mudford twins . . ." I winced. I hated being called the Mudford twins — as if we were sewn together like squares on a patchwork quilt. But I could forgive Mrs. Kiley because I liked her.

My sisters and I looked at each other, for we were as much surprised as the other kids.

Mrs. Kiley dismissed us for recess and suggested that we say good-bye to all our friends since this was to be our last day at Union School. As the day ended and the students left, Mrs. Kiley wished us good luck, saying that she'd miss us. She gave each of us a big hug. She was a large, plump lady, and her arms seemed to envelop me. It felt good to get a hug, and the warmth of it stayed with me for several minutes. The last big hug I could remember was from Mrs. Miller, and that seemed so long ago.

"I'm sorry I can't leave the door open for you so you can keep warm," she said as she turned the key in the lock. "But if you stand over here in this corner, you might be protected a bit from the wind. It's such a frightfully cold day, and I do hope your ride comes soon."

We waved good-bye and watched as she trudged away, adjusting her black wool scarf up around her face.

Chilled to the bone, we huddled in the corner against the red brick wall and waited patiently for Mr. Bender.

"D . . . D . . . Do you th . . . think he for . . . forgot he was supposed to pick us up?" Betty whimpered through chattering teeth.

"Naw, he probably couldn't start the old jalopy in this cold weather," Jean replied.

Joan crossed her legs and started wiggling up and down.

"I have to pee—real baaad—or I'm gonna wet my pants!"

"Me too," I said, wiping my cold, wet nose across my coat sleeve.

Struggling to pull down her thick undergarment from beneath her bulky winter coat, Joan squatted in the corner to pee while the three of us formed a wall in front of her. And when she finished we each took our turn.

"We'd better cover up our tinkle tracks so nobody sees them," Betty said.

"Don't see why it matters. Ain't coming back here anyway," Jean snickered. "Look, our old man's coming," she said, pointing toward the road. "See? He's got the horses and bobsled. I told you he probably couldn't start the car."

We kicked some clean snow into the corner to cover our mess and ran to meet the bobsled.

"Whoa! Whoa!" Mr. Bender yelled, yanking hard on the reins to bring the horses to a halt. "Hurry and climb on. We don't have time to waste!"

He had loaded some straw bales onto the sled, and we scrambled up onto them. As soon as we were on board, he gave a quick snap of the reins to the horses' cold rumps. "Giddyup!" he shouted. Bolting upright, the horses, with the cold, frosty air spurting from their flaring nostrils, shook their long manes and took off in a gallop down the main road. We lurched backward but managed to grab the twine around the bales to keep from falling off. As the sled passed by our school road, we figured we were on our way to the tobacco farm. We glanced at each other, nodded, and smiled smugly—knowing we had guessed right.

We rode for quite a while, down some unfamiliar side roads, across some fields, and finally down onto some railroad tracks. "Steady, girl! Steady, girl!" Mr. Bender called out to the horses as he tightened the reins and the bobsled bounced roughly over the tracks. "Whoa! Whoa!" he shouted as he drove off the tracks and jerked the horses to a stop in front of a white clapboard house with black shutters.

As soon as my boots were safely on the ground after that wild ride, I breathed a sigh of relief and looked around the place. I noticed the usual outhouse toilet; one large, red barn with a silo; a small, gray barn; a corncrib; and a henhouse — all familiar farm buildings. What puzzled me was a large, long A-shaped glass house near the railroad tracks. Beside it, perched high above on a wooden platform and held up by a wood frame structure, sat a big, gray-metal cylindrical tank. On the other side of the house were two large, green tarpapered buildings with huge doors on both sides.

Unable to curb my curiosity, I pointed to them and asked, "What are those strange green buildings?"

"Those are tobacco kilns. You'll learn more about them later. Off with you now."

I shrugged and walked away.

"Quick, let's get inside and look around," Betty said, tugging at my sleeve.

Not knowing any better, we dashed through the front porch door beside the circular driveway. As we opened the inner door of the porch, we found ourselves in the kitchen where Mrs. Bender was cooking on the wood-burning stove. "You came through the front door. From now on you are to use the back door!" she snapped, pointing to the door at the far end of the kitchen.

"Sorry," Jean muttered, as she turned her back and rolled her eyes at us.

We were surprised to see that the Benders had set everything up while we were at school, and Jean asked, "Can we look around?"

"Oh, I suppose so," Mrs. Bender said with some reluctance in her voice. "Just be quick about it."

Happy that Jean's boldness had paid off again, we followed her in single file as we wound our way through the house. We took a quick peek into Mr. and Mrs. Bender's bedroom at the far end of the house, then made our way back into the living room where we noticed a freestanding kerosene stove in the middle of the floor. It was nice and warm, so we stopped to thaw our hands.

"Come on, girls, get a move on," Mrs. Bender prodded. "I've got to get supper on."

We hurried through the dining room and out into the kitchen. Betty reached for the knob of a door leading off the kitchen, but Mrs. Bender stopped her. "Oh, there's nothing in there for you to see. It's just the laundry room." She pointed to another door and said, "That other door down there is the one you'll be using to go outside. There's a back porch there also." Pointing to another door, she said, "That room is Doug's, and the door next to it goes upstairs to your rooms."

It was obvious she was eager for us to get to our rooms, so we made a beeline toward our door. We took a quick peek into Doug's room as we passed by, noting how nicely she had fixed it.

Eager to look at our rooms, we pushed and shoved each other, trying to make our way up the narrow staircase. We stopped at the top to look around, and I suddenly felt chilled. "Brrrr, it's cold up here," I said, crossing my arms tightly across my chest as we checked out the bedrooms. There was a stovepipe in one of them, and I looked it over and saw wires wrapped around it to secure it out from the wall. "Guess it comes up from the kitchen stove," I said.

"Yeah, it sure does. It's warm, too," Betty said.

We crowded around it and tried again to warm our cold hands.

"Look over there," I said. "It's like the Steadman house. The boards on the walls don't meet the ceiling. Wonder if we'll see some furry friends again."

"Boy, I hope not," Betty said. "I've had enough broom whackings!"

Each room was furnished with a metal bed and a small chest of drawers. A piece of old linoleum was under each bed but barely covered the rest of the wooden plank floor. A naked lightbulb dangled from a cord in the center of each room. One lonely chair sat beside the hewn-wood stair railing in the front bedroom.

We grumbled about our rooms. These bedrooms weren't warm and cozy like the ones we had on the Front Road farm. "Well, at least we each have our own window," Joan said as we peeked out.

Because of the low, sloping ceilings, the windows were low and only a few inches above the floor. Kneeling down and poking our heads close, we blew our breath on the frost-covered glass until we had melted a hole big enough to see through. "This one looks out over the porch and down to the barnyard," Joan said. "Oh, look how far we can see down the road—almost a mile, I bet. This is gonna be our room!" she announced.

As she looked down to the driveway, Jean grinned and said, "We'll be able to see who's coming and going."

Betty and I ran to check our windows and found the view mostly blocked by the tobacco kilns. "Oh, yeech, we can't see anything except those stupid buildings," Betty grumbled. "What did he say they were?"

"He said 'tobacco kilns' and we'd find out later what they're used for."

"Look," Jean interrupted, "where does that cubbyhole lead to?"

We hurried over to investigate the strange black hole leading back off the railing.

"Beats me," I said, "but it's scary as hell. I'll never be able to sleep if they don't block it off."

"Fat chance they'll do that," Jean said with a huff, "really a fat chance!"

We waited in our rooms, wondering what was expected of us next, for it was getting dark now and our stomachs were beginning to growl.

"I'm so hungry I could eat the hind legs off a horse."

Joan had barely spit the words out when the door opened below. We were hoping it was a call for dinner, but we were disappointed when Mr. Bender made his way upstairs with a hammer in one hand and a few nails sticking out of his mouth. We watched as he went over to the far wall and hammered them in. "There, you can hang your clothes here," he announced as he made his way downstairs, bending his tall frame to keep from hitting his head on the sloped ceiling. Pausing on the bottom landing, he turned and hollered up one more command. "Now, don't go prancing around too much up here; it makes a helluva racket downstairs."

We stared at each other, not quite sure of what he meant. "Guess that means we have to stay in our beds, 'cause there's nowhere else to sit."

Just then the door opened again. "Your mom says you can come down for supper now."

As we hurried into the kitchen, we noticed only four dishes set out. I furrowed my brow and looked at my sisters. It was obvious that the Benders had already eaten. I couldn't understand the meaning of it, and it caused a strange feeling in the pit of my stomach.

• • •

Our lives on this new farm were fast changing as new rules were set out for us each day, making us very upset. Our first surprise came when Mrs. Bender told us that we would no longer be eating with the family but would be called for our meals when they had finished theirs. "Furthermore," she said, "I wanna remind you again that there'll be no yakking at the table, and you're to speak only when spoken to."

We grew unhappier each day, for they seldom spoke to us—not even saying good morning or good night to us—only scolding or cuffing the backs of our heads for one thing or another. They exchanged only a few necessary words with us each day.

The final blow came when we were told that we would be confined to our rooms or outdoors. "If you want to come out of your rooms to go outside or to come in the house, you are to knock first," Mrs. Bender warned. "Is that understood?"

Within a few short weeks in this new home, we found ourselves more cut off from the family and increasingly more fearful and lonely. Sitting huddled together in one of our cold beds, we discussed these new rules.

"Why do you suppose they won't let us eat with them anymore?" I asked.

"Maybe they want to eat up all the good stuff first and leave us the scraps," Jean replied. "Makes me so angry I feel like stompin' on the floor."

"Me too," added Betty. "And with Doug back home, they wanna make sure he gets his big belly filled first!"

"I think they just don't want us to overhear any of their conversations or know any of their business," said Joan. "Remember the Hunkie thing. They've treated us worse ever since that time. And besides, Mr. Bender can do a lot of cussing when he gets worked up."

"Yeah," Jean joined in. "You're right, Joan. They don't want us to know *any* of their business. Remember how she warned Mr. Bender about being careful what they say around us because little pigs have big ears?"

"They don't even care two cents about us! Betcha they just put up with us for the money they get!" Jean concluded, huffily crossing her arms over her chest.

• • •

In the winter months it was so frigid in these unfinished rooms that we had to sleep with our winter coats on top of our flannel nightgowns and chenille robes in order to keep warm. Most of the weekends when we were not forced outside in the cold, we had to spend our time in our beds, because there was no other place to sit.

Having no games, puzzles, or toys of any kind, we idled away our time reading or doing homework, balancing our books on our knees. Often, using paper from our scribblers, we played hangman, connect the dots, or X's and O's.

On rare occasions, Mrs. Bender would leave a Sears catalog on the steps for us. We drooled over the nice clothes and pretty shoes and then cut the catalog to pieces to make paper dolls.

During these long, cold evenings, my sisters and I would be bored to tears and hungry for some source of entertainment, so we would crowd together in Jean and Joan's bedroom near the warm stovepipe and chat. The lights were turned off from a kitchen switch, leaving us in near darkness long before we were tired enough to sleep.

In the evenings Mr. Bender often sat at the kitchen table, drinking beer while listening to a small, green plastic radio. We waited and prayed for him to turn it on so we could listen to it, too. Many times he would tune in to the Hit Parade that came from Wheeling, West Virginia, or Cincinnati, Ohio. Other times he would listen to Amos'n Andy, Jack Benny, Red Skelton, or mystery stories like

The Shadow or *The Green Hornet*. The Hit Parade was our favorite station. We would memorize the songs and sing them on our way to school. Jean and Joan had beautiful singing voices like our sister Muggs, but Betty and I could barely carry a tune.

As soon as Mr. Bender would click the radio on and the sounds began filtering up beside the stovepipe as if following a path, we'd yelp with joy and clap our hands. It was time to "listen down the stovepipe." Tossing the blankets aside, we would scramble out of bed and tiptoe over to the stovepipe, groping our way through the darkness. "Be careful, we don't want them to hear us. They're right below us, ya know," Joan would remind us.

Taking designated spots, we would lie with our bellies on the floor and position our heads around the stovepipe. We would press our ears as close to the stovepipe floor opening as possible, in order to hear most of the broadcast, being careful not to burn ourselves or, worse yet, bang the pipe with our heads.

"Oh, wow! He's got the Hit Parade on from Wheeling, West Virginyahh," Jean would say, trying to imitate the announcer.

"Quick, Bonnie," another would say, "grab a pencil and paper and copy the words down." For some reason my sisters assigned this job to me.

Soon the strains of "Chi-Baba, Chi-Baba" would drift up through the opening. "How do you spell that—quick, how do you spell it?" I snapped, as I hurried to copy down the words.

"Darned if I know; it sounds like gibberish to me," Jean said. "You know, the way the Hunkies talk."

"Shuuush!" I said. "It sounds nice to me. Wonder what it means . . ."

"I sure wish he would turn it up louder. I can barely hear it," Betty grumbled as she tried to wiggle her ear closer to the opening.

It was pretty cramped quarters for all of us, and finally a head banged against the pipe.

"Damn," Jean crabbed, "who hit the stupid pipe?" But before anyone had time to take the blame, Mr. Bender banged on the kitchen ceiling with a broom handle, sending us scurrying back to our beds.

Trying desperately not to touch the squeaky floor, we climbed onto the bed frame and squeezed through the metal rails of the headboard. No sooner had we dove into bed than he opened the door and bellowed up to us, "Get your damn heads away from that stovepipe, and quit your eavesdropping, or you're gonna get the shit beat out of you! Now, get the hell back in your beds!" He slammed the door with a loud thud that echoed up the stairwell.

"We'd better be more careful," Joan warned, "or we're gonna get another lickin' one of these days."

"Who gives a toot?" Jean snorted. "What do they expect us to do up here anyway, sit around and suck our big toes?"

We just had to laugh, but we were careful to muffle it with our blankets.

As we settled back into Jean and Joan's bed, Jean decided to make up a little hillbilly ditty for us to sing:

Gonna lissin down the stovepipe,
You betcha! Yessiree!
'Cause no amount of lickin's
Ain't gonna stop me.

True to our silly ditty, no amount of threats or whippings kept us away from the stovepipe. It was an escape from our lifeless world beyond our bedroom walls and was the highlight of our days. We felt cheated and sad whenever an evening went by and Mr. Bender didn't play the radio. The stovepipe was also like a good friend. It was always waiting to warm our cold hands or dry our wet mittens and socks as we hung them over the wires. Other times, after pulling our red ribbons through our mouths to wet them, we would pull them back and forth across the pipe to iron out the wrinkles. And, after spending long winter days in the woods helping to fell and cut trees to size for the stove, we would race upstairs to hug the warm stovepipe with our cold arms.

• • •

There were yet more changes in our lives. Mr. Bender caught Joan and me sneaking outside in the middle of the night to use the outhouse and decided to make short work of our nighttime trips. As we crowded in one of the beds to do our schoolwork, he opened the door and called to us. "One of you girls come down here right away!"

Jean ran at once down to the bottom landing while Betty, Joan, and I ran to the stair railing, anxious about what he could possibly want. We always feared the worst.

"Here," he said, "there'll be no traipsing in and out at all hours of the day and night to go to the outhouse. From now on you're to use this." He handed Jean an empty gallon paint can that had contained dark green paint. "You're to take turns emptying it every morning, and don't dare forget, or there'll be hell to pay. From now on this door will be locked."

Joan turned to me. "That old bugger is gonna lock us in!"

"Sure sounds like it." I shook my head in disbelief. *How can he be so cruel?* I wondered.

"He expects us to use this old thing?" Jean asked, curling her lip in disgust as she held the can up for us to see.

"Eeew! We had a nice chamber pot at the Millers', didn't we, Betty? Remember, it was all white with pretty red rosebuds on it."

"Yeah, and it even had a lid to keep the smell in."

"Where should we put it?" Jean asked, looking around the room to find a suitable spot.

"Here, let's stick it under Bonnie and Betty's bed where it'll be on the linoleum," Joan suggested as she bent down to slide it under our bed. "Oh, cripes, it won't fit! We'll just have to keep it at the head of the bed and hope nobody trips over it."

"What if we have to do number two? Are we supposed to use the can for that, too?" Betty asked. "That's really gonna stink."

"We'll cover it with an old Sears catalog. What else are we supposed to do?" Joan asked, throwing her hands up and slumping down on the bed.

"Well, it looks like we have only three choices: one, we use the can; two, we poop in our pants; or three, we stick our bums out the window," Jean said. "Take your pick."

"I'm sure we're supposed to use it for everything," Joan giggled.

After a few minutes of grumbling over this new set of rules, Joan asked, "Anyone have to pee yet?"

"I do," I said, scrambling out of bed to beat my sisters to the can. "I'm gonna be the first to try it out." Whipping up my nightgown, I settled down on the can as my sisters watch from the bed. "It's hard to sit on. It's too low, and I feel like I'm gonna topple off," I griped. "Maybe we could prop it up on something."

Jean—always quick to put me in my place, piped up. "For Pete's sake, princess, what do you want; someone to hold it for you?"

"Oh, you're such a smart aleck! Just wait until you have to use it." As I tried to get up off the can, the soft green paint around the rim caused it to stick to my backside. Realizing what was happening, I turned to my sisters. "Help, get this darn thing off me! It's stuck!"

My sisters took one look at me and doubled over with laughter.

"I think we should leave it there," Betty snickered. "It looks good on you!"

Joan was the first to feel sorry for me, coming to my rescue and pulling the can loose.

They all burst out laughing again. "Now what's so darn funny?" I snarled.

Pointing at my backside, Betty chuckled, "You've got a dark green ring all around your bum!"

I twisted as much as I could to see the green ring, wondering how I was going to get it off. Then, pouting and upset at their poking fun at me, I crawled back into bed as Jean and Joan left for their room. Covering my head with the blankets, I sulked and thought about how much I hated this place. I hated being locked in our cold rooms while the Benders sat beside a warm stove. I hated that we had to eat by ourselves and not be part of the family. I hated having to knock to go in or out of the house. I thought of how we would purposefully eat slowly just to warm ourselves and how Mrs. Bender would cuff our heads and tell us to get a move on and quit our dillydallying. Yanking the blankets off my head, I mumbled to Betty, "I don't like it here, Betty. I just hate it!" Banging my fists into my pillow, I buried myself deep into the center sag of the mattress and tried to sleep.

17

It Became Clear Now

Betty and I were thrilled to learn we'd be returning to the same school we went to when we lived with the Millers. Betty would be finishing up her third grade and I my fourth, and we were looking forward to seeing our school friends again. *Will they be surprised to learn that we have twin sisters?* I wondered.

Mrs. Bender kept us home the first two days to take us into the town of Simcoe to get shoes and boots and the clothes she'd ordered through the Sears catalog. This was our first trip into town, and having never known the joys of window-shopping, we were giddy with excitement as we peeked in the store windows on our way to the shoe store.

"You girls calm down and stop acting like a bunch of clowns!" Mrs. Bender crabbed as she marched us into the shoe store. "Now, behave yourselves and sit still while you're in here. Understand?"

We nodded.

Taking the first four available seats, we looked around at the beautiful assortment of girls' shoes on display, smiling and whispering to each other as we pointed out the ones we liked.

Mrs. Bender looked around for a few minutes and then sat down beside us while a salesman, who was nicely dressed in a suit and tie, pulled a few styles of shoes off the shelf and brought them over. My heart soared, for in his selection was the pair I liked. *Oh, please, let her pick those,* I prayed silently.

"So we're here to outfit these young ladies, are we?" he asked, smiling warmly at us.

"Young ladies?" No one had ever called us that except Mrs. Bender in her favorite warning: "Don't you get cheeky with me, young lady!" And so I sat up straight and squared off my shoulders the way Mrs. Miller had taught me.

Mrs. Bender shook her head and waved him away. "No, I don't want those. The girls are awfully hard on shoes, and I want something more durable—nothing fancy." She pointed to some shoes on the other side of the store. "Let's have a look at those over there."

"But those are boys' shoes, ma'am," the salesman said.

"Yes, I know. But I'd still like to look at them."

"Certainly, ma'am." Appearing puzzled, the salesman brought two pairs of heavy, thick-soled, black and brown leather shoes with laces. "Like these, ma'am?" he asked.

"Yes, the black ones will do nicely—perhaps a half-size larger because they have to make do for a good long time," she said, as he prepared to measure my foot. "I also want some galoshes to go over them. Now, if you will get them fitted up, we'll be on our way."

The biggest lump ever came into my throat as I put my foot on the strange-looking measuring tool. I wanted to throw up and cry. I could already hear the kids at school snickering and poking fun at us. I knew Mrs. Miller would never have put boys' shoes on us; I was no longer eager to return to our old school.

We sat stiffly in our chairs, the happiness draining from us as the salesman obligingly fitted us with boys' shoes and galoshes.

We then had to clomp around the floor until Mrs. Bender was satisfied with her purchase.

On the ride home, we sat silently in the backseat with the Sears catalog package crammed in beside our feet. *What's in it,* I wondered. *Is it more ugly school clothes?*

As we headed up the stairs, Mrs. Bender handed Jean the package. "These are your new school clothes. Put them on and come down so I can see how they fit."

"I hate boys' shoes!" I blurted out, hoping Mrs. Bender was still within earshot. "I'd rather go barefoot!"

"Me too," Betty chimed in. "It's too bad we aren't boys."

"Then she'd probably get us girls' shoes," Jean quipped as she ripped open the package, spilling the contents onto the bed. "Well, lookie here. We each got a pair of old ladies' bloomers." She held the bulky, blue flannel bloomers with elastic at the waist and legs, up against her midsection. We grinned at her. "Even a fart couldn't get out of these," she snickered as she peered down inside them.

There were blue, pleated tunics; short-sleeved white blouses with Peter Pan collars; dark blue cardigans; and long, brown cotton stockings.

"The tunics look pretty nice," Joan said, holding one up against me. "Too bad we have to wear boys' shoes with them."

"What in the world are these!" Jean exclaimed as she fished the last four items out of the package. "They look like boys' underwear." She tossed us each a pair.

"They are," I said. "They're long johns, like Doug wears. We've seen them hanging on the clothesline."

"Oh, yeech!" Betty scoffed, disgusted by the thought of wearing anything Doug would wear.

"Look at the silly flap in the back. I guess we unbutton this when we have to use the outhouse," Joan said.

Jean grinned. "Yup, it's a back door, all right. Sure beats taking all your clothes off in a cold outhouse."

We tried on all our clothes, but we were confused as to how to wear the stockings with the long johns.

"I think we pull them up over our underwear," Betty said, showing us how she was doing it. We did the same.

"This looks *so* ugly!" I grumbled, getting more upset by the minute. "My legs are all bumpy — like a warthog. I'm not gonna wear these. I'd rather freeze!"

"You'll wear them if you know what's good for you," Joan warned. "Besides, they'll go nice with your beautiful shoes."

"Hmm, I wonder how we're supposed to keep these darn stockings up," Jean said, rummaging through the package looking for garters. "Why don't you go and ask her what we're supposed to do."

"Go ask her yourself," Joan shot back.

Jean turned to me. "You go ask her."

"Uh-uh, you do it. She gave you the package."

"You're such a bunch of fraidy-cats," Jean scoffed, shoving us aside and stomping down the stairs. But when she got to the bottom landing, she stopped and looked back at the three of us hanging over the railing. She turned back toward the door and raised her hand as if to knock, but hesitated.

"Go ahead, knock," Joan said, hoping that Jean hadn't lost her nerve.

Jean hesitated, then knocked softly.

"What's the problem!" Mrs. Bender snapped as she opened the door, clearly annoyed.

"We don't have any garters to hold up our stockings," Jean said, trying her best not to appear timid.

"Wait right here. I'll be right back," Mrs. Bender said, pointing firmly to the spot where Jean was standing, to leave no doubt that she was not to set foot into the kitchen.

She returned shortly and handed Jean a bunch of old sealer rings she had used on canning jars. "Here, you'll have to make do with these. That's all I have. As soon as you're finished dressing, come back down so I can look you over."

"Sealer rings!" I complained, after Jean had handed each of us a pair. "These won't even fit around my ankles, let alone above my knee!"

We tried stretching the rubber rings as much as possible, but they still cut deeply into our legs, almost bringing us to the point of tears. We then went down to the kitchen for Mrs. Bender's inspection.

"They'll do fine," she said as we turned about in the middle of the kitchen. "Now, get them off and hang them up so they'll be ready for school tomorrow."

We raced upstairs, impatient to get the rubber rings off our legs. "Does she really expect us to wear these all day long? Our legs will be black and blue," I crabbed.

"Hey, these things might be more fun to play with," Betty said as she stretched one out and let it fly through the air, clipping Joan on the side of the head. Soon we were all running through the bedrooms shooting the rings at each other. After tiring of that, we played a game of ring-toss using the knob on the bedpost for our target. Our excited romping soon brought Mrs. Bender to the bottom landing. "What's all the racket up there?" she yelled. "Cut it out this minute!"

When the door slammed shut, Jean pressed her hands over her ears and groaned, "Damn, I didn't hear her open the door! I guess we were just havin' too much fun."

"Well, we have to have some fun," Betty lamented. "And these are the only toys we have to play with."

• • •

Later that day the Benders took us for a ride in the car to show us the route to school. "It's a straight shot from the farm, not more than a good mile's walk for you, so you shouldn't have any problem getting here," Mr. Bender said.

Betty and I recognized familiar surroundings as we passed through the small village of Woodsville and pointed out to Jean and Joan the Baptist church we attended, the Hoovers' store where Mr. Miller bought us candy, and the Miller house where we had lived.

Pushing Joan aside, I leaned close to the side window, straining my neck to get a better look at the house as we drove by. "Look, Betty, it looks just the same as when we left it!"

She nodded, and sniffled, "A . . . And there's where w . . . we used to skate." Her voice broke with emotion as she went on, "We ha . . . had so much fun; didn't we, Bonnie?"

I took her hand, gave it a squeeze, and then leaned back in the seat as I recalled the happy times we had at the Millers.

A few minutes later Mr. Bender pulled off the road and stopped at a large, two-story yellow house at the edge of the village.

"Hey, I know where we are," I said excitedly to Joan and Jean. "This is the Tillmans' house! We used to visit here with Mr. and Mrs. Miller."

I was wondering how the Benders knew them when Mrs. Bender spoke up. "Yes, I know. Mr. and Mrs. Tillman are my mom and dad. You may call them Grandma and Grandpa Tillman. We are only going to stay for a short while, and before we go in, I want to warn you to be on your best behavior."

As Betty and I hopped eagerly out of the car, I asked, "Do you think they'll remember us?"

"Yes, of course they will," Mrs. Bender replied, overhearing my question. "My mother was the one who told me about Mrs. Miller having to give you back to the shelter."

We now knew how we ended up with the Benders. Many thoughts and questions were swirling through my mind, but I said nothing as I hurried into the house.

The Tillmans seemed happy to see us again and greeted us warmly. "By Jove, you've both grown a tad since leaving the Millers," Mr. Tillman joked, as Mrs. Bender introduced Jean and Joan.

"We have time for only a brief visit," Mrs. Bender said. "We were only driving through to show the girls their new school route and let you meet the other set of twins. They'll be starting school first thing in the morning and still have some barn chores to do before supper."

• • •

We were apprehensive about starting back to school, making new friends, and meeting a new teacher. We began our daily routine by taking our washbasin downstairs where Mrs. Bender filled it with warm water from the stove reservoir. It was the same old enameled white basin with the red rim that she'd used for Betty when Doug hurt her, although it was now chipped and dented. Did my sister remember this basin? She never mentioned it and neither did I.

After the usual breakfast of bread and milk with a sprinkling of brown sugar on top, we were set to go out the door when Mrs. Bender wagged her finger at us. "Now remember, don't go stepping into any puddles with those new shoes, for they're all you're going to get for a good long time."

"She could have at least said good-bye or something," Joan grumbled.

"That'll be a frosty Friday," Jean retorted. "She never has anything nice to say to us."

Walking down the paved road wasn't as much fun as cutting through pastures, shocking ourselves on electric fences, dabbling in the creek, or hopping over cow pies; but the short distance through the village somewhat made up for it.

The first leg of our walk was quite boring, and we moaned about our garters hurting our legs and our too-big shoes causing blisters on our heels as they rubbed up and down with every step.

"I hate my bumpy legs. I bet no one else has bumpy legs," I complained.

"Oh, Bonnie, quit your bellyachin'," Joan chided. "You do more grumbling than all of us put together."

"Well, if anyone laughs at me, I'll spit in their eye or knock their tonsils down their throat," Jean said. "Just wait and see if I don't!"

I was beginning to care more about my appearance now and didn't want to be laughed at. "I don't care, I wanna look pretty, and so I'm pulling them up."

"You're what?"

"You'll see."

They gathered around as I rolled down my brown stockings and hiked up the legs of the long johns, tucking them under the elastic legs of the bloomers and leaving my legs bare. Then I pulled the stockings back up and adjusted the garters. "There," I said, patting down the bulky bloomers and smoothing my tunic over them, "my garters don't hurt as much now, either." I was pleased with myself and didn't care what they thought.

"You look a little fat," Betty said, "but it's not a bad idea. I'm gonna do mine, too."

I watched with satisfaction as my sisters did the same thing. Then we poked fun at our chubby thighs as we tried patting and smoothing down the bulkiness.

"We've got to remember to pull them down before we get home," Joan pointed out, "or we'll catch hell for sure."

Despite our grumbling about our clothes, we were pleased with our new tin lunch buckets—they sure beat the brown paper bags—but wondered why Mrs. Bender had bought them and what we had done to deserve them. We finally agreed that it was probably because we had to go through the Village of Woodsville, where more people would see us, as opposed to Union School, which was out in the country.

"I'm gonna check my lunch and see what we've got," I said, starting to open my lunch box.

"Why bother?" Jean shrugged. "Just 'cause it's a new bucket doesn't mean the food is gonna be different. It's probably the same old thing—beans, sliced potato, bacon grease, or brown sugar sandwiches and some soda crackers."

"I hope they're brown sugar sandwiches," I said, peering into my lunch box. "Those are my favorite." I pulled away the wax paper. "Aw, shucks, they're the leftover mashed white beans we had for supper last night."

"Darn good thing we wore these bloomers," Jean chuckled.

"But look," I said, "we've got soda biscuits with peanut butter between them. Wow, that's a first! I'm still hungry. I'm gonna eat mine now."

Excited about the crackers with peanut butter, my sisters unlatched their boxes, and we all munched down our crackers.

"Well, we've managed to eat most of our lunch now. We're gonna be starving before school's over," Joan sighed as she latched her bucket. "That wasn't very smart of us."

Once we had arrived in the village, Betty and I lingered in front of the Miller house for a few minutes, prattling on to Jean and Joan about our happy lives there, pointing out our bedroom window and telling them how hard we cried when we had to leave. I wanted to go around to the backyard and look around, but Joan said it would make us late for school. I felt sad and looked back over my shoulder at the Miller home as we trudged on toward school. But mixed with the sadness were happy thoughts of the beautiful clothes, pretty shoes, all the games and toys, and how I was never cold or hungry. Then my daydreaming was broken when Joan tugged at my arm and told me to get a move on or we'd be late for school.

No sooner had we stepped onto the school grounds than the bell rang and we hustled to get inside.

The teacher, Mrs. Anne Granderson, welcomed us, showed us where to put our lunch buckets, and assigned our seats. She was an older lady and was unusually tall. She had short, wavy gray hair that was held back behind her ears with gray combs. She wore gold-framed glasses that magnified the bags under her sharp blue eyes. On this day, she wore a plain, white, long-sleeved blouse and a woolen navy skirt. I noticed when she walked back and forth across the foot-high platform at the bottom of the chalkboard that her legs were quite bowed.

Several times throughout the day she turned away from the class to clear her throat in her handkerchief. The older kids wrinkled up their noses in disgust, but we younger ones just snickered behind our hands. She seemed pleasant enough, but the older boys in the eighth grade tried her patience until she either sent them out into the entranceway or called them forward for a strapping.

As the day progressed, she apologized to us twins for her inability to keep our names straight and decided to pin large name tags on us until she was able to fix them to memory. I hated those tags. *Just like an old cowbell,* I thought, and I was happy when they were removed a few days later.

Joan was right. After finishing up my two sandwiches at lunch, I was still very hungry. A little boy, who was a couple of years younger than I, sat on the top of his desk with his opened lunch box on his lap. I noticed that it was chockfull of food and everything was neatly wrapped in wax paper. I knew he was fond of me, because he had followed me around on the playground, trying to get my attention. And though he had a disgusting habit of picking his nose, he was a sweet little boy with a mass of curly brown hair and big blue eyes with long lashes.

Looking at my empty bucket, he unfolded the wax papers and pulled out a large sandwich made with peanut butter and jelly. "Would you like one of my sandwiches?"

My eyes lit up as I saw jelly and peanut butter oozing out along every edge. I wanted so desperately to take it—even just to taste it—but his bad habit kept coming to mind. And so, not wanting to hurt his feelings, I put my hands on my stomach to fake a stomachache. "No, thank you. I don't feel very good." I sank glumly down in my seat as I watched him rewrap the sandwich and put it back into his bucket.

The first day seemed to fly by as Betty and I enjoyed seeing our old school friends. Mrs. Granderson handed out the necessary homework in order for us to catch up with our classmates, and we went home loaded down with books and scribblers.

After finishing up the barn chores and our supper, we went back to our bedrooms to get our homework finished before the lights were turned out. We all sat around in a circle in Jean and Joan's bedroom, not just so we could get the warmth from the stovepipe but also because this room had the plasterboard that didn't meet the ceiling. That made it possible for us to get rid of our paper trash by poking it through the open space at the top.

We had frequently wanted to knock on the door and ask for a garbage bag, but fearful of being yelled at, we had always chickened out. Now Joan had suggested a simple way to get rid of our trash.

"I wonder where all this paper's going?" I asked as I shoved more of it through the opening.

"Who cares?" Joan said, grinning like she had just invented the lightbulb. "As long as it never gets filled up, we'll be okay."

• • •

When warm weather came and we'd shed our winter clothes and long underwear, our walks to and from school were more enjoyable. Never in a hurry to get home, we often dillydallied in the village, chatting with friends or hanging out in a small restaurant. Once in a while we worked up enough nerve to stop in and see Grandma and Grandpa Tillman, for our visits with them were so enjoyable, and we always left with a good feeling.

They were from England and still had English accents that we loved to mimic.

Grandpa was a veteran of the Boer War and World War I. He was a short little gent with full jowls, an impish grin, twinkling blue eyes, and a ruddy complexion. He sported a full, bushy moustache that he kept waxed and turned up slightly at the corners. A few wispy strands of hair still adorned the top of his bald head. In addition to smoking a pipe, he often chewed on a plug of tobacco and kept a small brass spittoon near the foot of his favorite chair beside the wood-burning kitchen stove. He often pulled up his right pant leg to massage the back of his calf. He had showed us the bruised swelling where a piece of shrapnel was still lodged. It looked pretty ugly, and we felt sorry for him.

Grandma was a short, boxy lady with a kind, wrinkled, Kewpie-doll face. Her long gray hair was braided and coiled in a neat knot at the back of her head, and a fine, gray hairnet kept it in place. A small pair of "Ben Franklin" glasses perched on her nose just below her gray-blue eyes. Her usual attire was a housedress covered with a full, calico apron. Her brown stockings were usually rolled like a doughnut around her ankles. A picture on the wall revealed that she had been a beautiful lady in her younger days.

They were an adorable and devoted old couple. She affectionately called him "Willie," and he called her "the missus."

Sometimes our visits caught Grandpa in one of his mischievous moods, and he would tell us some naughty little jokes, knowing full well that we wouldn't understand some of them.

"What are the three most important vegetables in the garden?" he asked us one day as we crowded around his chair. We each made some wild guesses but couldn't come up with the right answer.

"It's lettuce, turnip, and pea." Then he would chuckle, grin, and stroke his chin as he settled back in his chair. Then, after taking a long draw on his pipe, he would cradle the bowl in his hand while he thought up another one for us.

"Now, here's one for you. What are the three most important things on a stove?"

We looked the stove over thoroughly, hoping to solve the riddle. We attempted a few guesses but none of them were correct. "We give up, Grandpa. What are they?"

"Lifter, leg, and poker," he said with a grin of amusement.

Grandma slid her glasses farther down on her nose, peered at him over the frames, and gently scolded, "Now, Willie, you shouldn't fill their heads with your silly nonsense."

He paid no heed to her as he snapped his suspenders and continued on, amused by our innocence. "One more and we'll call it a day. This is a tricky one," he warned as he put his pipe aside and bit off a plug of chewing tobacco. "What's long and thin and covered with skin and God knows how many holes it's been in?"

"Oh, Grandpa, that's easy," I replied, happy to know the answer. "It's a snake."

"By Jove, you're right," he replied, as he slapped his knee and chuckled.

"Oh, Willie," Grandma piped in again, "you're such a naughty rascal. What on earth am I ever going to do with you?" Waving a hand at him as if to shoo him away, she continued her crocheting, shaking her head, knowing her efforts were useless.

Grandpa's blue eyes twinkled merrily as he wiped his hand across his mouth as if trying to erase his impish grin. He twirled the ends of his moustache, sucked in the sides of his cheeks to muster up a wad of tobacco juice, and then leaned over and spit a brown stream into the spittoon at his feet. He was always on target, and I marveled at his accuracy.

Before we said our good-byes, Grandma brought down a little white-porcelain shoe from the shelf of her china cabinet, cupping it carefully in both hands. It was filled near to the brim with pennies. Noticing me admiring the flowers on the shoe, she explained to us: "This was an anniversary gift from my Willie while he was stationed in Germany during World War I. You can each pick out two pennies—enough to buy your favorite sucker."

"Thank you, Grandma," we said in unison as we pocketed the money and made our way out the door. Those pennies were burning a hole in our pockets, and we could hardly wait for the next day to buy suckers. Our favorites were either a caramel or licorice B.B. bat. This was a popular treat, and the licking was good for a couple of hours.

Happy for the good time we'd had with the Tillmans but dreading what lay ahead, we would plod reluctantly homeward.

18

The Surprise of Our Lives

It was the spring of 1945. Jean and Joan were eleven and Betty and I nine when Mr. Bender made his first attempt at growing tobacco. My sisters and I could feel the excitement and nervous tension in the air as he called us out beside the greenhouse.

"You see all this junk and broken boards around here?" he said, motioning around the front of the greenhouse. "Well, I want it all cleared away to make room for the steam engine. The greenhouse has to be steamed today and the machine will be arriving soon."

"The steam engine?" Jean queried.

"Yes. It's coming to steam the soil to get ready for the tobacco seeds. Enough questions. Now, get a move on!"

So many curious questions were bouncing around in my head, but I knew enough to bite my tongue and get started cleaning up the junk. We'd seen the big monster-like machine chug down the highway before and were always fascinated, wondering what it was for. Now it was coming to our place. We could hardly contain our enthusiasm as we quickly cleared away the area so we could hurry over to our favorite viewing spot at the banks beside the railroad tracks where we could see far down the road. Here we sat, waiting and watching for the big machine to come chugging into view.

"There it is!" Joan yelled as soon as she spotted it.

Fascinated and amused, we watched as it clanged and clattered down the road. And when it came within a few hundred feet of us, we jumped up and down, waving our arms to catch the attention of the engineer. He gave us a few short, shrill blasts of his whistle, and we ran off to follow the machine as it rolled into the yard.

"Oooh, look at the big footprints!" Betty said excitedly as we examined the tracks the steel wheels had cut into the soft dirt. "We can play hopscotch on these."

"Good idea," I agreed, as we scouted around for some flat pebbles. It was so much fun playing in the warm, freshly churned earth with our bare feet, seeing who could jump the farthest between the cleat markings.

But soon Joan said, "Let's just play for a little while and then go and sit in the apple tree so we can watch them steam the greenhouse. We don't wanna get in the way because Mr. Bender's really grouchy today."

As we sat huddled together on the lower limbs of the apple tree, we saw two more men arrive to help. They lifted some huge metal pans from the machine and laid them over the black topsoil in the greenhouse. Soon the operator fired up the engine, and we giggled with joy as the silver steam started puffing furiously from the pipe stack.

A large, flexible hose was attached to the boiler and to the big silver pans. The engineer pulled a lever, letting the steam shoot through the hose. We laughed and swung our legs as the hose seemed to come alive and lurch into action like a giant worm each time the lever was pulled. Through the windows we could see the men moving the pans up and down the length of the greenhouse and wondered why all this preparation was necessary. Finally we figured it was to kill the weeds and bugs and soften the soil. It was a good day's work, and we were disappointed when all the excitement died down and the machine moved slowly out of the driveway.

Later on, Mr. Bender let us stand at the greenhouse doors and watch as he sprinkled what looked like black pepper over the soil. Each day we peered into the greenhouse and soon spotted the small tobacco plants poking through the black soil.

A large 500-gallon water tank sat on a high wooden platform beside the greenhouse for watering the plants. A hose ran from the bottom of the tank and connected to a sprinkler hose in the greenhouse. Mr. Bender watered the plants several times a day for about six weeks, and we had the responsibility of keeping the huge tank full.

Though most tobacco farms had motorized pumps to do this job, we had only a small, four-foot-high, forged steel hand pump. The water was pumped through a fifty-foot-long, one-inch-diameter pipe that ran underground and then up the side of the tank.

It was a full morning's work of steady pumping to fill the tank, two of us at a time working the small handle. It was a boring and difficult job, and we did plenty of grumbling. The water was used up in two or three days, and then we would have to refill the huge tank.

Mrs. Bender would tell us at breakfast when it was time to fill the tank again. And when her back was turned, we would look at each other and make faces.

We had to pump for so long that the steel handle would get hot and cause blisters on our hands. We rubbed them in the sand to cool them and dry off the sweat, and then we counted our blisters.

"I'll bet I've got the most blisters," Joan once said.

"Nope, I do," Betty bragged, "and that means I'm pumping the hardest."

"Wouldn't it be nice if they paid us a buck a blister?" I said. "We'd be rich in no time!"

Soon Mr. Bender called from the front porch door: "Quit your lollygagging and get back to work. That tank has to be filled before you get any lunch!"

"Why doesn't he come out and fill it himself?" Joan grumbled. "Maybe he'd realize how hard it is."

"I saw him pumping it one time," I said. "He knows how hard it is. Why do you think we got the job?"

"Yeah," Jean scoffed, "I'll bet he's in there swilling his beer while we're out here working our fannies off!"

The tank leaned a bit to one side, and we knew it was full when the water spilled over the low edge. "You know what?" Betty said. "Let's just keep on pumping after the tank is filled."

We knew that well water was scarce and at times the well got low, but we didn't care. We wanted to get even with them. So even after the water started spilling over the rim, we continued to pump away, grinning mischievously as it sloshed over and splashed into the rag weeds far below.

Mrs. Bender always kept a keen eye on us from the kitchen window to make sure we weren't goofing off. We knew she'd soon be shouting at us from the front porch, so we turned away from the tank and pretended we didn't see it overflowing. Her shrill voice soon cut through the air. "Stop pumping, for God's sake! You're wasting the water! Can't you see the tank's running over?"

We pretended not to hear her, making her yell again before looking her way, faking surprise as one of us pointed at the tank. When she called us in for lunch and we took our places at the table, she gave us each a clip to the back of the head along with a scolding for wasting the water.

We purposely looked at our blistered hands before eating, wanting her to see them. We knew she noticed, but she said nothing.

When the plants were large enough to be field planted, the tallest ones were pulled out of the greenhouse, put into trays, and carted out to the fields. A two-wheeled planting machine containing a fifty-gallon metal drum filled with a mixture of water and fertilizer sat on a platform between the wheels. On top of the drum was a seat for the driver, and behind the drum — low to the ground — were two seats for the planters.

Mr. Bender sat in the front seat and drove the horses that pulled the planter. Betty and Mrs. Bender rode on the back seats with their legs outstretched and their feet resting on a metal bar, the young seedlings on their laps ready to be planted. As Betty was short, the foot bar was moved completely forward. But even then she was barely able to reach it. Many times her foot slipped off the bar and she'd scream for Mr. Bender to stop the horses before her leg became tangled under the machine. Concerned that she might break her leg, we suggested to Mrs. Bender that Jean or Joan ride the planter, since they were taller.

"No, absolutely not," she said. "Betty's the quickest one of the bunch."

We grumbled about it, but she wouldn't listen.

The machine punched a hole in the dirt mounds every two feet or so and shot in a spurt of water. Mrs. Bender and Betty took turns dropping a plant into the hole. The machine then pushed the dirt up around the plant. If the horses weren't kept at a steady pace and went too fast, Mrs. Bender and Betty would be unable to keep up, and some of the holes would be left empty. Joan and I followed behind the machine with a six-quart basket full of plants, sticking plants into the empty spaces. Jean's job was to see that the four of us were well supplied with plants.

When Mr. Bender turned around at the end of the field to start down another row, it was Betty's job to quickly raise the lever, bringing the cutter up out of the dirt to keep from damaging it. It required all her strength. It was often hard for her to get it up in time, which made Mr. Bender jerk hard on the reins to bring the horses to a stop.

One day he turned and barked at her. "What the hell's the matter with you? Get that damn thing out of the ground before you break it!"

Shoving the plants off her lap, Betty jumped off the planter. "Plant your own damn tobacco!" she shot back, walking away in a huff.

Shocked by her bold behavior, Joan and I waited for Mr. Bender's fury to come full steam.

"She's gonna get the crap beat out of her," Joan whispered to me.

"Yeah, and she'd better come back if she knows what's good for her."

Much to our surprise, Mr. Bender called out to her. "Come on, Betty. Get your damn ass back on the seat. I'm sorry for yellin' at you. I'll try not to be so hard on you next time."

Scowling and dragging her feet, she returned to her seat on the planter.

"Wow, can you imagine that. He actually apologized to her," I chuckled.

"Yeah, guess he needs her. Besides, what does he expect from such a skinny little runt?"

Joan and I grinned at each other. This was the first time we'd heard him apologize for anything, and we felt proud that Betty had stood up to him.

It took a couple of weeks to complete the planting of twenty-five acres. We worked from sunup to sundown, stopping only to get a drink of water and to eat the sandwiches Mrs. Bender brought out for lunch. Many days we were kept home from school to get the planting done on schedule.

One day Mr. Bender found that there weren't enough plants to finish his crop and set out to buy a few extra flats from a family friend. As he headed toward his car, he saw Betty and me playing nearby and called to us, "You two wanna go for a ride? I'm going to Pete Butler's farm to get more plants."

We were thrilled and quickly climbed into the backseat. "Let's crouch down low," I whispered. "If Jean and Joan see us, they might beg to come, and he might change his mind." Once we knew he'd turned onto the road, we sat up and grinned.

We traveled several miles before pulling into the Butlers' yard and stopping some distance from the greenhouse where the workers were busy pulling plants. Then Mr. Bender turned to us and said, "You girls wait here while I go pick up the flats. You're not to get out of the car." He slammed the door and left.

We twisted and turned in the backseat to get a look at the farm. It had a large yard; a big, beautiful red-brick house; a couple of large greenhouses; and several kilns. We figured Mr. Butler must be a rich tobacco farmer.

Later we saw Mr. Bender and a strange woman coming toward the car, each carrying a flat of plants. *She must be one of Mr. Butler's workers,* I thought. As she approached the car, I got a better look at her. She was a short, wiry little lady. Her face was deeply tanned and weathered with overlapping wrinkles, but she was rather pretty. She had sharp, piercing dark brown eyes and full lips. A red, printed babushka, tied at the back of her neck, held her dark brown hair away from her face. Her untucked shirt and loose-fitting trousers were covered with dark topsoil from the greenhouse. She appeared chatty and happy as she stopped beside the car and set her flat on the ground.

It was then that Mr. Bender, with an amused grin, swung open the back door. "This is your mother. She wants to see you."

His words exploded in my head and were still ringing in my ears when the woman climbed into the backseat.

Betty and I pushed back against the seat, but she pulled us close, wrapping her arms tightly around us. "Oh, my babies! My babies! My little babies!" she cried.

Baby? I thought. *I'm not a little baby.* I pulled back a bit from her grasp, confused and overcome by the suddenness of everything.

But she pulled me close again. "Oh, my little bear, my little bear," she said over and over again as she showered me with hugs and kisses. I felt the sweat off her cheeks clinging to mine and the smell of cigarettes heavy on her breath.

"And you, my little one," she said, turning to hug Betty, "I never thought you'd make it this far. Let me take a good look at you both." Pulling back, she cupped her soiled and rough hands gently under our chins and looked lovingly into our eyes. "My, my," she said, "you've turned into such beautiful little girls. I've missed you sooo much!" She hugged and kissed us again and again until we were almost breathless.

Betty and I were tongue-tied, unable to find any words to say to our mother, so we just hugged her in return.

"Give my love to Jean and Joan," were her parting words, and then she was gone from our lives almost as quickly as she had entered it.

My throat was tight as I fought to choke back the tears, and my heart felt as if it had dropped into my stomach. I looked at Betty and saw that she was starting to cry. I took hold of her hand and gave it a gentle squeeze.

We sat silent and sad as we watched our mom walk away. Looking out the back window as we drove away, we saw her wave one more time before disappearing into the greenhouse. *Will we ever see her again?* I wondered.

As we left the Butler farm, Betty and I were fidgety and in a hurry to get home. We were eager to share the news with our sisters. Betty grinned. "Betcha they're gonna be really jealous of us," she said. And as soon as the car stopped, we tumbled out and ran excitedly to tell our sisters the good news.

"Guess what!" we called out breathlessly before we got to where they were playing. "We saw our real mother!"

They just stared at us with doubtful expressions on their faces. "Oh, baloney," Jean scoffed. "Yeah, you saw our real mother, and probably Roy Rogers and Trigger, too."

"We did! We did! Honest we did! Cross my heart and hope to die, we did!" I said excitedly, waving my arm back in the direction of the Butler farm. "She works for Mr. Butler, and Mr. Bender brought her out to the car to meet us. Isn't that right, Betty?"

Betty nodded, and then added, "She's telling the truth. We really did see her."

"Well, that was nice of the old fart," said Jean. "Boy, you must've really been surprised. I sure wish he would've taken us along."

"So what did she say, and what does she look like?" Joan queried.

"She looks sort of like you two, doesn't she, Betty?"

Betty nodded. "She didn't say too much. Guess she knew Mr. Bender was in a hurry."

We explained to them how everything happened so fast that we scarcely had time to catch our breath. We described to them what our mom was wearing and how she jumped into the car and hugged and squeezed us over and over again until we were breathless.

"She kept calling me her 'little bear.' I wonder why she called me that?" I asked, hoping Jean or Joan would remember.

"I remember her calling you that," Joan said, "but I don't remember why."

"It was probably because you were a little butterball, running around in diapers and drinking up all the molasses," Jean teased.

"Quit teasing her," Joan broke in. "What I wanna know is if she'll ever come to see us."

Betty shrugged. "I don't know. But she said to give her love to both of you."

That evening as we paraded across the kitchen floor toward the supper table, Mr. Bender stomped out of the house, leaving Mrs. Bender scowling and leaning against the stove. We'd heard them arguing from our rooms, and even though Betty had listened at the stovepipe and heard her hollering at him, she wasn't sure why. "I think she's mad at him for taking us to the Butler place," she reasoned. "I think I heard that name once."

As we settled into our chairs, Mrs. Bender managed to dash any hopes we had of ever seeing our mother again, as she said, "I understand you saw your mother today. Well, just don't get any silly notions in your heads that she'll be comin' to see you, for she's not allowed around here. Is that understood?"

We nodded and poked at our food.

"I guess that answers your question, Joan," Betty said as we made our way back upstairs. "She's never gonna let us see her again."

After supper, we sat around in bed, reliving the big event of the day. Knowing our mother worked just several miles away brought a measure of happiness into our lives.

19

A Narrow Escape

After the fields were planted and the young seedlings had taken root, it was time to look over each row again and check for plants that had died. The plants were tender, and sometimes the wind would break their frail stems or grubs would attack their roots. My sisters and I walked down the rows with a basket of fresh plants and a small spade. If a dead plant was found, it was removed, and we searched for the fat, white grub or wire worm that had killed it. When we found one, we stabbed it with our spade and planted a new plant.

Replanting lasted until all the acres were completed. And then we had only a few days' rest from the fieldwork before the weeds started growing around the young plants and the hoeing season began.

Work in the tobacco fields was for adults; not for children, and good money was paid for it. It was seemingly unending and backbreaking for us, but we dared not complain. But we certainly got angry and griped among ourselves.

Sometimes the hoeing got really tough, especially in the low-lying areas where moisture had collected, dried, and hardened, and the thick couch grass almost hid the young plants.

As we had no summer shoes, we went barefoot all summer. And many times while hacking away at the stubborn couch grass, we would whack our toes with our sharp hoes and slice them open. Not much thought or concern was given to our injured toes, and so we simply rinsed off the blood and went back to hoeing. If the cut was severe, we would tie a rag around the toe to keep the dirt out.

At times, the Benders might help with the hoeing if we were falling behind and the weeds were getting the best of the crop. But it was mostly our job.

To make things fun and get the work done faster so we could have some playtime, we would plan races. Starting at the head of a row, we raced to see who would be the first to get to the end. But no matter what we did to lessen the misery of it, hoeing was a hard and boring job. The rows seemed so long and the fields so big that we wondered how we'd ever finish.

It would take weeks to finish the crop. And when we thought we were all done, it was time to start all over again, for the weeds kept growing. When we complained aloud, Mr. Bender just told us to shut up and quit whining, adding that a hard day's work never killed anyone.

After a month or so, the hoeing would finally be finished, and Doug would return home to help his dad cultivate and spray the plants until they reached their full height of about six feet and were flowering on top.

• • •

It was July, school was out, and except for our regular evening barn chores of cleaning out the stables and bedding down the animals, we had more time to play and explore.

Our favorite place to go was a big wooded lot that ran for miles along neighboring farms, and there was no end to the adventures we were able to find there. To get there we would walk about a quarter mile down the farm lane that led from behind the barn into the woods. A large creek ran through the farm, winding its way through the woods, and we spent many hours playing in it.

There were thickets of raspberries, thimbleberries, elderberries, and many varieties of wild apple trees to satisfy our appetites. Our happiest days were spent in these woods. It was an escape from our fears, a break from hard work and the daily demands of the Bender family. We felt carefree and cheerful, and the Benders never seemed to mind how long we were gone.

Many times we toyed with the idea of running away but chickened out because we didn't know where to go. Other times we would get lost and had to listen for the sound of a train so we could find our way back to the railroad. From there we could find our way home.

Our biggest adventure in these woods was to visit the places where the neighbors had dumped their household trash and garbage. We spent hours prodding with big sticks and digging through these dumps, looking for hidden treasures while being ever watchful for snakes that might be coiled in empty cans.

We would squeal with delight when we uncovered discarded barrettes for our hair, colorful ribbons, old string beads, candles, matches, or used makeup. At times we found old Hollywood magazines to read and knew these could be easily smuggled upstairs under our clothes. Once we'd collected enough junk, we would rinse some of it in the creek, lay it out on the bank, and swap back and forth with each other.

One day Joan found our biggest and best treasure. "Oh, wow! You'll never believe what I found!" she yelled from the far side of the garbage dump. We all hurried over as she was wiping it off with her shirt.

"What is it?" we asked as she continued wiping it just to heighten our curiosity.

Finally she pulled it out.

"It's a mirror! See, it's a mirror!"

"WOW!" we cried in unison, our heads buzzing with excitement as we passed the shard of mirror back and forth to take a peek at ourselves.

"Shucks, all I can see is my nose," I said, peering into it.

"That figures," Joan giggled. "Here, hold it at arm's length — like this."

"Boy, we'll be able to fix ourselves up pretty when we go back to school," I said.

"In your case, it's gonna take more than a piece of mirror," Jean teased.

"And what boy are you fixing yourself up for this time?"

"Oh, shut up! I wouldn't tell you anyway. I was gonna give you a piece of my red ribbon, but I'm not now."

"Quit acting up, you two," Joan said, "and let's figure how in the heck we're gonna smuggle all our stuff upstairs past the big-eyed guard. You know how she gives us the once-over every time we go through the house."

"Yeah, old Eagle Eyes never misses a damn thing," Jean chipped in.

"I have an idea. Let's wrap it up tight in an old rag, and then you and Jean go upstairs first and open the window. Bonnie and I will stay behind and toss the bundle up to you," Betty suggested, happy she had thought of something first.

Agreeing that she had a good idea and hoping we could pull it off, we set about hunting for a good-size rag. Once our treasures were safely bundled up and our shadows were getting longer, we knew it was time to head home to do the barn chores.

We rounded up the cows from the outskirts of the woods and herded them up the lane and into the barnyard. Then, checking around to see if the coast was clear and seeing that Mr. Bender's truck was gone, we figured the time was right to carry out our scheme.

After knocking, Jean and Joan entered through the back porch door and crossed the kitchen to head upstairs. As they did, Mrs. Bender asked where Betty and I were.

"Oh, they're being poky. They'll be coming soon," Jean said, and Joan nodded.

"Well, okay, get on with you, then."

We carried out our plan without any suspicion from Mrs. Bender. Betty and I then made our way upstairs to join our sisters.

"Wheeew, we made it," Joan said. "That was scary!"

As we sat in bed looking over our collection of trinkets, we puzzled over where to hide it all so no one could find it.

We tied some of them on strings and dropped them down behind the plasterboard, securing the string with a tack. We could then pull them up like fish on a fishing line whenever we wanted to.

"Where do you think we can hide all the rest of the stuff?"

"We can slide our magazines under the linoleum," Betty said.

"Why don't we hide some of it back in the cubby hole? No one ever goes back there." I said. "But I ain't gonna go in there to do it!"

"She's right. Mr. Bender's too tall and Mrs. Bender's too fat. Our stuff should be safe there. I'll do it first thing in the morning," Jean volunteered.

With that settled, we waited in our beds for our supper call.

In the evenings when the lights were turned out, we would form a tent with a bed sheet over our heads. We would then light our smuggled candle, glue it to a tin can lid with some melted wax, and put it in the center of the bed where it gave enough light for us to read our magazines.

"We'd better be careful," Betty said, "or one of these days we're gonna burn the house down."

"Wouldn't it be great if we could just find a flashlight in the dump? Boy, we'd be all set," I said.

"Yeah, a flashlight and a mirror—what else could anyone possibly want?" Jean snickered.

• • •

There was a clearing in the woods where a large thicket of wild black and red raspberries grew in abundance along with thimbleberries. When they were ripe, Mrs. Bender made us a lunch of brown sugar sandwiches, put them into a paper bag, handed us a large bucket and four small wooden quart baskets, and said, "Here, I want you to go to the woods and pick the wild raspberries. And don't come home until the pail is full, for there's no use of my fussing about making jam with only half a pail. You can fill up a jug of water from the pump on your way. No fooling around. I expect you home before dark."

We weren't as happy about spending our day picking berries among the scratchy bushes as we were about eating the brown sugar sandwiches, for we all loved them.

"No one's gonna eat the sandwiches until we have the bucket half full," Joan ordered, clutching the bag close to her side as though she were our boss.

Joan and I paired off and picked around one side of the area while Jean and Betty did the other side, working our way toward the middle.

We threaded the small wooden berry baskets with binder twine and tied them around our waists, freeing up our hands so we could pick the berries, separate the bushes, and speed the job along. We reminded ourselves to watch out for the hornet nests, remembering how badly we got stung when we disturbed them once before.

As we picked, we hummed and sang all the songs we'd learned from listening down the stovepipe.

Joan and I worked away, filling our baskets and emptying them into the bucket. We seemed to be emptying ours faster than Jean and Betty, and since we'd lost sight and sound of them, we decided to search for them. We found them hiding under the bushes. One look at their red-and-black-stained mouths gave them away—they were stuffing themselves with all the berries they'd picked. We were angry and gave them a good chewing out.

"No sandwiches, you lazy bums, 'til you pick your share of the berries," Joan said.

"Well, it's hot, and I'm hungry and thirsty," Betty complained.

"So are Bonnie and I, but we have to get this pail filled, so let's get movin'. We don't wanna be back here all day."

Tired, hot, and weary, we eventually filled the bucket and lugged it up to the house to give to Mrs. Bender.

"Do you think she'll give us a treat for picking all these berries?" Betty asked.

"I don't know," Jean mused, "but I wouldn't hold my breath."

Joan knocked on the front porch door and handed the berries to Mrs. Bender.

She took the berries, and seeing that we had filled it to the brim, smiled at us. "Here," she said, reaching into her apron pocket. "It's some gum for you. Divvy it up among yourselves."

"Wow, there are two pieces each," Joan said, handing us our share.

We enjoyed getting chewing gum, because it was a treat that lasted us for a few days and was far tastier than the sealing wax she gave us off the jam jars. When we went to sleep at night, we stuck our wad of chewed gum on top of our bedposts, and heaven help anyone who swiped our wad after they'd thrown theirs away.

• • •

Although differences in personality sometimes made us bicker and squabble with one another, our isolation from the Bender family caused us to grow closer together, and we always managed to patch things up. We would enjoy trying to outsmart or outwit each other, but it was usually Jean who proved to be the wittiest.

As we began to develop and mature, our personalities, strengths, and weaknesses became more defined; and as time passed, we each began to have more in common with one sister or another. Though Betty and I had been together from the beginning, she began to identify more with Jean while I matched up more with Joan.

Jean was more vivacious and outgoing. She was a sassy daredevil with a devil-may-care-but-I-sure-as-hell-don't attitude. She was always quick with witty remarks, usually spiced with earthy, naughty language. She was brave enough to pick up a snake by the tail and chase us around the barn with it. She could roll with life's punches and shake off problems like a dog shakes water off its back.

Joan, on the other hand, was more withdrawn. Never one to seek attention, she was quiet, obedient, and level-headed. Mrs. Bender always sought her out when she had any instructions or orders for us. She was like a mother hen who always tried to keep us in line and out of trouble, and we always turned to her if we thought the sky was falling. In my mind, she seemed to take over where Muggs left off.

Betty was the bubbliest and prettiest. Her blonde hair, fair complexion, and sparkling blue eyes contrasted with the rest of us, who had tan skin, brown eyes, and darker hair. She was charming, likeable, mischievous, and flighty as a kite zigging and zagging in a March breeze. At the same time, she was emotional, high strung, and often ill. She had more health problems than the rest of us put together, seeming to pick up every "bug" that came along.

More like Joan, I was quiet and studious, and I had a strong sense of justice. I loved school and was happiest when I could lose myself in a book or had plenty of scribble paper to draw on. But I was often angry and rebellious and could become very stubborn and defiant when I felt things weren't right or if we were being treated unfairly. It was these two traits that got me in the most trouble and earned me extra whippings from the Benders. To sum it up, we were in some ways so different and in others so much alike.

• • •

The tobacco plants continued to grow, and the hay was soon ready to cut. Mr. Bender rode the hay mower while we followed behind with Doug, stacking the hay into neat piles. When this phase of haying was finished, the piles of hay were loaded onto a wagon. Mr. Bender would then jerk the horses to a stop and order us to hop onto the wagon so we could get to the barn and finish "making hay while the sun shines," as the saying goes.

Stabbing our pitchforks into the side of the hay, we would scramble up the back rack and on top of the pile. This was the most exciting part of the day, riding up to the barn, jiggling around atop the hay. We giggled and laughed all the way, hoping Mr. Bender wouldn't hit a hole and upset the whole load.

The barn was a big two-story building with large double doors on the upper level. The doors parted in the middle, sliding on tracks to the left and right. While Mr. Bender pulled the wagon up, one of us would hurry inside the barn, climb a ladder, and open the trap door that led to the haymow. Then we would go over to the big doors and slide them open. Mr. Bender would then stand on the wagon and heave the hay up with a pitchfork. Doug would catch it and toss it to one side or the other, and we would pick it up and move it to the back of the haymow.

This was hot, sweaty, dusty work, and we'd stop often to take a swig of cool water from the jug we kept nearby. Many times after Mr. Bender had unloaded the wagon, he would park it off to the side and head to the house for a cold beer while we finished stacking away the hay.

On one of these humid days shortly after my ninth birthday, I was working in the haymow and stopped to wipe the sweat off my brow with my forearm. Looking from beneath my arm as I rubbed it back and forth across my forehead, I suddenly realized that my sisters were nowhere in sight. Panic gripped me. I was alone with Doug. My heart began to pound as thoughts of the past raced through my head. *I have to get to that ladder before he sees me. It's the only way out.*

I worked my way slowly and cautiously toward the ladder, trying not to attract his attention. Then from the corner of my eye, I saw the open trap door. I tossed my fork into the hay and made a mad dash for the ladder. But I was too late. He'd beaten me to it. Standing rigid with his feet astride and the pitchfork outstretched in front of his body, he barred my way. "Well, now," he taunted with a wicked smirk, "just where do you think you're goin'?"

He had the same evil, lopsided grin on his face that he had the day he hurt Betty two years before, and I knew exactly what he had in mind for me. "I'm finished up here, and I'm going downstairs to help with the other chores!" I said, spitting the words at him.

"You'll go when I say you're finished!" he sneered.

"I'm going now, and you're not gonna stop me!" I fired back defiantly.

When he tossed his fork aside and tried to grab me, I backed away, almost losing my balance as I tripped over the hay. "Keep your grubby hands off of me, you bloody bugger!" I screeched, as he grabbed for me but missed.

With an evil laugh, he grabbed for me again. "Where do you think you're gonna go, huh? What're you gonna do?" he sneered, his eyes narrowing, his voice threatening. "It looks like I've got you cornered, and there's no way out."

My mind was racing, my heart thumping faster. He was right. He had me cornered. The only way out was to jump out the big doors, and he was certain I wasn't going to be that foolish. He grabbed my arm and twisted it, as he wrapped his leg around mine in an effort to trip me into the hay.

I fought against him with every ounce of strength in my body. The hard work on the farm had made me strong, and I kept fighting him off. Finally I wrenched myself from his grasp. But he came at me again, grinning from ear to ear, toying with me as if playing a game of cat and mouse.

As he grabbed for me again, I ducked under his arm and flew across the hay-strewn floor at breakneck speed to the barn door. Without a second thought, I jumped out, running in midair as the ground came up to meet me. I landed on all fours and was thankful that the grass was soft. I was shaken but not hurt. Righting myself, I turned to look up. Doug was standing in the open doorway, a scowl on his face, poised with a pitchfork in his hand as if ready to throw it at me.

Feeling safe now, I stared up at him, thumbing my nose defiantly, daring him to throw the fork. If he did, I knew I could dodge it.

Knowing that he had lost that round, he lowered the fork to his side, turned, and walked back into the darkness of the haymow. I thumbed my nose at him one more time and ran to find my sisters.

They were in the barnyard, mixing swill for the pigs. "Why on earth did you leave me alone in the haymow with that terrible jerk?" I demanded, still pale and shaking from my narrow escape.

"Why? What happened? What did he do?" Jean and Joan asked.

"He tried to get at me the same way he got at Betty, but I jumped out the door."

"You jumped out of the top of the barn?" they gasped.

I nodded. "That was my only choice."

"What do you mean, 'the way he got Betty'?" Joan asked.

Bit by bit, Betty and I told them how Doug had hurt Betty back at the old place before they came to live with us. I then warned them to be careful and to make sure they were never alone with him.

"Well, he better not try anything with me," Jean said, "or I'll knock his stupid block off!"

• • •

It was usually late in the day when Mr. Bender sent us back into the woods to fetch up the cows for milking and round up the ducks and geese from the creek and bring them into the barnyard.

"Here, cowbossie! Here, cowbossie! Here, cowbossie!" we would holler, cupping our hands around our mouths. Soon old Bessie's bell would ring, giving away their hiding place deep in the woods.

After rounding up several cows and a few young heifers, we'd clap our hands as we chased them up the lane.

We had lots of fun with the heifers since they were young and rambunctious like us. One of us would sneak up behind a heifer and grab hold of her tail. Then we would latch hands and have the "crack the whip" ride of our lives. The young heifer—bolting and with back humped—would kick her heels high in the air in a desperate attempt to shake us off, but we would hang on for dear life, our feet barely touching the ground as we raced to keep up with her. The heifer would always win, and we would be tossed off, laughing and giggling as we fell in the grass and rolled around like tumbleweeds.

Mr. Bender once caught us at our shenanigans, and we were severely scolded. But that was not enough to put off our fun. We would just wait until the cows were behind the barn, out of sight from the house, and then we would grab the tail again and be off for another joy ride. "We have to have some fun in our lives," we'd say to one another, trying to find good reason for our naughtiness.

One day Mr. Bender seemed concerned about old Bessie, and we stood nearby as he led her from the barn by her halter. He tied a rope to the halter, led her down the lane, and staked her out in the pasture near the blue salt block so she couldn't go back into the woods.

I wondered why he did this but knew that if I asked, he would just say that it was none of my business.

"Why do you think he tied old Bessie up?" I asked.

"I don't know," Jean said. "Maybe she's sick or something."

"She doesn't look sick to me," I said. "She just looks fat. I'm going over to pet her."

Joan yanked me back. "No, Mr. Bender said to leave her alone but to keep an eye on her. He muttered something about her calving or something like that."

"What does that mean?"

"I don't know for sure," she shrugged. "But I think it might mean she's gonna have a calf."

"Is the calf in her stomach? Is that why she's so fat?"

"I think so."

"But how will it ever get out? Will he have to cut it out?"

"How am I supposed to know? Guess we'll just have to wait and see."

"Maybe she'll lay a big egg just like the hens," Betty giggled.

We all laughed at the ridiculousness of that, but still we had no idea how the calf would get out.

A few days later as we were heading back to the woods, we noticed Bessie lying prone in the pasture, making low bellowing sounds. We couldn't be seen from the house, so we squiggled through the wire fence and made our way into the pasture. Walking barefoot through the dewy grass and watching for cow pies, we quietly made our way over to her, approaching from behind so as not to frighten her.

"Shuuush! Don't make a sound," Joan warned.

We were within a few feet of Bessie when we stopped short. It was then that we noticed it—a small leg sticking out from beneath her tail.

"Oh my God, what's happening to her?" Betty cried. "What are we gonna do?"

"I think she might be having a calf," Jean said.

"But how in the heck is it gonna get out?" I choked out, totally ignorant of any facts of life. "Is she gonna poop it out? One of us had better go and get Mr. Bender real quick."

"Who's gonna go? Not me!" Betty said. "Besides, I don't know what to say. You go, Bonnie. You can run the fastest!"

"Yeah, Bonnie, you go," Jean and Joan agreed.

I ran as fast as my legs could carry me, wondering all the way how to tell them what was happening to old Bessie. As

I neared the house, I got more nervous, and my mouth felt dry and dusty. I quickly put my tongue to the bottom of my mouth to find the "little well of water" Mrs. Miller often told us about.

Upon reaching the back porch, I stopped to catch my breath and then banged loudly on the kitchen door.

"Whaddya want now?" Mr. Bender shouted.

I opened the door and meekly poked my head inside. Mr. Bender sat at the table with a beer in his hand. The smell of onions frying on the stove filled the room.

"Well, speak up, for Pete's sake. What is it?"

"The c . . . c . . . cow has another l . . .l . . . leg," I stammered.

"The cow must be having her calf, Jim," Mrs. Bender said, as she shooed me away with her hand. "You best get down there."

Certain Mrs. Bender understood what I was trying to say, I quickly closed the door. And knowing something exciting was about to happen, I puffed hard to keep up with Mr. Bender as he wasted no time getting down to the pasture. As he neared the gate, he turned to me and commanded, "Round up your sisters and get back to the house!"

We plodded unhappily toward the house, glancing back over our shoulders, hoping to get a glimpse of the baby calf.

"I don't see why we couldn't stay and watch," Jean grumbled, kicking at every stick and small stone in her path.

I was wondering how the calf got into old Bessie's stomach and hoped Jean, who always had answers to my questions, could tell me. But even she was stumped.

The next morning after breakfast, we raced out to the pasture to get our first look at the baby calf. We snickered in amusement as it nudged and sucked milk from old Bessie.

20

A Sorrowful Walk Home

On rare occasions, when the Benders went away for the weekend, we could stay overnight with the Tillmans. These were the happiest days of our young lives, and we would sing and dance all the way to their home.

On one of these weekends, as we burst through the green wire gate that led to their house, we spotted Grandpa working away in his garden and ran over to greet him.

"Hi, Grandpa. Your garden looks like it's coming along nicely, but can we help you with it?"

"No, girls. Not right now. I'm a bit out of puff. We'll come out later when it cools down a tad." He pulled a blue patterned handkerchief out of his pocket and mopped his brow. "Let's go inside to see the missus and perhaps weasel a cool drink out of her."

I took hold of his hand and looked over the garden with him. "Why did you plant the garden in the shape of a V, Grandpa?"

"Because, little girl, it's called a 'victory garden' and the V stands for *victory*. I plant it to honor all the soldiers who fought and died in the wars."

206 • Bonnie E. Virag

"Did you remember to plant some 'lettuce, turnip, and pea'?" I joked.

"I surely did. So you didn't forget my little story, aye?" he replied with an impish grin.

We were giggly as we entered the house, each of us competing for his hand.

The Tillmans' home was so warm and welcoming. The front parlor had a walnut settee with a tall, three-legged coat rack nearby. On the wall beside the French doors leading into the kitchen hung a large picture of a fat, frumpy lady with a crown on her head. I was fascinated, wondering why Grandma hung a picture of such an ugly-looking lady on the wall.

A deep-red carpet covered the foyer and the stairs leading up to the bedrooms. Off the foyer, behind a set of double French doors, was a lovely living room with a tall, black organ. All the woodworking and furniture was in a dark walnut and looked so English, as if the room had popped straight off the pages of a Dickens novel.

Grandma welcomed us into the kitchen, picked up some papers from a nearby cot, and asked us to sit down. Never having shared much chatty conversation with the Benders, we were a bit shy and quiet until Grandpa loosened us up with his war stories and funny jokes.

Grandma brought out the family album to show us pictures of Grandpa in his army uniform as well as some of their lives growing up in "Merry Old England," as Grandpa emphatically called it.

The album had another photo of the ugly lady in the parlor picture, and so I asked, "Grandma, who is that lady? She looks so grumpy and mean."

"Well, now, my dear, that's Queen Victoria. She was the Queen of England when your grandpa and I lived over there. Grandpa fought for her during the Boer War."

"Yes, and a mighty fine queen she was, I might add," Grandpa said, beaming proudly, slipping his thumbs under his beige suspenders and puffing out his chest. "She was England's matriarch, holding the reins of Great Britain for many a year."

This bit of history didn't mean much to us, but the happiness radiating from their faces as they reminisced made us feel good.

Soon Grandma said, "It's getting nigh onto lunchtime and you girls must be hungry. How would you like to have some hot dogs and ice cream?"

We squealed with delight. It was so wonderful to have someone ask if we were hungry and what we would like to eat. Hot dogs and ice cream were a treat that we had only at Grandma's house.

"Here," she said, fishing around in her small change purse, "I want you to go to the store and get some groceries and a brick of Neapolitan ice cream. Don't tarry on the way back, or the ice cream will melt. Off with you now."

She needn't have worried, for we made it to the store and back in a flash with the ice-cream carton barely beginning to sweat.

After admiring the pretty table setting with the beautiful dishes and shiny silverware, we were feeling pretty special as we took our places at the table. Having made short work of the hot dogs, we waited eagerly for dessert while Grandma prepared a pot of hot tea for herself and Grandpa. Then, with mouths watering, we watched as she peeled away the cardboard box containing the strawberry, vanilla, and chocolate ice cream; divided it evenly into six pieces; laid them onto gold-rimmed, floral china dishes; and passed one to each of us.

We savored each mouthful, trying to decide which flavor we liked the best.

As Grandpa and Grandma lingered over their tea, Grandpa's strange-looking cup caught my eye. It was a floral china cup, but it had a bridge across the middle. "Grandma," I asked, "why is Grandpa's cup different than yours? It has a funny piece inside it."

"That, my dear, is called a moustache cup. Grandpa combs and waxes his moustache to keep it looking spry, and the little bridge you see there keeps the steam from getting at it and melting the wax."

Grandpa smiled and twirled one end of his moustache, and we grinned, always amused by his antics.

In the early evenings we would play checkers and dominoes before retiring to the living room to listen to Grandma play the organ. I was excited as she opened the French doors leading into the room. It was strange yet wonderful to step onto the soft carpet, look around at all the pictures on the wall, admire the heavy velvet drapes dressing the windows, and check out all of her figurines and knickknacks.

After taking in our surroundings, we settled into the plush sofa, sitting quietly and contented as Grandma played away on the organ.

Grandpa, sitting close by in a large, wingback chair, sang along to the music, stopping occasionally to puff on his pipe. Soon we were all involved, singing songs we never learned from the stovepipe: "When You and I Were Young, Maggie"; "The White Cliffs of Dover"; and "It's a Long, Long Way to Tipperary."

We did not want the fun to end, but as daylight dwindled and Grandma gently closed the lid over the keys, we knew it was bedtime.

We oooh'd and aaah'd the first time we saw the guest bedroom. It was so beautiful and inviting—so very different from our bare and unfinished bedrooms that my heart ached. There were two walnut-wood beds with a matching dresser and nightstand. A small washstand held a blue-and-white floral pitcher with matching basin. Fresh, white towels hung on a side rack, and lacy curtains adorned the window. Beside each bed was a large and colorful, oval-shaped, hand-braided rug that Grandma had made out of rags.

She had already turned the beds down for us, exposing the crisp white linens and large, fluffy pillows that were stuffed inside pillowcases edged with pink crocheted trim. Each bed had a charming, multicolored patchwork quilt. The scene was so inviting that we stood open-mouthed for a long moment, taking it all in.

"I'll leave you be now while you get your nightclothes on," Grandma said, "but I'll be back to check on you later. Oh yes, there's a chamber pot under each bed should you need it," she added.

As soon as she left the room, Jean checked under the bed and pulled out a two-handled, white porcelain pot, decorated in a tiny rose pattern. "Wow! Would you look at this? It surely beats our old paint can! I think I heard Grandpa call it a thunnn-der mug," I said with a giggle.

We all laughed. "Yeah, Bonnie, you'll probably feel like Queen Victoria sitting on it!" Jean sniggered. "We'll never be able to get you off it."

As we sat snuggled in our beds, we whiled away the time by picking out our favorite patchwork patterns by the light of the street lamp that radiated through the window, filling the room with a soft glow.

When Grandma returned to say good night and pull down the shade, I pleaded, "Please don't pull it down, Grandma. We like the lamp shining through the window."

"Yeah," the others chimed in, "we like it like that."

"Well, all right," she replied. "Just make sure you settle down in good time." She smiled, told us to have a good night, and then left the room.

It was good to hear someone wish us a good night's sleep. I was filled with a warm, secure feeling as I drew the cover up to my nose, breathed deeply, and inhaled the fresh, spring air in the sheets. "Isn't it wonderful here? I don't want the night to ever end," I said to Betty, but she was already fast asleep.

While washing ourselves in the basin the next morning, we shoved each other back and forth to catch a glimpse of ourselves in the large mirror while giggling at our tousled hair. "Boy, I'd love to have this mirror in our rooms. Sure beats that dinky little piece from the dump," Jean said.

"I don't even wanna think about home," Joan groaned. "It makes me too sad."

Just then Grandma called, "Breakfast is ready, girls. Hurry down while it's still hot."

We wondered what breakfast would be. We could smell the scent of something good wafting up the stairwell. We scurried downstairs, pushing and shoving each other, wanting to be the first in the kitchen to greet Grandma and Grandpa and find out what it was that smelled so good.

We weren't disappointed. Grandma had prepared us each a bowl of Cream of Wheat topped with a healthy sprinkle of brown sugar and cinnamon. Along with this came toast with jam and a cup of hot chocolate.

"This is the best breakfast ever, Grandma," I said, slathering my toast with jam.

"Oh now, I'm sure your mom gets a good breakfast in you, too," she said.

I didn't answer.

"Well, there's plenty of food," Grandpa said, "so fill up your boots. We don't want you going home with empty bellies."

When these weekends were over and it was time to leave, Grandma and Grandpa would give us each a hug and tell us we were always welcome. I wondered if they could read the sorrowful looks on our faces as we left their embrace. Then they would stand on the front porch and give us a good-bye wave as we made our way out into the street.

Sad and gloomy at the prospect of returning home to our barren rooms, we would trudge wearily home, grumbling about our lives with the Benders and wondering why they couldn't let us be part of the family.

21

Long, Hard Days

By late July the tobacco plants were as tall as Jean and Joan, who were over eleven years old and starting a growth spurt, or as Mr. Bender told them, "You girls are growin' like a couple of bad weeds."

"I wonder what they're gonna do with these big plants now," I asked Joan.

She shrugged her shoulders. "I dunno. I saw Mr. Bender breaking the flowers off on top, and he mentioned something about suckering them, I think."

"Well, you know who the suckers are gonna be," Jean sniped.

Joan had heard right. Mr. Bender called us out to the field early the next morning to teach us how to "sucker" the plants by removing the small shoots that were growing between the leaves and the stalks.

"Now pay attention, you kids. We gotta get all these little suckers outta here before they kill the plant," he said.

We watched as he slid his fingers down one plant, snapping off each sucker and then working his way up the next one. After suckering a few plants, he stood up and rubbed his back. "There, have you got the hang of it? It's too hard on my bad back, so I'm counting on you girls doing it. If you have any questions, I'll be topping the flowers off in the back field. Just be careful not to break any leaves. But watch for leaves with holes in them like this," he said, turning one over to reveal a big, green tobacco worm about the size of his finger. He plucked the worm off, and with one quick flick of his wrist, splattered it on the ground near our feet.

We jumped back as the juicy guts exploded in all directions.

"That's how you take care of these nasty buggers," he said. Then, noticing the sick looks on our faces, he quickly added, "There's no sense being squeamish—those damn worms can ruin a crop. Now lissen up. I expect you to get this field done today, so no goofin' off. Is that understood?"

We knew we weren't going to like this job, and as soon as he turned his back and headed down the rows, snapping off the flowers, we made faces at him.

"He sure doesn't expect much of us," Joan remarked as soon as he was out of earshot.

"We'd better get started or we'll never get all this done today," I said, looking over the area we needed to cover.

"And if we don't get it done, we probably won't get fed," Betty said, scanning the field and shaking her head resignedly.

We started off at a good clip, going down one plant and up the other, pinching off the suckers. The sap oozing from the suckers stuck to our hands, turning them black and sticky like fresh tar.

Soon we were all complaining about our sticky fingers and tried wiping them off on our shirts but to no avail. Then Joan discovered that we could get rid of the stickiness by rubbing our hands with sand, which we promptly did.

The hot sun was torturous, and by noon we were getting tired and beginning to slow down. We tried many ways to make the work seem easier in hope of making the day go faster. We sang songs, made up silly games, or talked gibberish back and forth, pretending we were foreigners. Other times we got lost in our thoughts.

I whiled away some of the time sketching clothes in my mind. When I came to the end of my row, I drew my ideas in the dirt with a stick to show my sisters.

"Look, I'm gonna have a dress just like this someday. I'm not gonna wear old rags and boys' shoes all my life. I'm gonna have high heels and silk stockings like Marge and May."

"Oh, Bonnie, you're just a dreamer!" Joan chided. "And where do you think you're gonna get all these beautiful clothes, I'd like to know?"

"You sure won't find them in the dump!" Jean scoffed, smearing out my dirt drawing with her foot.

"Yeah? Well, when I grow up, I'm gonna have lots of pretty clothes. You'll see!"

"Well, you'd better grow up fast, 'cause if we don't get this damn tobacco suckered, you ain't gonna live long enough to grow up!" she scoffed, as she drew my attention to all the work we still had to do.

"And if they don't feed us pretty soon," Joan said, "I ain't gonna live. I'm about ready to drop dead any minute!"

"Look," Betty said, pointing skyward, "you can tell by the sun that its way past lunchtime, and Mr. Bender went in a long time ago."

"Yeah, he did," I said. "And my stomach's growling so much I'm afraid it's gonna bite me. I'm gonna check the fence row to see if there are any berries."

I found no berries and broke some leaves off a large shrub. "Here, these are leaves the horses always eat. And if the horses eat them, why can't we?"

Examining the three-lobed leaves, Joan said, "I think Mr. Bender called them sassafras bushes."

"Well, you're a horse's ass if you think I'm gonna eat leaves," Jean snorted with disgust. "They'll probably kill you."

"I'm gonna try one," I said, taking a little nibble out of it. "It tastes pretty good — kinda like root beer and those striped humbug candies Mr. Miller used to give us. Remember, Betty?" I plopped the rest of it into my mouth.

Soon we were all munching down sassafras leaves.

"We'd better not eat too many or we might get sick," cautioned Joan.

We were getting angrier by the minute as we continued working and waiting for the Benders to call us in for lunch. At last, Jean was unable to contain her anger any longer. When she got to the end of her row, she grasped the last plant at the top with both hands and, in one swift downward motion, stripped it bare of leaves.

We stared at her as if she'd lost her mind, and then we quickly followed suit. When it was done, we stepped back and stared at our work of destruction, giggling hysterically at the four bare stalks standing at the end of each row. "Look's like the four of us," Betty quipped. "And they look hungry, too."

"At least I feel a helluva lot better," Jean quipped, standing as rigid as the naked stalk with hands planted firmly on her hips.

"But we'd better bury this mess right away," Joan warned. "If Mr. Bender sees it, we'll be skinned alive!"

We looked around to see if he was anywhere in sight. Then, getting a bit scared, we started furiously digging a hole big enough to bury the damaged plants. As my sisters continued digging, I pulled the stalks out of the ground and broke them into pieces across my knee. "You look like a pack of dogs trying to bury a bone," I mused, laughing as I tossed the stalks into the hole.

We kicked the leaves into the hole, covered it with sand, and trounced it down with our bare feet. We then smoothed out the disturbed dirt and started down our next rows that led toward the house. "Holy cripes, do you think he'll notice the missing plants?" I asked.

"Who gives a bloody toot," Jean snickered. "He sure ain't gonna find them!"

As we got halfway down our rows, we heard Mr. Bender whistling. Looking up ahead, I spotted him high on a ladder leaning against the kiln. "He's whistling and waving his hat at us. Guess he wants us to come in."

"Yeah, like an old turd bird on a perch!" Jean huffed. "Let's just pretend we don't hear him—make him come out and get us. Besides, I'm full of sassafras leaves now."

Soon he came walking down the rows. "We'd better get going," Joan said, waving her arms at him. "He's probably ticked off already."

"What the hell's the matter with you? Didn't you hear me whistling? Are you stone deaf?" he barked.

"Didn't hear a thing," Jean shot back, telling a barefaced lie.

"Well, keep your damn ears open next time. Get over there to the washtub and wash your hands. There's some sandstone soap to get the tar off, then get inside for your lunch. You'd better hurry because you still have a way to go before the day is over."

Our hands were now covered with black tobacco tar, and it took some hard scrubbing with the gritty soap to remove it.

"No use trying to get it all off," Betty said as she dried her hands on an old rag. "We're just gonna get them all black again."

When we sat down for lunch, Joan was able to see the clock in the living room. She held up her two fingers, indicating that it was two o'clock. *No wonder we're so doggone hungry!* I thought.

After lunch when we were headed out to the fields again, I grumbled that I was still hungry.

"Yeah, me too," Joan said, "but you'd get a clip to the back of the head if you dared ask for seconds."

I knew she was right. We often managed to get some smacks to the head for one thing or another, and Mrs. Bender was always close by to deal them out.

It took several more days of suckering and fighting heat and hunger before the miserable job was finished. During these days of working the fields, we found many clever ways to find food — often sneaking into a neighbor's field or garden to pluck some ears of corn, steal carrots or potatoes, or fill a dirty jar with milk from a staked-out cow. We counted ourselves lucky if we found a bush loaded down with elderberries or some wild grapes growing along the fence line.

Totally worn out by day's end, we would fall exhausted in our beds. And we'd be tickled pink when the job was finally finished; we would then have time to play in the woods.

• • •

During our first year on this new farm, we soon learned that work there was almost unending. Unlike the old farm, where all we had to do was pick apples, here, when the tobacco was done, the wheat was ripe and ready for harvesting.

Mr. Bender drove the grain-binding machine while we, along with Doug, gathered the sheaves by hand, stacking them into a circle to make a shock. The shocks stood for several days until the threshing machine, making the rounds to different farms, stopped by for threshing day. And it was a fast-paced day when the big thresher arrived and parked in the barnyard. We scrambled aboard the wagon along with Doug and headed out to the fields with our pitchforks. As Mr. Bender pulled the horses to a stop at each shock, we pitched the sheaves onto the wagon. By this time mice had taken up residence under the sheaves and scampered away as soon as we destroyed their homes, leaving behind their nest of newborns.

My sisters and I hovered around to admire the cute little naked babies. Doug, curious as to what had caught our attention, hurried over. "What are you looking at?"

"Some little baby mice. They're so cute. Their mother ran away," I sighed.

Without batting an eye, he stabbed them all with his pitchfork and then held the fork in the air for us to see their little squiggling bodies. We looked at him in total shock, horrified at his cruel act. I quickly snatched the two babies that were spared before he could stab them and tucked them into my trouser pockets.

"You miserable old meanie!" I screeched at him. "You have no feelings for anything!"

He laughed in my face as he scraped the dead mice off his fork with his boot and moved on to the next shock.

"Too bad someone didn't stick a pitchfork in him when he was born," Jean said.

"If we find another nest, we'll cover it up quickly before he spots it, and maybe the mother will come back," Joan suggested.

Beside the barn was an old rain barrel that caught the rain from the gutter drains. While the final load of straw was being threshed, we started toward the barrel to wash the prickly chaff off our faces and necks and noticed that Doug was already there. "I wonder what he's doing over there?" Betty asked. "It looks like he's trying to grab something."

"C'mon over here," he called. "I've got somethin' to show you."

We looked at each other and frowned. "Wonder what nasty idea he has up his sleeve now?" I asked.

As we sauntered over to the barrel, we noticed a large green frog squiggling in his grasp. "Quick, one of you run and fetch me a good straw from the straw pile."

While Betty ran to get a straw, the rest of us stared at each other, hunching our shoulders and wondering what he had in mind for the poor frog.

"Lookie here," he said, taking the straw from Betty's hands, "I'll show you a little trick."

I couldn't believe my eyes at what he did next. Inserting the straw into the frog's rear, he held the straw in his mouth and blew the frog up to twice its normal size. Its poor legs stuck out stiffly like twigs on a dead tree. Tossing the poor thing back into the barrel, he laughed heartily. "Look, a balloon frog!"

I gagged and backed away from the barrel, turning my head away from the horrible sight. "The frog's gonna die now," I said. "I hope you're happy, you miserable creep!"

"I wish someone would do that to you so you'd see how you like it!" Jean joined in, staring straight at him.

Doug hauled off to give her a good smack, but Jean, sensing what was coming, ducked under his arm. Then, totally disgusted with him, we dashed back to the barnyard.

Throughout the day, each wagonload of wheat sheaves would be brought up to the thresher and thrown off into the machine. As the wheat came out of the chute, we bagged it while the straw was blown out into a straw pile in the middle of the barnyard.

By late in the afternoon, when all the wheat was threshed, a huge pile of golden straw, almost as high as the barn, sat invitingly in the middle of the barnyard. As soon as the thresher left and Mr. Bender and Doug went in for supper, we flew into action. Climbing up inside the barn to the top of the haymow, we wriggled through a small hole at the barn's peak. Here we took flying leaps out of the top of the barn and onto the straw pile. Rolling off, giggling and laughing, covered head to toe with loose straw, we quickly clambered to the barn's peak to jump again.

When Mr. Bender returned to the yard, he saw the straw pile completely ruined and scattered all over the barnyard and took no time in figuring what we'd been up to. Breaking a switch off the nearest tree, he gave us all a sound switching and sent us off to get the pitchforks to clean up our mess.

"Old pissant," Jean grumbled. "For all the work we do around here, you'd think we'd at least be allowed to have a little fun."

Angry and sore from the switching, we cleaned up the mess—hating the Benders for being so mean to us and wondering why we always had to wait for our supper.

22

Night Plight

It was August and the start of the tobacco harvest season. Since this was our first year on the tobacco farm, my sisters and I were not too sure what it would mean to us. The day before the "big day," as Mr. Bender called it, we busied ourselves getting the tobacco tables set up beside the kilns and hauling out bundles of slats and wooden tying horses.

We were awakened about six o'clock in the morning by Mrs. Bender's shrill voice. "Hurry and get dressed, you girls. You're needed at the barn to help harness the horses."

We hurried downstairs for breakfast, but Mrs. Bender quickly shooed us outside. "You'll get breakfast later. We're filling a kiln today, and the workers will be here soon. So get a move on!"

We shivered in the frosty morning air as we hurried to the barn. Mr. Bender had the horses harnessed but quickly put us all to work. "Here, Jean and Joan, hook these whippletrees up to the boats, and you two," he said, nodding to Betty and me, "lead the horses up the tobacco field beside the house. We'll start priming there first."

I looked over the two tobacco boats. They were about six feet long, three feet high, and just wide enough to fit between the tobacco rows. They were made of wood and burlap with hinged flaps that could be dropped halfway down each side and ran on two wooden runners attached to the bottom of the boat.

"Get over here," Mr. Bender said, motioning to Betty. "This is gonna be your job. You'll drive the boat back and forth between the fields and the kilns." Handing her the reins, he went on, "Yell 'giddyup' when you want her to go and pull back hard on the reins and say 'whoa' when you want her to stop. If the boat's empty, you can ride inside, but when it's filled with leaves, you walk alongside to steady it and keep it from tipping over. And for God's sake, don't *ever* let go of those damn straps or they'll get tangled under the runners and cause all kinds of problems. Ya got that!"

She nodded, as she fumbled to straighten the reins in her trembling hands.

Betty looked dwarfed by the big horse, and I couldn't tell whether she was trembling from cold or fear. "Are you scared?" I asked. "You look like a midget beside that big horse."

"I'm scared to death!" she quavered. "It might be fun riding in the empty boat, but I'm afraid about bringing up the full boat. What if it upsets? I'm sure to catch hell!"

"Mr. Bender's gonna show us how to prime the first load before the gang gets here, so we'll help you out," I said, trying to calm her fears.

"The rest of you girls come on over here," Mr. Bender called, "and watch what I'm about to show you. You bend down and take off the first three or four leaves that look kinda yellow. Snap them off with your right hand and tuck them under your left arm. When you have as much under your arm as you can hold, then unload them in the boat. Have you got that?"

We nodded.

"Okay. Now each of you pick out a row and let's get started."

After filling the two boats, we drove them to the tables and began unloading them while Mr. Bender and Doug went in for breakfast. We were starving when we finished and hurried to the back porch to be called in for breakfast. It was then that the tobacco workers began arriving, and Mr. Bender and Doug rushed out the door, followed by Mrs. Bender. "Here," she said as she shoved several slices of bread into Betty's hand. "This'll have to tide you over until lunch. There's no time for breakfast now. The gang is here."

We just stood there, shoulders drooping, staring at each other in disbelief. "Darn it all. I'm hungry like a bear! And it's gonna be a long time before lunch," I groaned.

"They always have time for their bloody breakfast," Jean griped, grabbing a slice of bread. "Grrrr!" she growled, angrily biting off a piece and making us giggle.

Looking toward the kilns, we noticed Mrs. Bender wildly waving some tobacco leaves, motioning us over to the tobacco tables.

"Looks like they kinda need us," I snickered. We gobbled up our bread and hurried over.

Five men made their way out to the field to prime the leaves while Betty started the boat down between the rows. Jean, Joan, and I took our places at the tobacco table so Mrs. Bender could show us how to hand the leaves to the tyers.

Beside the table were two tying horses, as they were called— simply constructed wooden horses about three feet tall and notched at each end to hold a milled wooden slat about four feet long, two inches wide, and half an inch thick.

Alongside each tying horse lay a bundle of fifty tobacco slats ready to be grabbed by the tyer when needed.

The Benders' grown family came from town on this first day of harvest to help. Chuck and Doug worked in the fields with the other three primers while Marge and Jack did the tying. May, Jean, Joan, and I were the "leaf-handers."

Joan and I, facing each other, quickly snatched up three or four leaves with one hand, transferred them to the other, and handed them to Jack. He quickly wound a string tightly around the stems and tied them as he flipped them back and forth to each side of the stick. When the stick was full, he knotted it off at the end. Mr. Bender then removed it from the horse while Jack replaced it with an empty slat.

Jack was a very fast tyer, making Joan and me really hustle to avoid being crabbed at. Before the day ended, we were pretty much able to keep up with him.

Good money was paid to those willing to work in the harvest, and it wasn't difficult to pick up transient workers. Many Frenchmen from Montreal and Quebec, looking for good-paying priming jobs, arrived by carloads to the small towns. Jokes were often made by the local primers about how wimpy the Frenchmen were and how they frequently passed out from the backbreaking work and the hot August sun. Stories were often told that if enough money was wagered on them, you could talk them into eating a tobacco worm. After they were paid on Fridays, it was rumored that they'd spend all their hard-earned money on the prostitutes they brought with them. My sisters and I could only wonder about what all this meant.

The day usually ended around four in the afternoon, when enough sticks had been tied to fill the kiln. It was then that the primers trekked in, tired and thirsty, to hang the loaded sticks inside it. At this time Mr. Bender made a quick trip to the cellar to bring out a case of beer for the hired help so they could enjoy themselves once the job was done.

Each side of the kiln had large doors about three feet above the ground that opened upwards. A couple of sure-footed primers climbed inside to the top rafters of the building while two other men stood on the lower rafters. The filled tobacco slats were handed up to the men inside to be hung across the rafters for the curing process. As soon as the kiln was filled and the table empty of leaves, everyone grabbed a beer. It was a happy time after a hard day's work, and my sisters and I enjoyed the fun with the grown-ups. There were always lots of wild stories and dirty jokes — most flying right over our heads — but not wanting to appear stupid, we laughed anyway. Then it was off to the washstand where we scrubbed the horrible black tobacco tar off our hands and where Mr. Bender lined up the workers for the next day.

In front of the kiln was an entrance door, and on each side of the door was a large coal furnace. The furnace was connected to large tin pipes, almost a foot in diameter, running back and forth across the lower inside area of the building. Once the kiln was filled, the side doors were locked down, and the furnaces were fired up for the curing process. It took a few days of stoking the coal fires and careful checking of the temperatures before the tobacco turned a golden brown, ready to be removed and stored in the upper loft of the barn.

For this first tobacco curing, Mr. Bender hired a man from North Carolina to teach him how to maintain the furnaces to properly cure the tobacco. The "cure man" and his wife drove up from the south in a trailer home and parked it between the kilns. We learned their names were Marie and Robert. Marie sometimes helped with the leaf-handing, and I loved listening to her Southern accent. They had no sooner settled in than Mrs. Bender warned us that under no circumstances were we to bother them.

As we were playing outside one day, Marie waved us over to their trailer, and, ignoring Mrs. Bender's warning, we traipsed over to visit them. We settled down on the grass and listened to their fascinating stories about North Carolina.

"How old are you young'uns?" Marie asked.

"Joan and I are eleven, and Betty and Bonnie are nine," Jean said.

"I know ya'll are twins," she said, pointing to Jean and Joan, "but what about you other girls? Are ya'll sisters?"

"We're twins, too," I said.

"Two sets of twins in the same family? My goodness, ya'll must've kept your poor momma hoppin' when ya'll were little."

"She's not our mother," said Jean, biting her words and pointing toward the house. "Our mother's gone."

I looked at Jean, surprised by her remark, wondering what she meant by "gone."

"Oh dear, I'm sorry to hear that. Anyway, I think ya'll are a bit young to be a-working so hard. And you, little one," she said, looking at Betty, "I do declare, I get all jittery when I see you drivin' that big horse. You best be careful."

"I will," Betty promised with a smile, pleased with the concern for her safety.

We were still enjoying our visit when Doug, frantically waving his arms, yelled at us from the backyard. "Mom wants you in the house, right now!"

We said good-bye to Marie, and as we walked away, I asked Jean, "Why'd you tell her our mother's gone?"

"Because we ain't ever gonna see her anyway, so she might as well be gone."

I frowned and looked down at the ground.

Doug was walking toward us now, and Jean asked him, "What does she want? Did you go and tattle on us?"

The glint in his beady green eyes gave us the answer, and Mrs. Bender, her face flushed with anger, lit into us right away. "I thought I told you not to bother them!" she screamed. "You're not to go out there blabbin' your mouths off to them. What goes on here is no one's business. Is that understood?" She grabbed each of us by the shoulders, shaking us violently as she continued shouting.

"Well, she called us over," Jean protested, trying to defend our actions.

"Don't get cheeky with me, young lady," Mrs. Bender snapped, smacking Jean on the head. "Your dad pays them good money to look after those kilns, and I don't want to see any of you pestering them again. Now, get outside and keep your noses clean."

Jean couldn't resist slamming the door as we stormed outside, and immediately Mrs. Bender commanded, "You get back in here at once and close that door without slamming it. You're getting a little too big for your britches. One of these days you're gonna have to be brought down a peg or two!"

"Old battleaxe!" Jean sniped, as she joined us in the yard.

• • •

Early morning, when the dew hung heavy in the air, was the ideal time to unload the cured tobacco from the kilns. The dampness kept the leaves soft and prevented them from crumbling. Roused from our beds at four o'clock, we ran out to the barn to help harness the horses, hook them up to the wagon, and drive them up to the kiln.

Jean and Joan were almost big enough to climb up into the kiln among the joists and hand out the tobacco. But their legs weren't long enough to stride the two joists, so they straddled them, wrapping their legs around them to keep from falling, carefully balancing themselves as they removed the sticks.

Betty and I braced ourselves in the side door opening and held our breath as they climbed higher and higher up to the rafters and handed the sticks down to us. We had often heard stories of men injuring themselves if they lost their footing and fell on the pipes below.

"Careful, you girls. Don't fall," Mr. Bender yelled as they neared the peak. "I don't want you killing yourselves."

"We're okay!" Jean shouted back down.

Once the tobacco had cured, the sticks were light to handle. The four of us, working like a bucket brigade, handed the sticks to Mr. Bender to be loaded onto the wagon. When the kiln was emptied, the tobacco was taken to the barn and "booked" into neat piles for the stripping process during the winter months.

Some days, after the booking was finished, we'd hook the horses up to the tobacco boats and head straight to the fields to pick the tobacco for another day of kiln filling. We girls hated this early morning priming job. We wore only thin shirts, lightweight trousers, and no shoes, and the August nights were chilly, even though the days were scorching hot.

As we bent down to break the bottom leaves off, the cold wet dew dripped from the upper leaves and trickled down the backs of our necks. Tucking the wet leaves under my arm, I shivered and sniffled as I primed my row. I was tired, cold, miserable, and terribly hungry. Noticing my tears as we finished filling the boats, Mr. Bender snapped at me, "Oh, buck up, for Pete's sake, and quit feeling sorry for yourself. You ain't the only one who has to work around here! Now get in the house for your breakfast—all of you—before the workers get here."

"Hurry and eat your breakfast," Mrs. Bender commanded. "It's no time to be poky. The table gang will be here soon."

Rushing through our meal, we dragged our tired bodies back to the table for another day of kiln filling, waving to Betty as she drove off in the tobacco boat.

• • •

It was after supper on one of these long harvest days when my sisters and I climbed, sleepy and exhausted, into our beds. No sooner had I fallen into a deep sleep than Joan tugged at the covers around my head. "Bonnie, Bonnie, wake up," she whispered, shaking me.

I peered out from beneath the covers, sleepy-eyed and barely able to see her face in the darkness. "What's the matter?"

"I have to pee—real bad—and the pot's full."

"You're kidding," I moaned, sitting upright. "Who forgot to empty it?"

"I don't know. I guess we were all too busy. What are we gonna do now?"

It seemed close to midnight. The moon was full, and the pole light between the house and kilns cast some light into our rooms. There was no sound coming from downstairs, so we knew the Benders were asleep.

We woke up Jean and Betty, told them our problem, and quietly gathered in one bed to figure out what to do. Soon we were bickering over whose turn it was to empty the paint can.

"Who gives a toot?" I said. "It doesn't matter whose turn it is. It's filled to the brim. We're all gonna need it, and Joan has to go real bad!"

We knew they always locked the door at the foot of the stairs, so there was no way for us to sneak down through the house. "Should we wake up the Benders?" Betty asked.

"Hell no!" snapped Jean. "Mr. Bender will beat the crap out of us. He warned us already that we'd better not forget to empty it."

"What about dumping it out the window?" I suggested.

"No, someone pooped in it," Joan groaned disgustedly, "but we'd better think of something quick!"

"Hey, maybe we can hold your bum out the window, Joan," Jean said. The idea made us giggle, despite the predicament we were in.

"Oh God, don't make me laugh, or I'm gonna pee right here on the spot," Joan groaned again, crossing her legs tightly and diddling up and down.

"We gotta think of something really fast," I said. "Come on, Jean, you're always full of ideas. Put your thinkin' cap on!"

Jean furrowed her brow, pursed her lips, and then said, "Okay, I think I've got a good idea. Why don't we tie our sheets together, lower somebody out the window, and then lower the can down to them."

"Wow!" we exclaimed, looking at her in amazement. "That's a great idea!"

"Shuuush," I whispered. "We have to be really, really quiet. Their bedroom is right below us, you know, and we don't want them to hear us prowling about." Turning to Betty, I asked, "You're the lightest, so will you go?"

"Okay. But I'm scared. You've gotta promise not to let me fall!"

"We'll be real careful," Jean said. "But just make sure you hang on real tight."

After the two sheets were firmly knotted, Betty grabbed onto the tail of the sheet, winding it snugly around her right wrist. Then Jean and I boosted her out the small window, warning her to take it easy on the way down. We watched as she carefully maneuvered her body down the side of the house, landing safely below. Joan, tiptoeing across the room, brought the can over to us. "It's really full, so be careful you don't slop it."

Pulling up the sheets, we hurriedly tied the tail to the handle and gently started to lower the can down to Betty. She looked so tiny, standing in the moonlight, hugging herself, and shivering in the frosty night air.

"Hold it out from the house," I warned. "We don't want to bang the wall."

Soon the can was safely in Betty's hand. "Whew! So far so good," Jean sighed, rubbing her hand across her forehead.

Quickly untying the sheet, Betty made off to empty the can in the outhouse and was back in a flash. As she retied the sheet to the handle, we gingerly hoisted it up. We had no sooner pulled the can inside than Joan, snatching it from us, plunked herself down on it without giving us time to untie the sheet.

"Hurry, Joan, Betty's cold and waiting to get pulled up," I scolded, fearful that our scheme might be discovered at any time.

"Well, go ahead and untie it. I'm sorry, but I couldn't hold it any longer."

So far everything had gone smoothly. We didn't hear any stirrings from below, and we dropped the sheet down to Betty once again.

She wrapped it securely around her wrists and hung on for dear life as we pulled with all our might to haul her back up. Lowering her down was easy, but pulling her up along the overlapped siding of the clapboard house was far more difficult. Never in our wildest dreams were we expecting this part of our undertaking to be so tricky.

"You're hurting me!" she cried, looking up at us as her knees and knuckles scraped against the rough-edged boards. Even in the darkness, the tortured look on her face was clearly visible.

"She's getting all banged up," I said. "Slow down a bit."

Suddenly we heard a commotion downstairs and knew

we had awakened the Benders. Our hearts sank as we looked at each other. Jean chewed hard on the side of her lip as she pondered our next move.

"We woke them up," she whispered down to Betty, dangling halfway down the side of the house. "Hold on real tight! We're gonna pull hard and fast. Okay. One, two, three — pull!"

We yanked with all our might, and no sooner had her shoulders reached the sill than we latched onto her and pulled her, crying and moaning, into the room. Tears were streaming down her face as we looked her over. Her knuckles and knees were all skinned and bloody. Throwing our arms around her, we tried comforting her as we huddled against the bedroom wall, daring not to move, waiting, holding our breath, and hoping no one was going to come upstairs.

Soon we heard someone going out the kitchen door. Jean peeked out the window and saw Mr. Bender searching around the garage with a flashlight. We watched from the shadows of our room as he made his way out to the kilns and back. Coming back, he shone his light around the outside of the house and with one last motion, swept the beam across our window. Startled, we jerked back and sat motionless against the wall.

Jean took one more peek. "He's headin' toward the house."

"Do you think he saw us?" I asked.

"I don't know. I don't think so. But we better get back to our beds just in case he decides to come up and check on us. Pretend like we're sleeping."

We tiptoed back to our beds, and Mr. Bender didn't bother us. We were safe. We could breathe easy now.

In the morning I looked at Betty's scraped elbows and knees. She was pretty bruised and skinned up, and I told her that after breakfast we'd go to the pump and I'd help her get cleaned up.

"How do you feel?" I asked, and then added, "what if Mrs. Bender sees your sores. What will you say?"

"She won't see them. I'll put some long sleeves on and my trousers will cover my knees. And yeah, I did have a pissy time sleeping last night because I was sore all over."

It took several days for Betty's sores to heal, and we never again forgot to empty the darn paint can.

23

Cast Aside

Having to finish up the tobacco harvest, we were a week late starting back to school. Tired of all the hard work, I was thrilled to be back in school, enjoying the freedom of playing with friends, drawing and painting, and lugging books home to pass away the boring weekends. I was entering the fourth grade and was feeling quite grown up. I knew the teacher would be seating me on the right side of the school furnace along with the older kids.

I was feeling a little too grown up—perhaps a bit too big for my britches—because in November I managed to get myself in trouble when two boys were playing catch in class with a mitten, tossing it back and forth over Betty's head. On one ill-fated throw, the mitten sailed through the air and landed between Mrs. Granderson's bowed legs as she was preparing the day's lessons on the blackboard. Surprised and angry, she spun around, picked up the mitten, held it up, and demanded, "I want to know who threw this mitten!"

Everyone was silent.

Turning to the older students, she asked if they knew who threw it.

"Johnny, Walter, and Betty were throwing it around," an older student said.

Waving my hand frantically to get Mrs. Granderson's attention and casting the accusing boy a mean look, I blurted out, "Betty had nothing to do with it. Johnny and Walter were throwing the mitten, and it flew over her head. I saw it happen!"

"She did so," someone else piped up.

"I didn't do it," Betty protested, her voice quavering.

"Get up here at once—all three of you!" Mrs. Granderson demanded.

I was angry and upset as they marched to the front of the classroom. Watching as the teacher picked up the thick black strap from her desktop, I made one last plea for Betty. She looked so little and terrified as she stood in line behind the two boys. "Please, Mrs. Granderson, my sister didn't do it." But my plea fell on deaf ears as she prepared to administer punishment for the disruption.

The boys put on a brave front as they held out their hands, but Betty, white as chalk, lips quivering, started sniffling as soon as the teacher raised the strap. Whack! Whack! Whack! went the strap as she brought it down firmly three times to each boy's palm. Betty was last in line, flinching and crying out in pain as the strap met its target. She tried pulling her hand back, but the teacher grabbed it and held it outstretched as she finished out the rest of the punishment. I felt Betty's pain and was upset that I didn't ask to take the strapping for her.

Betty slid back into her seat, folded her arms on her desk, and laid her head down—her shoulders heaving as she sobbed aloud.

Eventually some of the older kids fessed up, admitting that Betty had nothing to do with throwing the mitten, and Johnny and Walter agreed.

"Well, I'm sorry I acted in such haste," Mrs. Granderson said. "Jean or Joan, would either of you like to come forward and strap me back for what I did to your sister?"

A few kids tried to egg them on, but they shook their heads.

She then looked at me. My stomach tightened as I pulled back against my seat. I was hoping she wouldn't ask me. "Bonnie, would you like to pay me back for what I did to your sister?"

I hesitated, not really wanting to strap her, but I was still upset because she didn't listen to me. And then I walked up the aisle, passed Betty's desk, and boldly took the strap from the teacher. Except for the sound of Betty's crying, the room went silent as she held out her hand. I swung the strap wildly, missing her hand more times than I hit it, waiting for her to tell me when to stop.

"All right, I think that's quite enough now," she said, taking the strap from me. "We've wasted enough of the day, so let's get on with our studies."

Noticing her rub her hands together a few times and knowing that I must have hurt her, I felt sorry and ashamed for what I'd done.

As we walked home from school, we talked about the strapping. "What if the Benders find out you strapped the teacher?" Jean said. "Mrs. Bender's gonna make mincemeat outta you! You shouldn't have done it, you know, but she should've listened to you."

"I know, but I was sooo mad!. Anyway, how's she gonna find out?"

"Oh, don't worry, she'll find out. Bad news travels fast. Besides, it's not every day the teacher gets strapped," she snickered.

"Well, I'm glad you stuck up for me, Bonnie," Betty said. "But I really didn't think you'd strap the teacher."

I was getting nervous now and wondered all the way home how Mrs. Bender could possibly find out. But Jean was right. As we dashed single file across the kitchen floor in a hurry to get upstairs, Mrs. Bender's sharp voice brought us to a quick stop, causing us to bump into one another like falling dominoes. "Hold it right there, all of you! Does someone have something to tell me?" she demanded, looking directly at me.

I knew by her cold glare and tight lips that there was no way to talk my way out of this. "Yes, I strapped the teacher."

"Well, there'll be no strapping of teachers while you live in this house. The rest of you get to your rooms while I deal with your sister!"

"But she strapped Betty, and Betty didn't do anything wrong," Joan protested, coming to my defense.

"I don't want to hear any of your poppycock. I swear, I've never been so embarrassed in all my life!" Mrs. Bender yelled as she opened the stairway door. "Now get to your rooms at once!" Then she grabbed Mr. Bender's belt from a nearby chair and gave me a whipping. Tossing the belt aside, she pushed me toward the opened door, shoved me through it, and warned, "Now, get out of my sight, and don't you ever pull a stunt like that again, young lady. Do you hear?"

Of course I heard, but I was too hurt and angry to answer her. So I just clenched my fists and banged them against the stairway wall as I made my way up the steps.

"I'm so sorry you got a whipping, Bonnie," Betty consoled as soon as my head cleared the top of the stairs. "I was hoping she wouldn't find out."

"It didn't hurt too much," I replied, showing them the red marks on my legs. "She used a belt. It wasn't quite as bad as a willow switch."

"Yeah, those darn willow switches really smart," Joan said. "You're lucky Mr. Bender wasn't home, or he'd have sent you out to get one."

"Do you suppose that's why they call it a *weeping willow*?" Betty speculated.

• • •

The beautiful fall days had flown away much too soon, and in crept the blustery, cold days of winter. Leaving the warmth of the schoolroom behind, we would hustle home before our fingers froze. Chilled to the bone as we entered our rooms, we would hurry over to the stovepipe to warm our hands and hang our mittens over the wires to dry. Then, snuggling down in the center of our beds, we would try to thaw ourselves out.

On one especially cold and blustery day as we huddled together to share our body warmth, I grumbled, "Why don't they put a kerosene heater up here like they have? And why doesn't the old bat let us come down and sit by the kitchen stove until we warm up?"

"It'll be a frosty Friday when she does that," Joan huffed.

"The only nice thing about winter is Christmas," Betty said, "and that's not too far away."

"I wonder what Christmas will be like and if the Children's Aid will send us something nice," I mused. "Do you think we'll get invited downstairs for the day?"

"Oh, for sure they'll let us down for Christmas," Joan replied confidently. "Everyone will be here."

• • •

A few more weeks passed before school let out for the Christmas holidays. As we sat in our beds, the smell of fresh-baked goodies wafted up beside the stovepipe. As we went down for our meals, we caught a glimpse of the decorated Christmas tree standing in the far corner of the living room.

Our excitement grew as Mr. Bender jingled some bells outside our stairway door on Christmas Eve. Giddy and silly, we chatted far into the night about what the next day might bring.

Returning to our bedrooms the following morning after a late breakfast, we took our places around the front window, waiting for family to arrive. Eventually we heard the sound of crunching gravel. "They're here! They're here!" Betty squealed excitedly.

We leaned nearer to the window, breathing hard on the glass to melt away the frost. Marge and May arrived with their boyfriends, followed by Doug and Jack with their girl-friends. Soon after, Chuck arrived with his wife, Dottie, and their small son, Mickey. Loaded down with gifts, food, and cases of beer, they stepped down from their cars and noisily entered the house.

Piling back into our beds, we waited and waited as the hours crawled by, eager for the moment when we'd be called down for the festivities.

As we listened to the cheerful sounds and bouts of loud laughter, we decided to tiptoe over to the stovepipe to eavesdrop. Lying on our bellies, ears pressed close to the hot pipe, we tried to pick up on what was going on. But the partying had moved into the living room, and the sounds were muffled. Someone started to play a guitar, and we wondered if it was one of the boyfriends. There was singing and laughing as the noise below became louder and louder. The hours were dragging by as we waited patiently in our rooms.

"I wish they'd call us down and have you and Joan sing for them," I said to Jean. "Remember how the people clapped so hard when you sang at the Christmas concert? These people don't even know how nice you can sing."

"Right now I wouldn't mind singing for my supper," Jean asserted. "I'm so hungry I could eat the bedpost!"

"Me too," Joan said.

Soon we could hear the clatter and tinkle of dishes and glasses and smell the food being prepared. But we were beginning to lose hope of joining the festivities, and our spirits were sinking. "When are they gonna call us down?" Joan moaned, making a fist and chewing on her nails.

"Do you think they forgot about us?" Betty asked, as she started to sob.

"I don't think so," I said, putting my arm around her shoulders. "But nothing surprises me anymore. We'll have to wait and see, but there's not much we can do about it anyway."

Late in the day the door opened and our hearts came alive. "You girls can come down for a bit," Mrs. Bender called.

Taking one last peek into our small piece of broken mirror, we tidied our hair and started down. But at the last moment I got cold feet and hesitated on the steps, nervous about facing everyone.

Joan tugged at my hand. "C'mon, Bonnie, it might be fun."

But I resisted. "Everyone's just gonna gawk at us." Then I relented, and following Mrs. Bender's lead, we filed into the living room and stood in a semicircle around the far end of the table beside the Christmas tree.

I felt so out of place in this strange room — a room we had never been allowed to enter and had only seen when we sat at the kitchen table.

"Well, say something, for heaven's sake. Has the cat got your tongues?" Mrs. Bender said in a sweetly sarcastic voice.

"Merry Christmas," Jean replied. "Merry Christmas," we all joined in.

"There, that's better," Mrs. Bender said. And then the others chimed in, "Merry Christmas, girls."

I felt terribly awkward and shy, not knowing how to carry on any sort of grown-up conversation. The room became unbearably quiet. It seemed like everyone was staring at us as if we were on display. I was feeling more and more like a sideshow freak and wanted to run back to my room.

Jean, embarrassed by her developing breasts, crossed her arms over them and turned away from the crowd.

Mrs. Bender bent down and picked out four brown paper bags from among the gaily wrapped gifts "Here are some Christmas treats," she said, handing us each a bag. "You can take them to your rooms now. It should tide you over until dinner."

Back upstairs, we climbed into our beds and looked into our bags. Inside were an orange, some gum, and an assortment of nuts. We quickly gobbled up the oranges and started on the nuts. We cracked the peanuts, pecans, and hazelnuts easily with our teeth but wondered how to crack the Brazil nuts.

"How on earth do they expect us to crack these darn things?" Betty asked, holding up one of the odd-shaped nuts.

"If we can figure out how to empty the pot, we should be able to find a way to crack these nuts," I said confidently. "What if we open the window and slam it down on them?"

"Don't be silly," Joan said. "It's too cold, and we're apt to break the glass. We have to think of something else."

She was right, and after looking around the room for something that might work, I said, "Why don't we lift up the bedpost, center the nut under it, and all of us sit on the bed?"

"That's worth a try," Jean agreed, and so two of us lifted the bedpost while Betty centered the nut under it. Then we slid back onto the bed, heard the nut crack, and felt the bedpost thud to the floor. But when we lifted the bedpost, we found the whole nut smashed to smithereens. We scraped the shattered bits up off the floor, sifted the pieces from the shell, and wolfed down the nutmeat. We were able to crack a few more before the door opened and Mr. Bender yelled up. "What the hell's goin' on up there? Are you trying to knock the house down, for Christ's sake?"

"No," Jean answered, leaning over the rail, "we're cracking our Brazil nuts under the bedpost."

"I swear I don't know what the hell you girls are gonna think of next! Leave the damn things until tomorrow when you can crack them outside with some stones," he said, slamming the door shut.

Jean turned to look at us. "Doesn't the old fart know we're hungry?"

We gathered up the shells and shoved them through the hole in the wall that had become our convenient trash disposal.

Just then the door opened again, and I grumbled aloud, "What now?"

"Here's your Christmas dinner," Mrs. Bender said as she set four plates on the bottom stair. "Put the dishes back on the step when you're finished."

Joan scurried down and slid the plates to us under the bottom rail. Getting back into bed and balancing our plates on our legs, we hungrily eyed our dinners. There was turkey, dressing, mashed potatoes and gravy, along with a generous piece of fruitcake.

"Yummy," Jean said, "at least we got a good helping of meat for a change."

"Yeah," I agreed, "but I wish she wouldn't put this horrible gravy all over my potatoes. I hate gravy. It tastes almost as bad as wallpaper paste. I'm never gonna eat gravy when I grow up."

"Oh, quit complaining," Joan said. "At least she gave us a decent slice of fruitcake."

"Well, I guess we found out what Christmas is gonna be like," Betty sighed as she prepared to take her dish down the stairs.

Jean frowned and tossed her pillow in the air. "Yeah, remind me not to get too excited next year."

•••

Early January was the time for stripping the tobacco off the slats and bundling it into bales ready for the factory, and a small section of the barn was walled off for this work. There was a steam room where the dried sticks of tobacco were hung to make the leaves soft and pliable. Doug was in charge of the steam room, removing the tobacco when it was ready and placing the sticks on the tying horse to be stripped.

In the evenings and on weekends, Mr. Bender let us strip the leaves off the slats while he sorted the tobacco into three different grades. Mrs. Bender gathered the leaves into small handfuls, wrapping the stems snugly with a soft leaf.

Comparing it with the rest of the harvest season, we didn't mind the six or so weeks of stripping. It was fairly light work, and we were inside, out of the miserable, bitter cold. And, as it was necessary to keep a good fire going in order to supply steam to the steam room, we were quite warm.

Often, Mr. Bender would bring his radio to the barn along with a case of beer that he hid under the table. This really tickled us to no end as now we could listen to the radio all day long.

One day, as we were cleaning out the barn stalls, Betty sneaked into the stripping room and snitched a bottle of Mr. Bender's beer. "Hey, look what I have," she said, waving it in the air for me to see. "I wanna see what it tastes like. Wanna try some?"

"You're crazy—you and your sticky fingers!" I scolded. "Mr. Bender'll beat the you-know-what out of you if he finds out you swiped his beer."

"Oh, for Pete's sake, it's just one bottle. I'll put it back when it's empty. He'll never know the difference."

"I think he hid the opener," she said, handing me the bottle. "You know how to break an apple over your knee; do you think you can get the cap off?"

Giving her a dirty look, I took the bottle from her. Positioning the edge of the cap along the top board of the cow's stall, I slammed my fist down hard on it, and the top flew into the air. Betty grabbed the cap, sticking it in her pocket. "Another checker for our checker board," she grinned. "Here, you wanna try the first swig?"

I was wise to her and shook my head. "Uh-uh. It looks like pee, and I'll bet it tastes like pee too."

As Jean and Joan gathered around, I said, "She's tryin' some beer." We all waited for her reaction as she gulped down a mouthful.

"Oh, yuck, it tastes terrible. How can he drink this gosh-awful stuff?" She handed the bottle to Jean, who took a big gulp. "Tastes more like horse piss," she said, screwing up her face and wiping her mouth off.

"How would you know what that tastes like?" I questioned.

"Well, I'll say that it tastes like what horse piss smells like when it's coming from the horse."

We passed the bottle around, taking small swigs until it was gone. I smiled and questioned why we were intent on punishing ourselves.

Betty then sneaked the empty bottle back where it belonged.

"Boy, I feel funny—like I'm dizzy or something," Joan complained, pressing her palms against her head.

"Me too," I said. "You think I'm drunk?"

We giggled and acted silly as we finished cleaning the stables.

"Don't you ever do that again, Betty," Joan said. "That yucky stuff is not worth getting a lickin' for."

24

A Crushing Blow

In the spring of '46, a Czechoslovakian family bought a large tobacco farm directly across the road. They had an eleven-year-old daughter named Marie. My sisters and I were happy to have a new friend to join us on our mile-long walk to school. She was a pleasant, pretty girl with slightly bucked teeth and one eye that turned a bit inward. Her hair was light brown with soft curls framing her oval-shaped face, but it was the pretty dresses she wore that made me a bit jealous. I was unable to keep from staring at them. I loved the pretty flowery fabrics, the lace-trimmed collars, the tucks and ruffles on every dress. Being tired of the boring navy blue tunics we wore almost every day, I longed to have pretty girlish clothes. The skirt backs on our tunics were so shiny and worn from sliding in and out of our school seats that Joan remarked, "If they get any shinier, we'll be able to use them as a mirror."

Once while admiring the fancy work on the front of Marie's dress, I pointed to it and asked, "What is that, Marie? It's so pretty."

"Oh, this?" she said as she touched her chest. "It's called smocking. My mother did it. She makes all my clothes."

"Your mother makes all your dresses? But how? They're so pretty."

"She orders fabric from Sears, makes a pattern, cuts it out, and sews it up."

"Don't tell her anymore," Jean quipped, "or she'll be cutting up the bedsheets."

"Yep, Bonnie's gonna do something like that when she grows up — that is, if she ever grows up," Joan joked.

"Just wait and see," I said, nudging her in the ribs, "I'll show you."

As we walked a bit farther down the road, Jean announced, "You know what? I'm gonna peek in my bucket to see what I've got for lunch."

I smiled, knowing full well she was curious to see what Marie's mom had packed.

Taking the bait, Marie opened her lunch bucket, and we all gathered around to sneak a peek. It was brimming with all sorts of good stuff. I drooled just looking at it.

She had a candy bar, a big piece of chocolate cake, meat sandwiches, and something wrapped in wax paper.

"What's that in there?" Betty asked, pointing to the wrapped food.

"It's a piece of breaded chicken," she said, opening up the wrapper a bit. "My mom makes it often."

"We've never had breaded chicken," I said.

"Chicken? What's chicken?" Jean asked. "Chicken at our house is as scarce as hen's teeth."

"Oh, we get it once in a great while — sometimes on Sunday," I said, "just not breaded."

"Sure, but by the time we get called down for dinner, it's mostly all gone, and we get stuck with the part that goes through the fence last."

Amused by Jean's silliness, Marie said to her, "Don't

worry. I'll let you all taste a piece on the way home. It's really good. But I sometimes get tired of it, and my mom likes me to eat all my lunch. She always packs way too much for me."

"What's in the thermos?" Betty asked.

"It's chocolate milk." She laughed. "Surely you know what chocolate milk is."

"Yes," Betty said. And as we strolled past the Millers' house, she pointed to it. "Bonnie and I used to live there, didn't we, Bonnie? And Mrs. Miller always made us hot chocolate."

I nodded in agreement as I looked longingly at the old home. Marie gave Betty a puzzled look but said nothing.

"I think the Benders need to get some jersey cows," Joan joked. "They probably give chocolate milk."

On the way home from school, my sisters and I got into a shoving match, each wanting to walk at Marie's side as we waited for her to open her lunch bucket. "I hope she didn't forget," I whispered to Joan.

After we had dropped a few hints about how hungry we were, Marie finally remembered her promise. Opening her bucket, she let us share the breaded chicken and some sandwiches. She was unaware of what she had started, for from that day forward we hung close around her, trying hard to keep on her good side, hoping for some leftovers. When she turned into her long lane we waved good-bye to her and Joan remarked, "Wouldn't it be nice to have a lunch like hers every day?"

"Sure would, but I was looking for the blood pudding," Jean said. "Remember, Mr. Bender said that they made blood pudding every time they killed a pig, and I wanted to see what it looked like."

"Sure, and he also told us the moon was made of cheese," Betty said, "so don't mention blood pudding, or you might hurt her feelings. She might get mad at us and never share her lunch with us again."

"You're right," Jean agreed with a sigh. "We sure don't want that to happen."

• • •

On our way to school one morning, Joan and I, straggling behind the rest of the group, noticed a gray coupe car coming toward us. We watched as it veered over toward the other girls as if to stop, then sped away and pulled up beside us, forcing us onto the shoulder of the road. We wondered what he wanted, thinking perhaps he was looking for directions. We were a bit nervous, as it had been rumored in school that Shirley, one of our classmates, had been grabbed on her way to school by some man in a car. As we edged back a few steps, he reached over and opened the passenger door. "Get in," he barked. "I'll give you a ride to school."

Joan and I looked at each other, confused, wondering why this big-bellied man with a bushy moustache and felt hat wanted to give us a ride to school when he wasn't even going our way. "But we aren't going that way," Joan hollered, trying to make herself heard over the sound of the rattling engine.

"Just get in!" he commanded sternly, picking up a small handgun from the seat and pointing it at me. Terrified, and without thinking, I stepped up onto the running board. As I started to climb inside, he leaned over to grab my hand. His large hand had barely touched mine when I caught sight of an axe and a large coil of rope on the window shelf directly behind his head. My mind went blank and I froze. Suddenly I was yanked off the running board as Joan pulled me away from him in the nick of time. I stumbled to the ground, but she jerked me to my feet. "Come on, let's get outta here! Run as fast as you can. We've gotta catch up with the rest of the girls in case he turns around!" Holding hands, we ran as fast as our legs could carry us. Joan, glancing over her shoulder, noticed him starting to turn around in the middle of the road and then deciding against it, seeing that we were catching up with the rest of the kids. We slowed a bit to catch our breath, and Joan said, "That old bugger was gonna snatch you! I'm sure of it. He didn't wanna give us a ride at all."

"I know. Thank God you pulled me away. You probably saved my life," I gasped, explaining to her what I saw in his car.

Catching up to our sisters and Marie, we told them what happened. "He almost got Bonnie!" Joan exclaimed, her voice trembling. "She was halfway in his car!"

"He started to pull over here, too," Marie said. "Do you think he was the same man who picked up Shirley a few weeks ago?"

"I doubt it," Jean said. "From what I heard from the older kids, it was a young guy who grabbed her, forced her into the ditch, and raped her. But he was caught, taken to jail, and got thirty lashes — or something like that."

"I don't know what 'rape' means," Joan confessed, "but it must be really bad."

Arriving at school, we rushed to tell the teacher what had happened to us. She then talked to us about the dangers of getting in cars with strangers. Looking at me, Mrs. Granderson said, "I'm sure you'll be forever grateful to your sister for protecting you from harm. Heaven only knows what might have happened to you."

"Yes, I will," I replied, linking my arm to Joan's. "I'm glad she was with me. I was so scared. I'm glad she yanked me away in the nick of time."

• • •

Another season of tobacco growing arrived, and my sisters and I were filling up the water tank again, hating every minute of it. Within a few weeks the field planting began, and Betty had to work on the planting machine again. We were happy that she had grown some. Her legs were now long enough to reach the footrest, so we didn't worry too much about her.

Once, during a break in the planting day, my sisters and I were sitting on our beds when we heard the muffled sound of an engine outside. We knew this meant a car had arrived, so we made a mad dash for the window. As we knelt and crowded our heads together, we watched curiously at the activity below. Noticing four people in the car, we looked closer as the driver and passenger stepped out and walked toward the front porch. Joan let out a squeal of delight, "Our brothers! Our brothers are here! They've come to see us!"

As we pressed our noses against the window to get a better peek, Jean, bubbling with excitement, remarked, "Oh my God, she's right! That's Hank and that's Bobby! I'd recognize them anywhere!" Tears of joy began welling up in our eyes.

"Look, Betty!" I said, moving aside to make more room for her head. "That *is* Bobby! Look how big he is. Remember he told us he'd look for us?"

Throwing our arms around each other, we bounced joyfully up and down on our knees. We were so thrilled to see him.

Then Betty asked, "Who are the people in the backseat, Jean?"

"Could be Jim. And that's our mother beside him."

"How do you know that's our mother? All I can see are her legs."

"Those are her legs. I just know it. I'm positive it's her."

As we peered through the porch window below, we saw Mrs. Bender open the front door. Watching our brothers' faces and hand motions as they appeared to be explaining their reason for stopping by, we quickly tidied our hair in anticipation of being called downstairs.

"Shuuush. Let's listen," Joan said. "I can't make out a word they're saying."

After talking for a few minutes, the boys got back into the car.

"What's going on? What are they doing? Why are they getting back into the car?" Betty cried out.

"She's sending them away! She's sending them away! She's not gonna let us see them!" Joan wailed, burying her face in her hands.

We shoved our heads into the window again, frantically waving our hands, hoping they'd see us. But they didn't, and the car pulled back out onto the highway.

"You're right. They're leaving. I don't believe it! How can she be so mean?" I covered my mouth with my hand, trying to stop the hurt inside.

Our hearts and spirits sank. Feeling like wounded animals, we moved away from the window and sat with our backs against the wall, too numb and sad to speak. Betty began sobbing softly, and Joan moved closer to her and put her arm around her shoulder.

"I can't believe she wouldn't let us see them. Old battleaxe!" Jean snarled, banging the back of her head against the wall. "Why doesn't she just rip our guts out?"

"I wonder how they knew where to find us?" Joan asked.

"Our mother works for Pete Butler, so perhaps she told them," I said. Then, hoping for some encouraging words, I asked Jean and Joan, "Do you think we'll ever see them again? Will they ever come back?"

"I doubt it. She'd just chase them away," Joan lamented.

Sitting still and glum, we heard the stairway door open. "You can get your fool heads out of the window now. Your brothers are gone!" Mrs. Bender yelled, her harsh words rising up the staircase, breaking through the stillness and stabbing our hearts like a hot poker. Heartbroken, we drifted slowly back to our beds. Our moment of excitement had been cruelly crushed, and we were too sad to talk or play anymore. I threw myself across the bed and banged my fists on my pillow. "I hate her! I hate her!" I cried. Tossing the pillow over my head, I covered myself in darkness and tried to smother my feelings. I ached so much to see our brothers and our mother, and Mrs. Bender's heartlessness at chasing them away was just too much for me to understand.

We were filled with anger and resentment as Mrs. Bender called us down for supper.

"Well, I guess I took the wind out of your sails," Mrs. Bender said as we made our way to the supper table. "From now on when someone drives up, I want you to keep your noses out of the window. Is that understood?"

When we didn't acknowledge her remark, she raised her voice, "Did you hear me? Answer me!"

We only nodded, stubbornly maintaining our silence.

• • •

At the request of the Children's Aid Society, Mrs. Bender rounded us up to take us to Dr. Archer for a physical checkup. We lined up in the examination room in nothing but our underpants while he held the cool stethoscope to our bodies. After weighing us, he turned to Mrs. Bender and asked, "What do you feed these girls for breakfast?"

"Oh, they usually have a big bowl of bread and milk."

"Bread and milk?" he inquired. "Is that all?"

"Why, yes," she replied, shifting in her seat.

"Well, they're going to need something a little more substantial. They're growing girls now and need a hearty breakfast—something that'll stick to their ribs. I suggest that you start their day off with a big bowl of porridge."

"All right," she said, nodding in agreement.

I looked at my sisters, wrinkling my nose and pushing out my cheeks as if I wanted to puke. They grinned at me.

As expected, the next morning's breakfast consisted of a big bowl of cold, lumpy porridge with a dusting of brown sugar. Settling into my chair, I took one look at the lumpy mixture and knew I wasn't going to like it. After scraping off the top part with the brown sugar, I couldn't eat any more.

As soon as Mrs. Bender left the room, I looked at my sisters, who seemed to be getting their porridge down, and asked, "Do you want some of my porridge?"

They shook their heads, and Jean whispered, "Be brave, Bonnie. Eat your own mush."

That did it for me. "I can't eat this stuff." Quickly grabbing handfuls of it and stuffing it into my trouser pockets, I dashed outside before Mrs. Bender came back into the room.

When my sisters finished and came out to the yard, they found me at the chicken coop, feeding my porridge to the chickens.

"Are you tryin' to fatten them up?" Betty joked.

"Yeah, but this stuff might kill 'em first."

"Oh, it wasn't that bad, but I still like bread and milk better," Joan said.

After emptying my pockets I walked down to the creek, washed out my trousers, laid them over the wire fence to dry in the sun, and sat shivering on the banks while watching my sisters poke around in the creek, trying to scare the frogs from their muddy homes.

"Are you gonna do this every day?" Joan asked with a giggle.

"I dunno. I hope she gets tired of cooking it and goes back to bread and milk."

We suffered through a week or so of cold, lumpy porridge before we were given a new cereal called "puffed wheat." Mrs. Bender bought it in big paper bags that were almost two feet tall. She kept a bag beside the kitchen stove, and we were always happy to see it there.

After she started serving the puffed wheat to us for breakfast, we'd practically fall over each other to get down the stairs to the breakfast table. At last we had something really delicious to eat.

As we were enjoying our puffed wheat breakfast one morning, a knock on the front door got Mrs. Bender's attention. "Hmm, I wonder who that could be this early in the day?" she muttered. It was her uncle Jake, and she invited him inside. He was a grubby, scruffy old man with a long, straggly gray beard. Mr. Bender always called him the hermit. We knew that he lived alone in a tumble-down shack hidden by a grove of pine trees over on the front road. As he made his entrance into the kitchen with his walking stick, Mrs. Bender asked him to take a seat directly behind Betty. He removed his stained, weather-beaten hat and perched it on his knee. The smell coming from his clothes was so strong that I wondered if it were possible to hold my nose and eat at the same time.

"These young'uns of yours are getting mighty big, Mary," he said in a croaky voice.

"Yeah, they're growin' like bad weeds," she replied. Motioning with her head toward the bag of puffed wheat, she asked, "Would you like a bowl of cereal or perhaps a cup of coffee?"

"What's that stuff?" he asked, pointing his walking stick at the bag's label. "Is it the newfangled cereal they just came out with—that puffed wheat junk? My goodness Mary," he said, stretching his neck to peer into our bowls, "surely you ain't feedin' the girls that stuff? Why, one good fart and—

poof! — it's all gone! Why, it ain't nuthin' but a bag of wind."

At that, my sisters and I clamped our hands over our mouths to muffle our giggles.

"All right, that's enough now, girls," Mrs. Bender said. "Get on with your breakfast and make it fast."

We gobbled down the rest of our breakfast and hurried outside to play, still giggling over Uncle Jake's funny remark. "I sure hope she doesn't change her mind and stop giving us puffed wheat for breakfast," I said, "because I could eat that stuff 'til the cows come home."

25

A Dumb Mistake

Behind the house and close to the garden fence was a large stump we called the chopping block, and it came in handy for many uses. Aside from using it for a stand to hold a tub of water for the tobacco workers to wash their tar-covered hands, Mr. Bender used it for splitting kindling for the stove. Sometimes he would kill a chicken for Sunday dinner by laying its head across the block and chopping it off.

This day the stump found a new use. Mr. Bender had been smelt fishing at Lake Erie and had lugged home two bushel baskets full of smelt. "C'mon over here, girls. I'm going to teach you how to clean these little suckers." Plunking the baskets down beside the stump, he said, "Watch carefully now."

He picked up a fish, sandwiched it in his hand, removed the back fin, and laid it across the stump. Flipping it from one side to the other, he ran his blade up toward the head, scraping off the clear, silvery scales. He then chopped off the head, held onto the tail, jabbed his knife into the belly, and slit it open.

Turning to my sisters, I clamped my hand over my mouth as the yellow stuff inside spilled onto the stump. My thoughts flashed back to the muskrat incident and I wondered if Betty's did too.

"Now, scrape out all this nasty stuff and wash the fish in a pail of water," he said. "Bonnie, you go fetch a couple of pails of water from the pump."

After gutting a few more to make sure we got the hang of it, he handed us each a knife. "There, go to it. This should keep you out of mischief for the day. Be careful you don't cut your fingers."

As he strode away, we looked at each other and screwed up our faces. We weren't happy about this disgusting job.

"Well, we ain't gonna get this done just sitting here looking at each other," Joan said. "Let's get busy."

"Yeech," I groaned, cringing as I scraped the guts off the stump. "They sure smell stinky. Look, they're still alive. Look at them flopping around."

"Yeah, I hate to kill the poor little critters," Jean said. "They never did anything to me."

Betty grabbed the first fish, laid it across the stump, and was doing fine until she slit open the belly. Once the guts tumbled out, she stabbed the knife hard into the stump, covered her mouth with her hand, and fled to the outhouse.

Jean rolled her eyes and shook her head. "Well, there she goes again, puking her guts out."

Joan stared for a moment at Betty running for the outhouse, and then she said, "You know what? I'm gonna find a small board for her. She can cut off the back fins and remove the scales, and then we'll do the rest. Otherwise, she'll be in there all day."

"Good idea," I agreed, as I started toward the outhouse. "I'm gonna check on her."

"Come on out, Betty," I called, banging on the side of the outhouse, you can do the scaling. We'll split them."

Pale, clutching her stomach, and taking short breaths, she reluctantly trudged back to the stump.

"This is such a yucky job," I said, "so I'm gonna sing. It won't make the job go faster, but at least it'll help to keep my mind on something else."

"Well, I'm gonna plug my ears," Joan said, screwing her face into a disgusted frown. "You couldn't carry a tune in a bucket!"

Betty, recovering a bit from her nausea, joined in with, "Go ahead, Bonnie, start singing. Maybe you'll scare the fish away and we won't have to clean them."

"I don't care what you say. I'm gonna sing anyway," I proclaimed, stubbornly refusing to let their teasing stop me.

Swim little fishy, swim on,
Swim little fishy, swim on,
There's nothing in the brook,
And you're bound to catch a hook,
So swim little fishy, swim on.

It really was a good diversion, so soon my sisters joined in. "I'm not sure that's the way the song goes," Joan said, "but who gives a darn. Let's sing it again."

We did, and just as I had hoped it did make the disgusting job a little more pleasant and the time seemed to go faster.

It took the better part of the day to finish cleaning and washing the fish and hosing down the area before Mr. Bender returned to cart them into the house.

"Betcha we're gonna be stuck with this job every time he goes smelt fishing," I grouched.

"I heard him say that they run in the springtime, so maybe this'll be it," Joan said.

"I sure hope so," Betty said with a shudder, "'cause I'm sick of being sick."

We wondered what Mr. Bender was going to do with all the fish, but Joan told us that he planned to wrap them up and take them to the storage freezer in Williamston.

"Do you think we'll be having these for supper?" Betty choked.

"Probably," said Joan.

Joan was right. Fried smelt was on our supper plates for the next several days. But we didn't mind. They tasted quite good, and much to our surprise, Mrs. Bender even asked if we wanted seconds.

• • •

Our second summer on the tobacco farm had arrived. School was out, the crop was planted and hoed, and with the exception of the barn chores, my sisters and I had some free time. Back to the woods we went to poke around in the neighboring dumps, collect old pots and pans for our makeshift restaurant behind the barn, and take long hikes down the railroad tracks, balancing ourselves on the rails to see who could go the farthest without falling off.

When the trains came whizzing by, we would wave and flail our arms at the engineers, who would give us a blast on their whistle as they passed.

One day as the train slowed for some stray cows that had wandered onto the tracks, we saw a man jump from one of the cars. As we watched him regain his footing, he threw a stick with a bundle tied to it over his shoulder and began making his way into the woods. "Look," Jean cried, "that's a hobo. We better get the heck outta here!"

"Do you think he might hurt us?" I asked.

"I don't know, but I sure ain't gonna hang around to find out."

The man turned and looked our way, then started coming toward us.

As we ran barefoot up the tracks, the sharp cinders cut into our feet. And so we veered off toward the woods, hid for a while in a farmer's cornfield, then dashed for home — frightened, gasping for breath, and ever so glad to be safe.

"Boy, that's the first time I ever saw a real hobo," Betty said. "It's gonna be a long time before I go that far down the tracks again!"

"That's for sure," I agreed. "I think we'd better stick to playing on the hill."

"The hill," as we called it, was a grassy overhang behind the barn and out of view of the house. It was our private playground. During the summer months we spent many happy hours playing in the sandy side of the cliff, digging holes so deep that we felt certain of reaching China. Or, getting more adventurous, we'd take turns curling our bodies inside old tires and rolling each other down the hill. This daring adventure often ended up with painful results if we crashed into a fence. We fell out of the tire either laughing or moaning, depending on where the tire decided to stop.

During the winter months the hill served as our toboggan run. Using pieces of heavy box cardboard for sleds, we sped lickety-split down the hill, racing to see who could go the farthest and marking out our finish lines in the snow with the heels of our boots.

I was the last one to leave the kitchen one summer day when Mrs. Bender told me that she and Mr. Bender were going visiting and we were to play outside. My sisters, knowing I'd be running at full speed to catch up to them, decided to play a trick on me. They put a piece of cardboard over a fresh cow pie on the slope of the hill, knowing full well I'd be tempted to step on it. They guessed right. No sooner had I plunked my foot on the cardboard than it flew out from under me, landing my bottom smack into the middle of the cow pie. I was furious with them as they stood laughing their fool heads off at the bottom of the hill.

"That was a mean and dirty trick!" I snapped at them while hurrying to the creek to wash out the stinky green dung before it dried.

Joan came over to console me as I sat on the bridge, sulking and waiting for the sun to dry my trousers as they hung over the wire fence. "We really didn't think you were gonna land in the cow pie. We were just placing bets on whether or not you'd step on the cardboard."

"It sure surprised me when I went flying like that. Now this is the second time I've had a green fanny."

We grinned at each other as she patted my hand. "You're not angry with us anymore?"

"Naw. But I might try to pay you back."

We laughed. And then she asked, "What did the old biddy have to say when she put you out of the house? Did you do something wrong?"

"No. Not this time. She said they're going away and will be back by lunchtime. I saw their truck heading toward Woodsville."

"Maybe they're going to visit Grandma and Grandpa Tillman. Sure would be nice if they'd take us with them."

"That'll be the day. They never take us anywhere. And besides, us little pigs might hear somethin' we're not supposed to hear."

Hours passed, and we were getting hungrier by the minute. "Look at our long shadows," I said. "It's gotta be close to four o'clock."

"When are they ever coming home to feed us?" Betty whined, rubbing her tummy. "Pretty soon I'm not even gonna have a shadow."

Jean suggested that maybe we could get into the kitchen and swipe some bread, but I shook my head, telling her that I saw Mrs. Bender locking the house up.

"Well, my stomach's already touching my backbone," Jean groaned. "If I get any skinnier, I'll be able to slide under the damn door!"

"Yeah, I can picture that," I chided. "And it'll be your last piece of bread if you get caught! But there's gotta be something we can find to eat before we starve to death." And then I thought of something. "Hey, what about some eggs? We can sneak into the chicken coop and get some eggs."

"You wanna suck eggs?" Joan asked, giving me a disgusted look.

"No, I don't wanna suck eggs!"

"Why? You sucked one before," Joan chimed in.

"Did not! You lie!"

"Did so," Jean and Betty joined in simultaneously.

"Soooo, I was hungry, and besides, you dared me. Right now, I'm gonna find that old fry pan from the dump, wash it out, make a fire, and scramble them up."

The teasing was over now and Betty agreed that scrambling up some eggs was a great idea. "I still have some of Doug's matches left."

"You mean they *were* Doug's matches — until you swiped them from his room when you made his bed."

Reaching into her pocket, she pulled out the book of matches along with a small square packet.

"What's this?" I asked, taking the packet to examine it.

"I don't know," she said, smiling sheepishly. "I found it along with the matches."

"There's something round in there," I said, sliding the packet between my fingers. "I wonder what it is?"

"Got no idea. We'll figure it out later," she said, slipping the packet back into her pocket.

We hurried about getting all the necessary items together before setting the dry leaves and twigs on fire. Joan cracked several eggs into the heated pan while I stirred them with an old fork.

As we were sitting around the fire and enjoying our first mouthfuls, Betty noticed the Benders' truck coming down the road. Jumping to her feet, she screamed at us, "Oh my God, they're coming back! What are we gonna do?"

"Quick, grab some sand and put out the fire!" I cried.

We all rushed to the side of the bank to scoop up handfuls of sand. As we tossed it on the fire, thick, black smoke began curling in the air. We looked at each other, realizing what a foolish thing we'd done.

"Shit!" Jean growled. "That wasn't such a good idea. We're really in for it now. They couldn't miss those smoke signals if they were blindfolded!"

"We better get rid of all the evidence before Mr. Bender gets out here," Joan warned. "Let's dig a hole and bury everything in it."

No sooner had we smoothed over the holes and patted them down than Mr. Bender came tearing around the corner of the barn, his face twisted in anger. Taking long strides, he came to where we were sitting side-by-side on the edge of the bank, dangling our legs, trying to pretend innocence. "What the hell's going on here!" he barked.

"W . . . W . . . We were just burning some paper," I stammered nervously.

"Where are the matches? Who in the hell has the matches?" He held out his hand as he searched our faces, waiting for an answer.

Betty stared down at the ground. She wasn't about to say anything.

"There was only one left in the packet and I threw it in the fire," I said, covering for her. "I found the matches in the garbage dump."

He stared at me coldly, not knowing whether to believe me or not. "I swear to Christ, we can't leave you kids home alone for one minute unless you get into one fool thing or another. Next thing I know you'll be burning the damn barn down! Now get to the house, all of you, and bring in some switches from the willow tree."

Burning with anger, we gathered up four switches and brought them into the house.

"Put them down there," Mrs. Bender said, pointing to the empty wood box beside the stove. "You can eat your supper first."

I'd enjoy my food more if I had my switching first, I thought.

After we finished eating our sandwiches, Mr. Bender retrieved the switches from the wood box and shuffled them back and forth before settling on the one he figured to be best for the job. I was filled with anger as I watched him toy with the switches before settling on the sturdiest one. I wanted to get it over with and the sooner the better.

We were cowered close together, none of us wanting to be the first, when Mr. Bender pulled Jean from our midst. Jerking her body forward to avoid the full sting of the switch, she screamed and cried out in pain. "Ooow! Ooow!" she screamed as the switch found its target.

Once he had broken her down, he grabbed Joan. She started crying after only a few hits, hoping he might ease up sooner. She was right; she got fewer hits than Jean.

Betty and I were the next in line for punishment. "Be brave, Betty," I whispered, squeezing her shoulder. "Cry really fast."

Finally it was my turn, and after he was through, we stood near the doorway rubbing our bodies, still feeling the burning sting of the switch and watching as Mr. Bender gathered up the switches.

"Here," he said, handing the switches off to Joan, "you can toss these away. And I'm warning you that you're not to go into the barn except for doing chores. If I catch you in there, you'll get another whipping. Is that clear?"

We nodded, as we continued to rub our backsides.

Holding the back door open, he waved the back of his hand at us. "Now, get outta here!"

"Old fart!" Joan snarled, flinging the willow switches as far away as she could.

"Why can't we play in the barn anymore?" I complained. "We always had so much fun playing hide-and-seek in the haymow, and it was warm in the winter."

"Because he's afraid we'll burn the stupid thing down. You heard what he said," Jean replied. "And guess what. We ain't gonna get any supper either because she called that our supper, remember?"

Boiling with anger and resentment, we plodded back to our hill.

When we were out of sight of the house, Jean asked Betty to show her the strange packet she'd taken from Doug's room.

She pulled it out of her pocket and began to tear it open.

"What is it?" Jean asked, bending down to sniff it.

"God, Jean, do you have to smell everything first?" I chided.

"Yep. You can tell a lot by smell."

"Then what does it smell like?"

"I'm not sure, but it looks like some kind of balloon."

Turning to Joan, Betty asked, "What do you think it is?"

Joan scratched her head, staring at the strange thing in Betty's hand. "Let's fill it with water and see what happens."

After we'd taken it to the pump and filled it with water, Betty held it up and exclaimed excitedly, "Look, we have a water balloon!"

She had some difficulty tying a knot in the end of it, but when it was done we formed a circle and began tossing it back and forth. "It's like a wiggly pig," I squealed, trying to hold onto it.

We had several minutes of enjoyment that took our minds off our whippings, before it slipped from my grasp and exploded on the ground, splattering water all about. "Well, I guess that's the end of that," I lamented, as I squished it into the soft dirt with my heel, fearful someone might find it. "But it was lots of fun while it lasted."

"Maybe I'll find another one someday," Betty said as we plunked ourselves down on the warm grass.

"*Find?*" Jean snickered.

• • •

We were playing in the sand a few days after our whipping when Mr. Bender's whistle penetrated the air—his signal that he wanted us for one thing or another. Our minds raced as we grumbled aloud wondering what trouble we were in now. We met him in the lane, and he told us that we were needed at the house.

As we approached, we saw the little English girl from next door who often peered at us through the fence while we worked in the fields. Her mother and Mrs. Bender were standing beside her.

"Don't tell me we're gonna have to play with her," Jean whispered. "She's too young. Besides, she looks like a spoiled little brat."

"Come here," Mrs. Bender called. "This is Sondra. Her mother's going away for a while, and she wants to play with you."

I looked back at our sand hill and then turned to her mother and said, "We're playing out in the sand hill. Is it okay if she plays there with us?"

"Yes, that's fine," she said as she turned to leave.

As we held her hand and walked to the sand hill, Sondra chatted away about her birthday party. "I'm six years old now, and this is what me mum got me for me birthday." She held out from her neck a shiny gold chain with a cross attached to it. "Do you loike it?"

We were amused by her strong English accent as we gathered around to admire her necklace. "Why, I'd give me right 'awnd if I could 'ave one just loike it!" Jean mimicked. We snickered behind our hands.

Seeming to ignore our making fun of her accent, Sondra asked, "How old are you?"

"Jean and I are twelve," Joan replied.

"And a 'alf," Jean cut in. "Bonnie and Betty are ten."

We dug in the sand and skipped rope with Sondra for a while as we tried to keep her amused. A couple of hours or so had passed when her mother returned for her and we went back to play on our hill.

Shortly thereafter, Mr. Bender's whistle interrupted our fun again. "What now?" I exclaimed, tossing my little shovel down in the dirt.

As we hurried back to the house, Mrs. Bender waved us to the front porch door. "Sondra's mother phoned to say that one of you girls had stolen Sondra's necklace; that you had taken it off her neck. So which one of you has the necklace?" she snapped, holding her hand outstretched.

We looked at each other, shrugging our shoulders. My stomach tightened.

"Who'd she say took it off her neck?" I blurted angrily, upset that we would be accused of doing that after all we had done to be nice to the girl.

"She didn't know. She just said that one of you must have taken it."

"None of us took it," Joan protested. "She probably lost it and blamed us just so she wouldn't get a spanking."

"Well, one of you took it, so you'd better own up to it. Her mother said it had a special safety latch and couldn't have come off by itself. When you come in for supper, you'd better have it!"

"That little lying snot nose!" Jean fumed as we made our way back to the hill. "I hope she never comes back again 'cause I sure ain't gonna play with her."

"She probably lost it, got the dickens from her mom, and decided to blame us," I said. "But we'd better dig in the sand and see if we can find it, or else we'll be in for another whipping!"

Hoping to get lucky and prove the Benders wrong, we dropped to our knees and began to sift through the sand where Sondra had been playing. Soon Betty jumped up and cried out, "I found it! I found it! Look, here it is!"

As we ran over to examine the necklace, Betty held it up by one end. "The darn thing's broken, that's why it fell off her stupid neck!"

Happy to be off the hook, we were racing back to the house to show Mrs. Bender that we had found the necklace when Jean brought us back to reality. "Yeah, well, you know what? I'll bet we'll be accused of breakin' it."

But to our surprise, when Betty handed the necklace to Mrs. Bender and Jean explained that it must have broken and fallen into the sand while Sondra was playing, she seem pleased. She told us that she would phone Sondra's mother right away and for us not to wander off because our suppers would be ready soon.

We breathed a sigh of relief as we climbed up the apple tree to wait for supper.

Although Sondra came to the fence a few times to chat with us as we worked in the fields, we chose to ignore her. Finally she stopped coming.

26

Twins, Twins, and More Twins

One day May came home for a visit and called us onto the back porch. Pointing to a long, low bench, she told us to sit down and then said, "You girls are getting quite big now, and I want to show you how to pretty yourselves up a bit so you'll look nice when you go back to school. Here, Joan, tear these old cloths into strips. And Bonnie, you come and sit on this stool. Now, all of you watch what I'm gonna do."

She had our full attention until Mrs. Bender opened the kitchen door. "For heaven's sake, May, what are you teaching them now?"

"Their hair is at a nice length for curling, so I'm showing them how to do it up in rags like I do. It'll sure beat that short, bobbed look that Dad gives them. They look like a bunch of mushroom heads!"

We snickered at that, but she was right. We were the only girls with short, cropped hair and bangs, and I envied the other girls with their pretty ringlets, soft curls, and braids.

"Well, do as you wish. But I don't want them getting any fancy notions in their fool heads and goin' boy crazy on me." That said, she returned to the kitchen.

May then pulled the comb through my tangled hair, separating several strands. Moistening them with water, she rolled them under the rag strip and tied it in a knot on top. After finishing a few curls, she handed me the comb. "Here, you do the next one, and the rest of you try putting a few in your hair to see if you've got the hang of it."

When she was satisfied that we knew how to do the curls, she handed me the torn strips. "Count them out and plan on putting about twenty curls in your hair. Have fun."

"Thanks, May," we all said as she left us and headed toward the kitchen. Passing the comb back and forth, dipping it into the water jar, and rolling and tying as we had been shown, we giggled with excitement at the thought of having curls. Soon we had wound up our hair.

"Boy, we look like a bunch of rag-mops," Jean said, laughing as she looked at herself in the hand mirror May had left with us.

"Let me have it before you crack it," Joan teased, snatching the mirror from her.

After we had poked fun at ourselves, I returned the mirror to May. We then went out to sit in the sun to let our hair dry.

"I can hardly wait to take the rags out and fix my hair," Betty said.

"Me too. I just can't wait to get boy crazy," Jean sneered, mocking Mrs. Bender's sarcastic remark.

Joan then pointed to the kiln. "Let's go sit over there where it's nice and sunny."

• • •

Shortly after May's visit, Mrs. Bender called Joan to the foot of the stairs, handed her four new dresses, and said that we should put them on and come down so she could see how they looked.

"Wow!" Joan exclaimed as she hurried excitedly up to our rooms. "Look what we got—some pretty new dresses!"

We bounced off our beds, eager to try them on.

"It's so pretty," I said, laying mine out on the bed to admire it. "It looks like the dresses the little angel-girl stickers wore that we got for Sunday school attendance."

"Oh, you and your silly stickers. That was so long ago," Jean chided. "And besides, it's gonna take more than a pretty dress to make you look like an angel."

"Oh, don't be such a smarty-pants," I snapped.

"Stop bickering and let's put them on," Betty cut in. "I can hardly wait to see how we look!"

The dresses were white satin with a white sheer overskirt, embroidered with tiny flowers. A long, pink, satin sash ran through loops at the side, and small buttons ran down the back to the waist. Ripping our clothes off, seeing who'd be first to get into her dress, we quickly poked our heads through the neck openings.

We took turns buttoning each other up and tying our sashes into pretty bows at the back. When we had finished, Betty sighed, "I wish we had a mirror so we could see ourselves."

"Some new shoes and stockings would be nice, too," I joined in. "I wonder why she got us these. Do you suppose May or Marge is getting married?"

"Yeah, like they'd invite us to their wedding," Joan sniffed. "But let's get downstairs and find out what's goin' on. Gotta be some good reason why they got us these nice dresses."

After looking us over, Mrs. Bender rested her chin in her hand and remarked, "Well, I'm quite pleased with my choice. Now take them off and keep them neat, for tomorrow you'll be wearing them. Your grandma has a friend who's celebrating her seventieth birthday along with her twin brother. They want to get their picture in the newspaper, and in order to make it interesting enough, Mum suggested that you girls join them so there'll be three sets of twins in the photo. You can put some curls in your hair tonight." Handing us each a small bag, she added, "And here are some white stockings to go with your dresses."

The next day we fussed and fussed with our new outfits and our hair. The very thought of having our pictures in the paper seemed so strange that we could hardly believe it.

When it was time to go, Mr. Bender spread a blanket in the back of his pickup truck. "Doug took his car, so you'll have to ride in the truck," he explained, as he boosted us up over the tailgate.

As he took off down the road, we ducked down low to keep the wind from messing up our hair. When we arrived at the place where the party was being held, Mr Bender stopped the truck and helped us down into the yard, saying that he'd be back to pick us up in an hour or so.

Someone brought us some red pop and cookies and we sat down on a blanket to enjoy the treat. We'd never had pop before and seldom had a cookie, so we savored every bit of it. Soon a young girl came by to let us know that the photographer was ready to take the picture.

Within a few days the photo appeared in the newspaper under the heading "Twins, Twins, and More Twins." Mrs. Bender showed it to us during supper and commented, "I think it turned out quite nicely."

Later, as we were on our way outside, Doug, who was perched on the porch step, put out his foot to trip us and taunted, "I'll bet you think you're all movie stars now."

"Oh, you're just jealous because you weren't in the picture," I sassed, thumbing my nose at him. At that he jumped up and started chasing me.

"Run, Bonnie, run!" my sisters yelled.

I ran around the outhouse to escape from him, but he went the other way and stuck his foot out just in time to catch me across the stomach and kick me backward onto the ground, knocking me out. My sisters came to help me, shaking me until I regained consciousness. By then Doug was gone.

"He knocked you out cold," Joan said. "Jean was gonna tell on him, but he threatened to beat the crap out of her if she did."

"I'll be okay," I said, letting her help me up as I clutched my sore stomach. "But someday he's gonna get a taste of his own medicine!"

"Yeah, and it can't come soon enough!" Betty added. "Someday he'll get paid back for all the mean things he's done."

• • •

As we had new dresses and the weather was nice, Mrs. Bender decided to start sending us to the Baptist church to attend Sunday school, and she purchased some new straw bonnets to go with our dresses. After we'd put on the bonnets and tied the ribbons under our chins, Betty pulled out the mirror from its hiding place so we could see ourselves. And after we'd all had a look, Joan said, "Does she really expect us to wear these silly baby bonnets? We're way too old for them."

"I look like Little Bo-Peep," I said, holding the piece of mirror at arm's length for another look at myself. "And I've messed up all my curls, too."

As we filed into the kitchen, Mrs. Bender remarked, "Well, I must say you do look quite spiffy. Here's a penny for each of you for the collection plate."

"Spiffy?" Jean scoffed as we left the house. "More like stupid."

"Quit your crabbing," I said. "From her, that was a compliment."

We felt so ridiculous in our bonnets on the way to Sunday school that Jean decided not to wear hers. "There's no way I'm gonna wear this dumb thing," she grumbled as she removed her bonnet. "The good Lord himself would probably laugh at me. I'm just gonna carry it."

"Well, that'll look stupid," Joan warned, "and some old gossip will probably squeal on you."

At that I got what I thought was a brilliant idea. "Why don't we find a good spot to hide them—maybe under the bushes in the ditch? We can pick them up on the way home."

Searching the side of the ditch, we found some dense underbrush. As Betty and Joan held the bushes back, Jean and I shoved our bonnets deep inside. Then Joan looked around for something to remind us where we had hidden them. "Right across from that big maple tree," she finally said.

"Yeah, but we'd better pray it doesn't rain and someone offers us a ride home," I said. "And besides, how would we ever explain what happened to our bonnets?"

"I doubt that'll happen," Betty said. "The sky looks pretty clear, and I can't imagine anyone giving us a ride home."

We took our places in the back corner pew along with a few of the kids from school. And when my friend Rosemarie slid in beside me, I looked longingly at her black Mary Jane shoes with gold buckles and pretty white anklets with a tiny pink flower adorning each side. I remembered the time she'd taken me home for lunch and how her mother tidied the bow on her braids as she was about to leave. She'd given each of us a cookie and then kissed her daughter good-bye. As we held hands and walked back to school, I fought back my tears and confessed how much I wished I could have a mom like hers.

Our Sunday school teacher pulled the curtain around us, closing us off from the church crowd. She welcomed us and told us that her name was Inga. *Inga,* I thought to myself — what a nice name. She read stories from the Bible, stopping occasionally to explain the meaning of some things.

She was the most beautiful young lady I'd ever seen, probably about twenty years old. I was so fascinated by her that instead of listening to her lessons, I found myself watching her every movement. *She's so pretty,* I thought.

A wooden, blue-felt-lined collection plate was passed around. Noticing that the girls from the village had put shiny nickels and dimes on the plate that shone off brightly against the blue fabric, I felt embarrassed as I laid down my dull, brown penny. *It looks dead next to theirs — and they never did a lick of hard work,* I thought.

As the curtain was pulled back and class was dismissed, I stayed behind, sitting quietly in the far corner of the pew. Soon someone slid in beside me. It was Inga. "What's the matter, Bonnie?" she soothed. "You look so sad. Why, your lower lip's so long I could almost pin it to the corkboard."

When I just smiled and remained silent, she laid her white-gloved hand on mine and went on, "What's troubling you?"

Fighting back tears, I confessed, "I only have a penny to put in the plate, and all my friends have shiny nickels or dimes."

"Well, pennies are precious, too. Have you heard the song, 'Pennies from Heaven'?"

I nodded, holding my gaze on the floor, still ashamed for having had only a penny for the offering.

"Well, remember that God doesn't love things just because they're shiny or bright. It's the giving that counts with Him, no matter how much." She took hold of my hand to lead me from the pew. "Church is getting out now, so why don't you hurry and catch up to your sisters." She smiled and patted my shoulder. "And don't forget that God loves you and your penny!"

Saying good-bye and feeling so much better, I ran to catch up to my sisters. "Isn't our teacher beautiful?" I panted. "I wanna look just like her when I grow up."

"Well, you'd better get a move on or you ain't gonna make it," Jean teased.

We gathered our bonnets from beneath the bushes and tied them back on our heads. We got away with this for a few Sundays without any problem and were happy when the bonnets became too tattered to wear anymore.

• • •

Mrs. Bender seemed jittery one morning as she tidied things up in the kitchen and rushed us through our breakfast. As we got up from the table, she said, "Just stay put for a while. I want to have a few words with you, and I want your full attention. So listen up. A lady from the Children's Aid is dropping by for a visit, and I'm giving you fair warning that if she talks to you, there's to be no blabbing about anything or running off at the mouth. Just answer a simple yes or no to her questions, smile, and be pleasant. Remember, it's no-body's business what goes on here, so just keep your big mouths shut." She folded her arms and glared straight at us. "Have I made myself perfectly clear?"

We nodded, and then she said, "Now, get outside, try to keep yourselves halfway decent, and stay close to the house. Oh, and tuck those shirts inside your trousers."

"Now I know why she gave us clean clothes this morning," Betty said, shoving her striped shirt inside her beige trousers.

Mrs. Bender's nervousness had rubbed off onto us. Being fearful of saying the wrong thing, we ran and hid behind some trees when the lady's car pulled into the driveway.

Mrs. Bender was quick to meet her at the door and invite her inside.

Several minutes passed before Joan, peeking out from behind a tree, gave us the high sign that they were coming our way. Then Mrs. Bender's crackling, high-pitched voice pierced the air. "C'mon out, girls," she called. "Where are you?" Turning to the Children's Aid lady, she said, "They're being a bit silly. They like to play hide-and-seek. They're quite immature for their age, you know."

Upset over her insulting remark, I came forward to meet the lady. Jean and Betty followed, but Joan, being more timid and shy, required some coaxing. "Come on out," Jean called as she went over to the tree, took her hand, and brought her over to us.

"Mrs. Bender tells me that you girls enjoy being on the tobacco farm and that you're able to earn quite a lot of spending money," the lady said. "I'm sure you must be pleased about that."

We glanced at Mrs. Bender, who was standing slightly behind the lady, nodding her head ever so slightly at us—a clear warning that we'd be sorry if we mentioned anything unpleasant about our situation there.

"Yes," we said, nodding our agreement.

"She also tells me that you enjoy helping her in the kitchen now and then, and she's teaching you to cook?"

As we were never allowed in the kitchen except for meals, we glanced again at Mrs. Bender. She nodded another "yes." We obeyed her silent message; smiled and nodded at the lady.

"Well, it seems like everything's coming along fine," the lady said, smiling approvingly. "And I understand that you're all doing quite well in school. Keep up the good work." She shook our hands, looked us over from head to toe, and then added, "You're becoming such nice-looking young ladies." With that she turned and left us standing there, angry inside for what we had been made to say and wondering if she sensed that we were lying to her.

As soon as the lady had left and Mrs. Bender had gone inside, we ran off to the bank by the railroad tracks where we could grumble aloud without anyone hearing us and without fear of being punished.

Jean plunked herself down on the warm bank and immediately grumbled, "Boy, what a bunch of big fat lies we had to tell. I'm so angry I could spit nails!"

"I think she needs her mouth washed out with soap. That's what Mrs. Miller threatened to do to us if we ever lied. Didn't she, Betty?"

Betty nodded. "And now she's teachin' us to lie."

"Yeah, and I wonder where all the money is we're supposed to be making?" Joan chimed in, picking up a piece of cinder and hurling it down the tracks. "Leaf handlers get ten dollars a day and all we get is a measly five pennies every now and then!"

"And what about boat drivers?" Betty added. "They make good money, too. I wish I had the nerve to tell that lady everything and see the look on her face!"

"There's no use stewing about it," Joan sighed, as she lay back in the warm grass. "She's gone, and we probably won't see her again for a long time."

The shrill whistle of a train took our minds off our problems, and Betty rushed over to lay a penny on the rail. We then waited eagerly for the train to come rumbling past so we could wave at the friendly engineers.

Seeing us sitting on the edge of the bank, they gave us a short blast of the whistle and waved their blue-and-white-striped hats. Jumping up, we waved wildly back. As the train sped by, we counted the boxcars, placing bets as to who could come closest to the number.

When the train had passed, Betty rushed to look for her flattened penny. "I found it! I found it!" she said, squealing with delight. "It's really warm."

She held it out proudly for us to see. "And look how big it is!"

"Just because it's bigger doesn't mean you can buy more with it," Jean quipped. "In fact, it's probably worthless now."

The Children's Aid Report stated:
It was difficult to draw these girls out.

27

At Last, a Promise Kept

Mr. Bender made frequent trips to Port Ryan to visit the hotel bar or purchase a few cases of beer. On one such occasion while we were suckering in the fields, he waited for us at the end of our rows. "Look," he said, "I have to slip into town, but if you hustle and get this field finished, then I'll take you to the movies later today."

"The movies! You'll take us to the movies?" we squealed with delight, jumping around like grasshoppers. We'd never been to a movie, but many of our friends had, and we'd listened with envy as they talked about them.

"Yes," he replied, "but the suckers are getting pretty big, sapping all the juice from the plants. We can't let them get away from us. Did you bring your jug of water?"

"Yes, it's over there," Betty said, nodding toward the bush where she'd put it to protect it from the hot sun.

"It looks like you're all set then. Oh, and don't forget to look for worms." He turned and strode away.

"Boy, that's a lot of work he expects us to do. Do you think we can get it done?" I asked.

"We'll have to work our tails off," Joan replied, looking over the field. "Sure wish they'd come and help out."

"Ain't gonna happen," I said, looking out across the field and shaking my head defeatedly, "so we better stop whining and get a move on or we won't get to the movies."

"I wouldn't put much stock in his promises," Jean grumbled. "I'll betcha dollars to doughnuts he doesn't take us at all."

"Well, that's a pretty safe bet when you don't have either," I said.

We worked hard and fast, challenging each other as to who'd reach the end of her row first, and we were fast running out of energy as it neared noon.

"When is she gonna call us in for lunch?" I complained, as my stomach began to rumble. "Doesn't she know we're hungry?"

"It seems like they're always forgetting about us," Joan complained. "But I think it's more like they just don't care."

"Out of sight, out of mind," Betty replied. "If you can believe that!"

Joan looked toward the house, hoping to catch a glimpse of Mr. Bender waving us in for lunch. "Oh, cripes, old Pete Butler's car is there again. We'll never get fed now. They'll drink and talk for hours."

"I'm gonna get some leaves to eat," I said, making my way to the fence row and counting the rows we still had to do. "We've got only twenty more rows to go before we're finished. Anyone want some leaves?"

"You're gonna turn into a horse if you keep eating all those sassafras leaves," Joan teased, as she pulled one from my grasp.

"But it sure beats going hungry, and besides, I kinda like them."

We had finished our work, had scrubbed ourselves at the tub, and were waiting for Pete Butler to leave when Mrs. Bender called to us from the back porch. "Here are some sandwiches for you girls." She hesitated a moment and then said, "Oh, yes, I almost forgot. Jim's tied up and says he can't take you to the show today—perhaps another time."

We took the sandwiches and stared with long faces as she quickly closed the door.

"Miserable old fart!" Jean snapped, as she stuffed half the sandwich in her mouth. "Ain't ever gonna believe him again—not that I ever did."

Walking over to the shady side of the implement shed, we sat side-by-side, backs against the wall, and finished our sandwiches. We were so mad about the broken movie promise that we sat and sulked for at least an hour.

A few days later when we had finished the whole crop, Mr. Bender finally found time to take us to see a Roy Rogers movie. He bought our tickets, gave us some spare change for popcorn, and headed off to the hotel. Once the movie was out, we waited for some time in the parking lot, visiting with some friends from school until he came to pick us up.

Staggering and smelling of beer, he helped boost us over the tailgate and into the back of the truck. Then, staring into our faces as if we'd done something wrong, he questioned, "Who were those boys you were yakkin' to?"

"Just some kids from school," Jean replied, giving him a puzzled look. "They were at the movies, too."

"Well, just don't go getting any silly notions in your fool heads," he said, slurring his words as he climbed into the cab.

Confused by his remark, we looked at each other and shrugged our shoulders.

"Got no idea what he meant by that," Jean muttered, puckering out her bottom lip as Mr. Bender steered the truck onto the road.

"What's the matter with him?" Betty asked. "He's driving all over the crazy road. I hope he doesn't run into the ditch!"

Soon we were being tossed from one side of the truck to the other. Terrified that we might get thrown out, we lay on our bellies, clinging to each other until we reached home. When the truck came to a stop, we rubbed our sore bones and helped each other over the tailgate. "Wow! That was some joy ride!" Jean exclaimed.

We nodded in agreement, happy to be home in one piece, as Mr. Bender staggered into the house.

• • •

The tobacco leaves had ripened, and harvest time was upon us again. Betty was back to her boat-driving job, and Jean, Joan, and I back to leaf-handling.

On many of the harvest days, Mr. Bender was either unable to round up enough workers or unable to pay them. At other times there wasn't enough ripe tobacco, so we'd only be able to fill half a kiln. This meant an extra workday for all of us, and we were happy when we had a full gang. On days when we weren't filling a kiln, Mr. Bender occasionally loaned us out to another small tobacco farmer, for we had now become pretty good leaf handlers. We noticed the man paying him at the end of the day and figured that he used this money to pay his own hired hands. Since we had done the work, we grumbled among ourselves, angry that we didn't get any of the money.

• • •

Betty gave us the scare of our lives one day while we were busy at the tobacco table. As she was bringing in a heaping boatload of tobacco leaves, loud road traffic spooked the horse. At the same time, Betty's frightened screams cut through the air. "Whoa! Whoa! Whoa!" she cried, yelling at the top of her lungs. Looking up from the table, we saw the panicked horse, nostrils flaring, galloping headlong toward the kilns. Betty's feet were barely touching the ground as she tried bravely to keep up with the runaway animal, yanking hard on the reins to stop it. The boat—with leaves flying through the air—was rocking dangerously back and forth, almost tipping over. The thought of the heavy boat falling on top of her and dragging her to her death was a real possibility.

"Let go of the reins! Let go of the reins!" the table gang screamed. But I knew she was too afraid of being punished if she did.

"Let go of the damn reins!" Mr. Bender yelled as he ran toward her.

She dropped them at once, jumping out of the way and landing in the soft dirt just as the boat flipped onto its side. The horse, dragging the boat behind him, ran crazily around the kilns until Mr. Bender managed to bring it under control.

I ran to see if Betty was okay. "Next time let go of the stupid reins!" I scolded, putting my arms around her trembling shoulders. "You could've been killed!"

"I didn't know what to do!" she cried. "I was so scared!"

"You stay and unload the boats, Betty," Mr. Bender said. "I'll take over the driving for the rest of the day."

As the primers came in to enjoy their cold beers and hang the kiln, Doug decided to show off, wanting to make fun of my sisters and me in front of all the workers. "Hey, girls, you know what? There's a circus in town, and I went to see the freak show. And guess what. I saw your relatives. They're the strangest looking creatures. They've got baboon faces with pointed heads and red hair. And they're kept on a chain in a cage. The keeper said they're your brothers and sisters, and they're a bunch of dunces."

Everyone laughed, thinking it was funny. But I was growing angrier by the minute. Finally I couldn't take it anymore. "That's not true, you big liar!" I yelled, running and lunging into him with clenched fists, hoping to land a good punch to his big belly. Holding me at arm's length by the top of the head, he laughed mockingly as I flailed wildly away, unable to reach him.

Everyone was enjoying our little skirmish. But knowing I was no match for him, I gave up and backed away. As I did so, I shrieked, "You don't even know my brothers, and they're probably a lot smarter than you! You big dummy! So there!" Sticking my tongue out at him, I ran to seek shelter in the outhouse, feeling totally humiliated and angry with the whole bunch of them.

28

A Bitter Cold Day

As we had to finish up the harvest, we were a week late starting back to school. By now we were quite good at setting our hair as we prepared for our first school day. Sitting in a circle in our bed, passing around the only comb we had, we spit on our fingers to wet our hair before winding it up in rags. We'd giggle at each other again as we looked at our rag-mop heads, but our efforts paid off in the morning when we combed out our curls. Clipping in the barrettes that we'd salvaged from the dump, we passed around the mirror shard for a final glance before heading downstairs.

As we entered the kitchen for Mrs. Bender's inspection, I was hoping she might tell us how nice we looked, but instead she was more concerned with how clean we were as she checked behind our ears and the back of our necks. Messing up my nice hairdo, yanking my ear, and giving me a swat to the back of the head, she remarked, "Get up stairs and wash that filthy neck. You've got enough dirt there to plant a garden."

I ran pouting back upstairs, and soon my sisters were hot on my heels. "What's the matter if my stupid neck is dirty? Hair's gonna cover it anyway," I huffed.

"Besides, it ain't gonna do much good washing it," Jean grumbled. "The doggone water's dirtier than our necks!"

"Yeah, we used to get to take a bath in that big washtub when we lived on the old farm, but here all we get is a pan of water," I said. "Guess we got too big for the tub."

"Well, she's probably worried the health inspector might be coming around. She doesn't want another note from the teacher, either. We'd better hurry, though. The school bell will be ringing and we'll be late."

Tired of the miserable and demanding harvest work, I was looking forward to my first day of school — playing with friends, drawing and painting, and lugging books home to pass away the boring weekends. What I wasn't looking forward to was our new teacher. Our friend, Marie, had told us we now had a man for a teacher. That bothered me, for I'd never had a man teacher.

"I'm Mr. Daryl Williams, your new teacher," he said as we waited for our seat assignments.

Daryl — what a silly name — and he looks so strict, I thought.

He was a tall man with thinning, reddish brown hair, pushed forward to form a slight wave on the right side of his head. He was square-jawed with green eyes and a large nose. He sucked constantly on tiny, black licorice mouth mints called Sen-Sens to mask his bad breath, rolling them around with his tongue until black saliva pooled at the corners of his mouth. Invisible clouds of stale cigarette odor seemed to surround his dirt-brown suit.

"I have your names and grade levels here," he said, looking at a sheet of paper. "Hold up your hand as I call your name." After getting that straightened away, he asked for our ages.

"Joan and I are twelve, and our sisters, Bonnie and Betty, are ten," Jean said when he called her name. I thought it odd that he seemed to be looking directly at me as he assigned our seats.

He appeared a bit cocky, hooking his thumbs beneath his suspenders as he strode up and down the rows, checking our work.

At the end of the first school day, he walked a few blocks with us, parting ways when he arrived at his boarding house. He boasted to us that he was a "two-thousand-dollar-a-year" teacher. Our eyes lit up. We couldn't imagine such a great amount of money and tried to figure how much we'd have if the Benders had paid us. Jean picked up a small twig and began scratching numbers in the roadside dirt, hoping to figure it all out. "Oh, it's too darn complicated, but I betcha we should have been paid as much as that or more."

"That's for sure," I grumbled, "and I know Mrs. Bender's storing it away in a mason jar to give it to us someday." The irony of that wasn't the least bit funny, but as we couldn't do anything else, we giggled at the silliness of it.

Mr. Williams seemed to enjoy picking on me, or so I thought. Arithmetic was not my best subject, and I absolutely hated it. During math class one day he strode over to my desk and said, "Stand up, Miss Mudford, and tell me how to find the circumference of a circle."

I jumped up, my mind whirling. I hadn't the slightest idea, so I stood quietly and as still as a road sign.

"Well, well, speak up, young lady, I can't hear you," he said, cupping his ear in an attempt to ridicule me and putting his face so close to mine I could see the spidery red veins that lined the sides of his nose. The older kids started to snicker, and I could feel my face turning red. "I don't know how to find it," I said indignantly, staring directly at him.

"Well then, Miss Mudford, you can just stay in at recess until you learn how to find it."

I sat at my desk, watching as the other kids ran eagerly out of the classroom, leaving me all alone with this miserable old man. I cringed as he leaned over my desk, rested his left arm on my shoulder, and took the pencil from my hand. I could smell the licorice Sen-Sens on his breath as he flipped through the pages of my scribbler.

Turning to a blank page, he drew out a circle and explained the equation to me. Once he'd finished tormenting me, he turned me loose. "You're free to go now, but be prepared to answer the question tomorrow," he warned.

I glanced at the wall clock and saw that I had two minutes left to play. Happy to be free of him, I flew out the door.

• • •

Winter was fast approaching, and since we had outgrown our winter coats, Mrs. Bender ordered new ones. They were all the same — full-length, green-and-black tweed coats, with fur collars and large black buttons down the front. "This coat is so big on me I could hide a snowman inside," I complained as we made our way to school.

"Oh, don't worry about it. You'll grow into it," Joan said, shaking her head, mimicking Mrs. Bender's remark. "But they are kinda nice, and warm, too."

"Wish she would've got us different colors," Betty complained. "How are we gonna tell them apart?"

"We'll have to ink our names in them," I said, hiking the fur collar up to cover my cold ears.

The winter of 1946 was very cold and snowy, and on the way home from school, we enjoyed running and jumping feet first into the snow-filled ditches, burying ourselves up to our armpits. Arriving home, we would hurry to our rooms to remove our cold, wet clothes and hang our stockings and mittens over the stovepipe wire and our long johns over the stair rail, hoping all would dry before the Benders let the stove die out for the night.

Happy that our new coats were plenty roomy—as they fit better over our nightgowns and robes—we would put them on before snuggling into bed. We knew by morning it would be freezing cold. Many times the water in our washbasin would form ice crystals and our windows would look like Jack Frost had painted a woodland scene on them.

Sometimes we would get up in the morning to find that our long johns were frozen stiff as a board. One morning Joan and I took ours to the nearest corner to see if we could get them to stand on their own, but they kept buckling in the middle and toppling over. "Well, they ain't gonna co-operate," she chuckled, as she picked them up off the floor.

Betty didn't share in our fun. "Boy, jumping in the ditches was a lot of fun, but how in the heck are we gonna get these frozen things on now?" she grumbled.

"The pipe's getting warm!" Jean squealed. "I think she's started the fire. We better see if we can thaw these things out a bit before putting them on."

We had learned through hard experience to deal with the inconveniences and hardships the Benders had forced on us; we dealt with this one by pulling the frozen legs of the underwear back and forth across the stovepipe to thaw them out before struggling to get them over our shivering, naked bodies.

"I ain't gonna jump into any more snowbanks," Betty said, grimacing as she buttoned up the front of her long johns. "It ain't worth it."

Perhaps feeling sorry for us one bitterly cold night, Mrs. Bender called us to the foot of the stairs and gave us two mason jars filled with hot water to keep our feet warm. Her kind deed was short-lived as the bottles rolled off the bed during the night, meeting the floor with a thundering thud and waking the entire household. We got no more hot-water bottles after that.

• • •

On many cold weekends as we huddled down in our beds, we would make our own set of playing cards and several of our own games. We made a checkerboard out of cardboard and used beer caps we'd collected in the stripping room as our playing pieces. We were outgrowing our paper doll cutouts and now spent more time in our beds playing hangman, connect the dots, and X's and O's. Some days we'd be bored to tears as we waited for the evening when Mr. Bender would turn on his radio. And so one day I suggested that one of us should ask Mrs. Bender if she had any magazines we could look at to pass the time away.

"Oh, sure. Why don't you go and ask?" Jean said.

"No, I'm not gonna do it. She'll probably bite my head off. You ask. You're the oldest."

"It was your idea, not mine," she shot back. "So go ahead and ask if you're brave enough."

I shifted my weight back and forth as I descended the stairs, trying to muster up the courage to knock.

"Go ahead, knock," my sisters prompted, as they leaned over the stair railing to see whether or not I had the courage to follow through on the idea. As it turned out, I didn't. Frustrated, and certain that my request would anger Mrs. Bender, I turned and ran back upstairs. "I'm too scared. You do it, Joan," I pleaded. "She likes you best."

We dillydallied for several minutes before Joan got up the courage to ask. Hurrying down the stairs, she rapped quickly on the door, knowing that if she hesitated she would lose her nerve.

"What do you want now?" Mrs. Bender snapped. "You've just managed to interrupt my radio program."

"We thought . . . I mean w . . . we wondered if maybe you had some old magazines we could look at," Joan stammered.

There was a moment of silence, and then, "Go back to your room, and I'll see if I can round some up."

Joan returned to the top of the stairs. "I think I annoyed her. But it isn't nice that she can sit and listen to her programs while we sit up here gettin' bored to death."

Several minutes passed before the door opened and we heard the sound of magazines being flopped on the step. We pushed and shoved, each wanting to be the first to get to the magazines. But it was Betty who broke ahead and got to the bottom of the stairs first. "Wow, she gave us some old movie magazines!" she exclaimed, shuffling through them, tickled that she had gotten to them first.

We browsed through the magazines for days, ripping out pictures of our favorite movie stars and tacking them to the bare walls.

At other times when we were bored with being confined to our beds, we'd tiptoe over to the frost-covered window; we would then blow our breath on the window to melt some holes big enough to peek through. Now we could watch for cars to come down the road and bet our collected beer caps on who could guess the color of the next car.

Sometimes our moving around annoyed the Benders, and Mr. Bender would open the door and yell at us. "Hey, you kids, get your coats on and get the hell outside! You're making too much damn racket up there!"

He did this on one of the most brutally cold days of the year, and we shivered as the snow crunched noisily under our feet and our breath hung motionless in the frosty air. It had been cold enough in our bedrooms, and now we were outside in the freezing weather. As we made our way toward the barn, I stopped to feel the side of the brick smokehouse to see if it was warm. Whenever Mr. Bender was smoking meat, we'd crowd together against the brick walls to warm ourselves. But that day the walls were cold. Our teeth were chattering and our insides shaking as we wrapped our arms close to our bodies and shoved our hands up our sleeves in a desperate attempt to keep warm. Knowing we were no longer allowed to go inside the barn where we might nestle in the haymow, Jean suggested that we go into the corncrib.

As we climbed inside, the mice that had been nibbling away on cobs of dried field corn, scampered away to hide.

"We're not gonna be much warmer in here," I complained. "The wind is blowing between these boards."

"Well, I don't know where else to go," Jean said, "and besides, I'm damn hungry."

Grabbing a corncob, she twisted it in her hand until several hard kernels gave way. She popped them into her mouth. We looked at her in disgust, knowing that the mice had been nibbling on them.

"What does it taste like?" Betty asked.

"Like corn, silly, but you have to let it soften up in your mouth before you can chew it. Here, try some." She wrenched off a few more kernels and passed them around.

"I'm so da . . . damn cold I'm sure my teeth will break if I ch . . . chomp down on anything," Joan chattered. "M . . . My goose bumps are already riding piggyback."

"M . . . Mine. . . too," I stammered, feeling that any minute my bones were going to crack from the bitter cold.

Betty began to whimper. "Wha . . . What should we do? I'm sure they've forgotten about us again. We've g . . . gotta go and ask to come in! And I g . . . gotta pee, too!"

"You're g . . . gonna have to hold it because it's too cold to p . . . pull your pants down to p . . . pee, and besides, it'll be an icicle before it hi . . . hits the ground," Joan managed to get out between chattering teeth.

It was a weak attempt at humor, but somehow we managed to get a laugh out of it.

Finally Joan got the idea that we could squeeze ourselves into the hog-loading crate under the apple tree. "Ma . . . Maybe they'll see us there and call us in before we fr . . . freeze to death!"

The crate was a small wooden structure made of four-inch-wide boards. The floor ramped upward with two long legs at one end — just high enough to reach the back of a truck and wide enough to load a large hog.

"Y . . . You go first," I said to Jean, as I snuggled my arms across my chest. "And hurry. 'Cause I'm fr . . . freezing!"

"Okay, bu . . . but don't squeeze against me, because if I fart, it's g . . . gonna be a snowball!"

"Oh, d . . .don't make me laugh or m . . . my face will crack. And besides, I f . . . feel like a snowball already," I chattered, nestling close to her.

Betty could no longer fight back her tears, so Joan wrapped her arms around her, telling her to climb in next to me. Joan offered to get in last and maybe that would help keep her warm. "You're s . . . such a skinny little runt," she added, "and you d . . . don't have an ounce of f . . . fat on your bones."

Once we were all packed inside, trying to keep each other warm, Joan suggested that we think up nasty names to call the Benders, just to pass the time. We would see who could come up with the best one.

Brrrrr," I shuddered, "my brains are so frozen I d . . . don't think I can dream up anything."

Our shared body warmth was easing the chill a bit now, and Betty let off with, "What about 'snot nose' for her?"

"Or 'fart face,'" I added.

"That's a good one," Joan said with a snicker. "Now, what about him?"

"Let's stick with 'turd bird,'" Jean said. "That's still the best because he always whistles when he wants us for something."

It seemed like an eternity before the front porch door opened and Mrs. Bender's shrill voice carried out on the icy wind. "You girls can come in now!"

"She's gonna have to chop us out. I think we're frozen in here like a block of ice," I said.

Crawling stiffly out of the crate, too numb to run, we plodded toward the house, so full of bitterness that we stomped through the warm kitchen without even giving them as much as a glance. Hurrying over to the stovepipe and wrapping our arms around it, we moaned and groaned as we tried to warm ourselves. Jumping into bed, sneezing and sniffling, we rubbed our aching fingers and toes, trying to get the blood flowing again.

"Mean SOBs," said Jean. "If I never get that cold again, it'll be too damn soon."

• • •

Christmastime arrived again, but it didn't bring much joy for us. We were called down for our usual ten-minute display, given our bag of fruit and nuts, and sent back to our cold rooms. May was nice enough this year to give each of us a tiny plastic cosmetic case containing a small bottle of jasmine toilet water and a bar of perfumed soap.

"Boy, we sure can use this stuff," Joan said, opening the perfume and dabbing some behind each ear.

"That was nice of May to get us something," I said. "But why do they call it toilet water? Are you supposed to use it in the toilet?"

"Beats me," Jean said. "But it sure smells nice. I'm saving mine for when we go back to school."

As she'd done the previous Christmas, Mrs. Bender set our dinner on the stairs, and we hurried down to pick up our plates. Soon Christmas was over, the smell of spices was gone from the kitchen, and a new year had begun.

I turned eleven this year. I was becoming more interested in boys, and there was one in particular that I liked. His name was Ronald Simons, and he often rode his bicycle beside me most of the way home. And one day he asked if I would like to have a puff on his cigarette.

"Sure," I said, trying to show off, "what do I do?"

"You just suck on it and then take a real deep breath to inhale the smoke—like this," he said, demonstrating. He then passed the cigarette to me.

I did exactly what he told me to do, and no sooner had I inhaled than it seemed as though my chest was going to explode. I started choking, coughing, and sputtering—tears welling up in my eyes as I fumbled to hand back his cigarette.

"You inhaled too deeply," he chided with a laugh. "You'll probably never get the hang of it. Only boys know how to smoke a cigarette."

"It's not funny," I sputtered, "and besides, it tastes terrible!"

• • •

Ronald came down with mumps in the late spring and was out of school for several days. I missed him and decided to write a nice note to cheer him up. It took me all evening to write it. The next day I asked Billy, a neighbor friend of Ronald's, to deliver it for me. He agreed.

Billy's desk was beside mine, and the next day while Mr. Williams's back was turned, he leaned over toward me and whispered, "I wasn't able to give Ronald the note because my mom didn't want me to catch the mumps."

He then started to pass the note back to me, but my fingertips had barely touched it when it caught the eye of Mr. Williams. "Well, well, what do we have here?" he sneered as he came down the aisle toward us. "I'll just take that, thank you." Snatching the note from Billy's hand, he strode back toward his desk, reading it to himself. He then spun around to face the whole class, waved my note high in the air, and announced loudly, "My, my, it looks like someone doesn't have time to learn the circumference of a circle but has plenty of time to write love letters."

I stared blankly at my desktop, embarrassed and red-faced. Then, as if to totally humiliate me, he stepped up on the platform and, like a minister in a pulpit, read my note out loud for everyone to hear.

My embarrassment turned to angry defiance. I sat stiffly with my arms boldly crossed and stared straight at him, my eyes filled with hate for this miserable man.

Then, to shame me further, he turned my note to face the class, grinned, and pointed to a small drawing at the bottom. "Oh, and would you lookie here. She's even drawn a cute little picture of a broken heart with tears pouring from it. How sweet!"

A few kids snickered, but some felt sorry for me.

Apparently not getting the laughter from the students that he expected, he came over to my desk, plunked the letter down, held his large hand on it, and announced, "And you, young miss, are expelled from school for three days."

A groan arose from the class, and I glared at him as he walked away.

My sisters tried cheering me up as we walked home from school. "That was a mean thing he did to you," Joan consoled. "It was a really nice letter, and he had no reason to expel you for three days just for writing it."

"I think he was pissed off because you didn't bawl your eyes out," Jean said.

Betty seemed concerned and wondered what we were going to tell the Benders.

"I don't know," I sniffled. "I just wanna run away and never come back! I don't know why he always picks on me."

Joan took my hand and tried to console me. "We sure ain't gonna tell them anything, or Mr. Bender will tar and feather you."

Happy the Benders didn't find out about my expulsion, I left for school each morning as usual and then spent the day hiding in the woods at the edge of the playground. My sisters came to stay with me at recess and lunchtime, but someone must have squealed on me, for my time wasn't yet up when Mr. Williams called me back into the classroom.

29

The Invitation

My sisters often teased me, saying that "trouble" was my middle name, and if I couldn't find it, it would find me. And it found me one day as I was searching for five pennies I had saved and hidden under the corner of the linoleum, thinking they were safe there.

We had decided to pool our pennies to see if we had enough to buy a box of icing sugar from the Hoover store. This was one of our favorite treats and a good value for our money. We would moisten our fingers, stick them into the box, and then suck them clean. The box would last us all the way home. We would then stomp on it to flatten it, smuggle it upstairs, and shove it through the hole in the wall.

I jumped off the bed to get my pennies from their hiding place and found that they were gone. "Who took them?" I asked, searching my sisters' faces for signs of guilt. Jean and Joan looked innocent enough, but Betty didn't. And after all, we did share the same room, so I asked her if she had taken my pennies. She shook her head.

As I climbed back onto the bed, Joan confronted Betty point-blank: "I'll bet you took them. Did you see Bonnie hide them there?"

Betty shook her head but looked guilty.

Joan didn't let up. "You took them. I just know you did. You're pretty good at snitching things . . . like Doug's matches, for instance."

That convinced me. I leaned over and bit Betty's leg.

"Yee-oow! That hurt!" she screamed. "I'm telling!" She sprang up, flew off the bed, bounded down the stairs, and banged on the door.

The rest of us looked at each other, surprised at her actions. Bothering Mrs. Bender was something we were always afraid of and seldom did.

"What's the matter *now*?" Mrs. Bender snapped, clearly irritated by the interruption.

"Bonnie bit me!" Betty blubbered.

"Get down here this minute, Bonnie!" Mrs. Bender yelled up the stairwell.

Betty looked at me with apprehension as I passed her on the stairs, and I gave her a dirty look.

"You're such a big tattletale," Jean said to Betty when she was back upstairs. "You really made her mad, and Bonnie's really gonna get it."

Mrs. Bender grabbed my arm, yanked me into the kitchen, and kicked the door shut behind me. "Like to bite, do you? Well, I'll show you how to bite, young lady!"

"B . . . B . . . But she stole —"

Before I could finish getting my words out, she sunk her teeth deep into the fleshy part of my upper arm, biting down so hard and holding me in a vicelike grip for so long that my stomach knotted and I squeezed my eyes shut, trying to block out the pain.

"That should teach you a lesson!" she barked, finally releasing me. "Now get back to your room, and I don't want to hear another peep out of the whole lot of you!"

"What did the old battleaxe do to you?" Joan asked as I returned upstairs. Then noticing me clutching my arm, she exclaimed, "Holy crap! Don't tell me she actually bit you!"

"She did! She bit me really hard!" I moaned, uncovering the bite mark for my sisters to see.

"That looks awful! It's already swelling up and turning blue," Jean said. "I can count every one of her teeth marks."

"Look, she even drew blood," Joan noted, giving Betty a nasty look. "Wow, that must have really hurt."

"It hurt like the dickens, a . . . and it still hurts — worse than a whipping!"

Ashamed for having caused my suffering, Betty apologized. "I'm sorry. I really didn't think she'd do something mean like that. And I didn't take your pennies. Honestly I didn't. Maybe Mrs. Bender found them. She snoops around up here sometimes, you know."

By morning my arm was black and blue and terribly swollen — the red teeth marks still clearly visible.

"Boy, I wish the lady from the Children's Aid was coming today," Jean grouched. "You could show her your fat arm."

"I doubt it," Joan added. "Mrs. Bender would lock you up out of sight with the cows."

I purposely rolled the sleeve of my shirt up on top of my shoulder as we went down for breakfast the next morning so Mrs. Bender could see how badly she'd bitten me. She just glanced at it and walked into the dining room.

As I was leaving to go outside, she called after me, "You can roll that sleeve down any time now."

As we walked away from the house, Joan warned, "You'd better not pull that stunt when she calls us in for lunch, or she might chomp down on your other arm."

"Just let her try it!" I spouted off through clenched teeth. But I had no idea what I would've done.

• • •

During the last few weeks of the school year, the soles of my shoes started breaking away from the upper part and flip-flopped noisily as I walked along the road.

"You know what your shoes sound like?" Jean chuckled. "Like cow flops hitting the barn floor."

"Yours are gonna sound the same way pretty soon," I said, pointing to her shoes. "See, they're coming apart too."

"You're right. Let's tear them all a bit more so Mrs. Bender'll have to get us some new ones. Besides, they're so small for me now that they curl my toes."

"Yeah, mine too. Marie said her brother's getting married in June and she's gonna ask her mom to invite us to the wedding. She said they're hurrying to get a new barn built and that the reception—whatever that is—will be in there. Maybe Mrs. Bender will get us new shoes then. After all, we've had these for over two years."

"I wouldn't hold my breath," Betty said. "We'll be lucky if she'll let us go to the wedding. They're not crazy about foreigners, you know."

That night we tore our soles down a bit more, hoping for new shoes in case we might be allowed to go to the wedding. We knew Mrs. Bender noticed them the next morning, but she said nothing.

After supper she told us that we wouldn't need our shoes for the weekend and to leave them on the landing. The next day Mr. Bender told us to bring our shoes to the tool shed. We watched as he slipped the toe of each shoe over an anvil and tacked the sole back into place. Doing a quick rub inside with his hand, he handed them back to us. "Here, these should hold you for a while longer."

As we walked to school on Monday, Jean and I became painfully aware that a few tacks had missed their mark and were pricking our toes.

"Damn, he did a lousy job," Jean grumbled. "Good thing the bottoms of our feet are as tough as nails." We walked with crimped toes throughout the day.

"Do you think we should tell him?" I asked Jean that evening.

"Naw. He's probably having his beer. Follow me."

Sneaking into the tool shed, she found a long chisel and hammer, slipped the chisel inside each shoe, and hammered down the offending tacks.

"Thanks, sis," I said, slipping on my shoes. "Just a few more days of school, and we'll be rid of these ugly things."

A few days later Mrs. Bender called us in from our play. "Tidy yourselves up. We're going to town to get some new shoes. You've been invited to the Nowinski wedding."

"Can we go? Can we go?" Betty squealed, jumping up and down.

"Yes, I've talked it over with your dad, and he says it's okay with him. It's this coming Saturday, and you can wear your Sunday school dresses. You'll be getting new clothes for fall, so there's not much use of getting you anything new until then."

"Yippee kyayea, yippee kyayea," Jean sang as we headed up the stairs. "We're goin' to a wedding!"

The fact that we weren't getting some new clothes for the wedding was disappointing news, but the thrill of going to the wedding was so exciting that we could hardly stop talking about it.

As we flopped joyfully onto the bed, Joan asked, "Do you think maybe she'll break down this time and get us some girls' shoes so we'll look nice for the wedding? After all, we ain't little kids anymore."

"Heck no," Jean replied. "I wouldn't hold my breath. She'll probably get us the same old boy shoes. Just you wait and see."

As it turned out, Jean was right. Terribly disappointed with more of the same old boy shoes, we lugged them upstairs and angrily shoved them beneath our beds.

On the day of the wedding, we fussed over ourselves, made certain not a hair was out of place, and then waited eagerly for Mrs. Bender's call.

"It's time for you to go now," she said. And as we hurried out the door, she called after us. "And just remember, there's to be no blabbin' about any of our business. Have you got that?"

We nodded, but we still hadn't yet figured out just what she meant by "our business."

We walked hand in hand as we strolled down the long lane to the Nowinski wedding celebration. "Do you think we'll be eating blood pudding?" I asked, turning up my nose. "They're sure to have it at the wedding."

"Betty will eat some." Joan kidded.

"Yuuuck!" Betty gagged, giving her a sick look.

"Oh sure, her face is already as white as the Cliffs of Dover just thinking about it," I teased, remembering the song Grandma often played on the organ.

Marie greeted us at the barn door. "Come on in. Let me show you around."

We followed her around like puppy dogs, gazing at all the beautiful decorations—streamers cascading from the beams and colorful balloons floating everywhere. Marie then led us into a smaller room that seemed to be filled to the rafters with cases of beer and pop. We stood wide-eyed in the doorway as we took it all in.

"Wow!" I exclaimed, "I've never seen so much pop in all my life."

"Come on," Marie said, "pick out a bottle of your favorite pop before we sit down to eat."

"We don't have pop at home," I confessed shamefully. "So we don't have any favorites. What's yours?"

"I like the red pop. It's cherry flavor."

We all picked cherry, and then she led us out to the tables.

For a long moment I just stood there staring in amazement at the long tables covered with white cloths and loaded down with food. It was hard to believe my eyes. There were bowls of soup, plates stacked high with breaded chicken, potatoes, vegetables of all sorts, fancy rolls and breads, and foods I had never seen before.

"These are cabbage rolls," Marie explained. "And this, of course, is your favorite—breaded chicken." She then pointed to one dish and said, "And this is blood sausage. But it's not my favorite food."

We stared blankly at it for a while, remarking that it wasn't at all like anything we had imagined.

She then led us to a large, round table and said, "And this is the pastry table."

We were tongue-tied. Never before had we seen so much food—and all those yummy-looking pastries! Our eyes nearly popped out.

"It all looks sooo good, I'm gonna try everything," Betty said, her eyes as big as saucers.

"Even the sausage?" I asked, giving a playful nudge.

After dinner was over and everyone was dancing, we listened to the music while stuffing ourselves with delicious pastries and gulping down bottles of cherry pop. I was sure that no princess had ever had a more enjoyable feast.

On our way home we chatted about the great time we'd had and agreed that it was the happiest day of our lives.

"I have never been this stuffed in all my life," Betty exclaimed as she rubbed her belly. "The Benders won't have to feed me for a whole week."

"And did you see all the presents they got?" I asked. "That table was piled sky-high with them!"

"Do you think we were supposed to take something for them?" Betty asked.

"I don't know," Joan said. "But I was surprised the Benders let us go. Sometimes they can be okay, I guess."

"Naw. They probably just wanted to get rid of us for the day," Jean sneered, then added, "But I do think they should have sent a present, or somethin'."

"Yeah, probably. But I'll bet they've never seen a feast like that," I added as we headed up the lane, sad to see the day end.

• • •

Although they lived in town, Doug and Jack often came to help during harvest time. We were never happy to see Doug, but we were fond of Jack. He was tall, slim, and handsome. He had black wavy hair and was in his early twenties. Doug was now probably twenty years old. Both of them were dating girls in town. Often on Saturdays after a long day's work, they would sit on the back porch steps before getting dressed for their dates, soak their feet in a bucket of warm water, and offer us a quarter to wash them.

We hated to wash Doug's feet, but at the same time we couldn't pass up the quarter. Jim was always honest and would pay up, but Doug would often renege on his promise, so we tried to wheedle the quarter out of him before we did his feet.

It was during one of these times that Mr. and Mrs. Bender were going away for the weekend and left the boys in charge. Jack called us in from outside, saying that his parents had made macaroni and cheese for us.

We were happy about this, for most of the meals Mrs. Bender made were just to fill our stomachs, but macaroni and cheese was one we really enjoyed.

As we gathered around the table ready to dig into our macaroni, I sensed that Doug and Jack were planning something. Sure enough, they dug into their noses, pulled out boogers, held them over our plates, and threatened to drop them into our food. I was ready to throw up as Jack dangled a one-inch snotty booger over my plate and taunted, "How'd you like this in your macaroni? Betcha it would taste pretty good."

"Yeah, Jean, how would you like some?" Doug joined in, tormenting her the same way.

"I'm not eating this stuff," I said, angrily pushing back my chair and bolting from the table.

Doug shoved me back down and said, "You're gonna eat it!"

"I'm telling on you," I threatened.

"We're just funning with you, for Pete's sake," Jack said. "Get on with your supper."

Sitting in silence, we picked away at our macaroni — the joy of eating it completely gone. I was so disappointed in Jack but knew this was Doug's idea.

As we left to go upstairs, I saw Doug wink at Jack and sneer, "You think we should try takin' 'em?"

A shiver went through me. I didn't know what he meant, but it frightened me.

"Naw," Jack said, shaking his head. "Leave them alone."

Later on that evening we watched from our window as Jack drove away. We were alone with Doug now, and it was only a few minutes before he opened the door. "I want one of you girls to come down here and help me wash clothes."

"We're not coming down. Do it yourself," I shot back.

"Well, I'm gonna need some help. Jean, you come on down."

We didn't answer, and he eventually closed the door.

"I'll go see what he wants me to do," Jean said as she started down the stairs.

We followed, begging her not to go.

She opened the door, peeked out, and asked, "What do you want?"

"C'mon in here," he said, motioning to her from inside the laundry room.

I could see that sly grin on his face again. Grabbing Jean by the back of her shirt, I yanked her away from the door and slammed it shut. "You're not going in there with him! He's mean, and he'll hurt you!"

"Good for you, Bonnie," Joan said. "He's a creep. You can't trust him."

30

Dire Consequences

We were playing around the tobacco kilns one warm sunny day when Harry Gee, a young schoolmate about fourteen years old, pulled his bike into the yard to chat with us. "What are you girls up to?"

"Oh, we're just playing games," I replied. "Where are you off to?"

"Just bikin' around. I thought of riding up to Williamston to see if I could find some boys to play baseball."

"You've got a nice bike," I said, toying shyly with the streamer dangling from the end of the handlebar.

"Don't you have a bike?" he asked.

"No, none of us do."

"Well then, would you like to take mine for a spin?"

"No. I'm too short to ride a boy's bike, but Jean can ride a bit."

He looked at Jean. "Would you like to ride it?"

"Sure, if someone will help me out onto the road."

Jean threw her leg over the crossbar and settled shakily on the seat. "I'll go about half a mile down the road," she said as Harry steadied her and gave her a little push.

We held our breath as she wobbled a bit and then took off flying.

As she came back into view, a dog was running along beside her and nipping at her legs. Quickly pulling onto the grass, she toppled off the bike as Harry threw a stone at the dog.

"The damn thing bit me," she said, hoisting up her pant leg. "See?"

"It's bleeding!" Joan said. "You'd better go wash it off at the pump."

When Jean returned, Betty asked Harry if he wanted to play hide-and-seek.

"Sure. Sounds like fun."

"Okay, I'll be the seeker," Jean volunteered.

"More like a peeker because you always peek," Joan teased.

Jean went to the nearest tree, covered her eyes, and started counting to ten as we scattered to find good hiding spots.

I told Harry that I was going inside the kiln where it is dark, to hide under the pipes. "She'll never find me there," I added. He agreed, and followed me into the darkened kiln.

"Ready or not, here I come!" Jean called out.

She easily found Betty and Joan, but it was some time before she opened the kiln door to discover Harry and me.

Scrambling out from beneath the pipes and shoving Jean aside, we made a dash for the tree, waving at Mr. Bender as he passed by on his way back from the hotel in Port Ryan. He pulled into the driveway and disappeared behind the house.

A few minutes went by, and we were about to continue playing when he came tearing around the house. I could tell by his long strides, the curl of his fingers, and the stern look on his face that he was really angry with us. *What did we do wrong?* I wondered. Jumbled thoughts went racing through my mind as I thought over everything we had done that day.

I looked at my sisters and saw that they were also frightened.

"He's mad as hell about something," Jean muttered as Harry headed toward his bike.

"What the Sam hell's goin' on here? And just what the hell do you think you're doing here, you little son of a bitch!" he barked at Harry.

Before Harry could answer, Mr. Bender grabbed him by the arm and gave him two hard kicks to his backside. "Now, get the hell off my property and don't come back again to mess with these girls!"

At that, Harry hopped on his bike and pedaled furiously down the road without looking back.

What Mr. Bender had done made no sense, and we looked blankly at each other, shrugged our shoulders, and shook our heads. We had no idea what we'd done wrong or why he was being so cruel.

Turning to us, he demanded, "I want to know what the hell that boy was doin' here and what was goin' on in the kiln."

"Nothing was going on," I replied, mincing my words. "We were just playing hide-and-seek."

"Don't lie to me, you little bitch. I know exactly what you were doin' in there! Now, get the hell in the house—all of you," he barked as he picked up a tobacco slat lying beside the kiln. He broke it over his knee, held onto the longer piece, and tossed the other toward the kiln. I watched as it bounced off the side of the building. We knew he was going to use that stick on us and that we were in for a severe thrashing. We were terrified.

"We weren't doing anything wrong! Honestly we weren't!" Betty pleaded, tears streaming down her cheeks as she tried to keep up with him.

"Shut up!" he snapped. "I don't want to hear any more damned excuses!"

There was no use talking because he wasn't about to listen. And so we held tightly to each other's hand as he shoved and cuffed us toward the house.

"Get inside!" he barked as he held the door open.

Frightened and shaking as we stumbled into the kitchen, Mrs. Bender just leaned against the stove and stared disapprovingly at us.

Whatever did we do wrong? I wondered, as my eyes met her cold gaze.

Mr. Bender grabbed my sisters one by one—first Betty, then Joan, and then Jean. Holding their arms with one hand and swinging the thick stick with the other—showing no mercy, he beat them as they danced around on their toes to avoid the harsh sting of the slat as it hit their backsides. Once he had broken them down and they cried out in pain, he let them go and reached for me. I pulled back against the kitchen door, but he grabbed me and yanked me toward him. I clenched my fists and gave him a defiant stare, seething with anger at the thrashing he'd given my sisters.

"Oh, so you wanna play games, eh?" he snarled, swinging the stick in the air and sticking his face so close to mine I could smell the beer on his breath. "Well, I'll teach you who's boss around here!"

I cringed every time the stick stung my backside, but I steeled myself, determined not to give him the satisfaction of seeing me cry.

My sisters, still shaking and sobbing from their beatings, cried out to me, "Cry, Bonnie, cry!" They knew it was the only way to get him to stop. But I wasn't about to give in. I set my jaw and tightened my stomach muscles. *There's no way this old bugger's gonna get me to cry. He can beat the stuffing out of me. I don't care!*

Then Mrs. Bender's voice seemed to come from a distance. "That's enough, Jim. I think you'd better stop."

"Well, someone sure as hell's gotta beat this rebellious streak out of her." He growled, giving me a final whack before he threw the stick into the firewood box. "Now get the hell to your rooms! And let me tell you something: if I see hide or hair of that boy here again, I'll beat the livin' daylights outta him too!"

As we made our way up the stairs, I rubbed my backside and felt the painful welts popping up under my thin trousers. I started to cry.

"Why are you crying now? You should've cried when he was beating you, and he would've stopped sooner," Joan cried, putting her arms around me.

"I wasn't gonna give him the satisfaction. Besides, I didn't do anything wrong!" I cried as I banged my fist on the stair wall.

"You're so darn stubborn," Jean sniffled. "I wish you'd smarten up."

"I don't know why we stood there like we were rooted in the ground. We should've just taken off and made him chase us," Betty grumbled.

"But we didn't do anything wrong, and I still don't know what set him off," Joan said.

"What does he mean by 'messin' around' anyway?" I asked.

"Darned if I know," Jean said. "The bloody old bugger's drunk again, so who knows what crazy ideas go around in his head."

"I'll ask Harry when we go back to school," I said. "Maybe he knows."

"I think we'll be lucky if he even speaks to us," Joan sighed resignedly.

We then looked at our welts and checked the dog bite on Jean's leg.

"It looks pretty nasty. Do you think you should show Mrs. Bender?" Joan asked.

"Oh sure! And get another beating? It's only a mosquito bite. It'll go away."

"Now who's being stubborn?" I argued.

I lay in bed that night on my stomach, staring into the darkness, still smarting from the pain and knowing we'd done nothing wrong to deserve such a horrible beating.

Hardly two days had passed before it was clear that Jean's leg was infected. It was inflamed and appeared to be three times its normal size.

"God Almighty, girl," Mrs. Bender exploded when she saw it, "why didn't you say something about it before? Now we're gonna have to take you to the doctor. I swear, you girls haven't got the brains of a mosquito!"

• • •

It took a few days to get over our anger toward the Benders, so in the mornings after finishing up our barn chores, we hurried off into the woods to have fun poking through the garbage dumps. Another grueling harvest was only a few days away, and we were hoping to find some ribbons or bobby pins for our hair before the start of the new school year.

Mrs. Bender never seemed to mind how long we were gone, knowing that there were plenty of fruits and wild berries for us to eat and that she wouldn't have to feed us lunch. Many times we wandered so far away that we had to climb the highest tree to look for the barn silo in order to find our way home. We always kept our eyes peeled for hunters or hoboes and hid deep in the thickets if we heard male voices. Carefree and happy, we enjoyed these trips into the woods.

One day, after much digging and poking around in the dumps, we found some stuff for our hair and some old jewelry. With our pockets full of these treasures, we headed home, chasing the cows up to the barn on our way. It had been well over a year since Mr. Bender had cut our hair, and it had grown to shoulder length, giving us many styling choices. We could pull it back into a ponytail, sweep it high on our heads, or work it into short braids. And using the rusty bobby pins I'd found, I could pin my hair full of wild flowers.

The week just before school began and before Doug returned to town after helping in the harvest, he came up behind me and yanked a flower from my hair. "Are you trying to look pretty for the boys?" he sneered, reaching out to mess up my hair.

"Aw, shut up," I snarled, turning my back on him and walking away.

"Well, you're gonna get it all cut off anyway before you go back to school," he yelled after me, "because Mom says you're all gettin' boy crazy."

His remark stabbed me like a knife. Clamping my hand over my mouth, I gave him a dirty look and ran to the barn to tell my sisters. *Surely they aren't gonna cut my hair off,* I thought. *I'd rather have another beating!* The very thought of them doing this just before the start of the new school year made me sick. I loved my hair — it was my prized possession. I thought of my friends at school. Rose Marie had beautiful red hair with neat braids tied at the end with pretty bows. My best friend, Shirley, had bouncy ringlets, and Marie, the neighbor girl, had soft, naturally curly hair. "Why can't they leave my hair alone? It's mine, not theirs. They have no right to cut it," I grumbled to myself.

"Guess what?" I cried to my sisters. "Doug said Mr. Bender's gonna cut our hair before school starts because we're getting boy crazy. Do you think he's lying?"

"I doubt it," Jean replied. "After that incident in the kiln, it sounds like something he'd do, the miserable old so-and-so!"

"And just when we got it looking nice and long enough to chew on," Betty said, putting a few strands into her mouth as she often did when upset.

"Well, he's not hacking mine off," I said, planting my hands firmly on my hips. "The train will run off the tracks before he gets his miserable hands on my head!"

"Maybe he'll just trim it a bit," Joan mused.

It was the next day when Joan, the last away from the breakfast table, came to break the news. "Mrs. Bender wants us to stay put in the backyard because Mr. Bender's gonna cut our hair."

"You're kidding!" I said, not wanting to believe my ears. *Please don't let it be true.* I wanted to throw up.

"Do you think we can talk him out of it?" Betty asked.

"Naw, you know what he's like," Jean replied. "Lightning would have to strike him dead first."

Mr. Bender came out with towel, scissors, and whisk broom in hand and motioned for one of us to sit on the old stump we had gutted the smelt on and where he chopped off the chicken heads. *I wish he'd just cut my head off.* I was getting terribly anxious now and glanced nervously at my sisters.

"Who's first?" he demanded. "Get a bloody move on. I don't have all day."

We pulled back, but he grabbed Betty and plunked her down firmly on the stump and threw the towel around her shoulders. Mrs. Bender then came out the back door with a large hand mirror—the same one May let us use when she taught us how to curl our hair in rags.

"Does she really think we wanna look at ourselves after he cuts all our hair off?" I whispered to Joan.

She hunched her shoulders as she chewed on her bottom lip.

I watched with panic welling up inside as Betty's beautiful blonde curls fell onto her shoulders and then tumbled to the ground. After cutting her hair straight across the bottom of her ear, across the back, and below the other ear, Mr. Bender then combed some hair from the top of her head over her forehead. Holding it in position with his left hand, he made a shabby attempt to follow the line of his hand to cut the bangs. Whipping the towel off her, he whisked some loose hair from her neck as Mrs. Bender handed her the mirror.

"I look terrible!" she grouched, handing back the mirror. "My bangs are all crooked!"

"Oh, they look just fine. Don't be so darn fussy," Mrs. Bender snapped.

I then turned to her, shook my head, and said defiantly, "He's not cutting my hair!"

"Well now," she said, "aren't we the cheeky one. We'll just see who rules the roost around here!"

Joan squeezed my hand as if to tell me to be quiet, and then without complaining, she took her place on the stump. She was always so obedient, but I was getting angrier by the moment as I watched my sisters being shorn like a bunch of sheep.

"He ain't gonna cut my hair," I protested, nudging Jean. "I won't let him. I'm gonna hide!"

"You're crazy!" she said, as I ran off to hide in the outhouse. Latching the door behind me, I sat between the two seat openings, drew my knees up to my chest, and hugged them in silent defiance. I knew I was going to pay for my stubborn behavior sooner or later, but I was too angry to care.

Soon Joan rapped softly on the outside wall of the toilet and whispered through a small knothole, "You'd better come out, Bonnie. He's almost through with Jean, and you're next."

"I ain't coming out!" I said through clenched teeth.

"Please come out," she pleaded. "He's gonna beat the crap out of you if he has to come in after you, and he sure ain't gonna beg."

"I don't care. I'd rather be dead. I'm staying right here!"

Joan went silent, and only seconds passed by before I saw Mr. Bender's blue coveralls flash through a crack in the boards and heard his heavy footsteps stop at the door. Then I threw myself back against the wall as his booted foot came crashing through the door, sending the shattered wooden lock flying toward me and ripping the door off its top leather hinge. Without saying a word, he grabbed me by the scruff of the neck, hauled me roughly off to the stump, and plunked me firmly down on it. I looked for Mrs. Bender, but she was nowhere to be seen.

"So you wanna be contrary, do you, you young whipper-snapper? Well, I'll show you who's boss around here!" he barked as he angrily snapped the towel before throwing it around my neck.

I could feel my stomach coiling as he picked up the scissors and recklessly chopped off my hair to mid-ear length and then hacked away at my bangs. I knew by the shocked look on my sisters' faces that he was getting even with me for my defiance. I clenched my teeth as he continued hacking away.

Mrs. Bender returned to the yard just as he whipped the towel off my shoulders. "Goodness' sakes, Jim, what've you done? You've gone and butchered her hair!"

"Well, someone has to teach her a lesson. One of these days I'm gonna kick her in the ass and leave my shoe there!"

After feeling my bobbed hair, I jumped off the stump and quickly grabbed a fistful of my curls from the ground. Holding them close to my chest, I ran crying to the barnyard. The cows had worn a small groove in the side of the straw stack, and I crawled inside and sat down, looking longingly at the hair in my hand. "I hate the old bugger. How can he be so mean!" I moaned.

A jersey cow on her way to the watering trough stopped briefly and looked curiously down at me. *She feels sorry for me, too,* I thought. She had large, soft brown eyes with nice long, thick lashes and a thatch of thick curls tumbling over her crown between her shorn horns. I smiled weakly at her. "You lucky cow; you have more hair than I do."

I reached out to pet the side of her face, then watched as she moseyed over for a drink.

Joan, finding my hideaway, snuggled in beside me. "I expected to find you bawling your eyes out," she said.

"I was, but old Bessie over there made me laugh. She has more hair than I do."

"Your hair'll grow out in no time," she consoled, laying her arm across my shoulder.

"Yeah, but in the meantime—and it sure is the *mean* time—I look like the village idiot. I'll be the laughing stock of the whole school!"

"If anyone dares laugh at you, I'll give them a black eye. And what're you gonna do with that," she snickered, poking her finger in the ball of hair nestled in my lap. "Did you think you could glue it back on your head?"

"No, I just hated to part with it." I forced a smile and added, "But that's a good idea."

We tried to laugh at the ridiculousness of it all but could find little humor in what had just happened to us. "I hate it here, Joan!" I cried. "I just hate it!"

"We all do," she sympathized, "but we can't do anything about it." Pulling me up out of the straw, she wiped off my wet cheeks with her hands. "Your hair'll grow back in no time, you'll see," she reassured me again. Grabbing my hand, she tugged me. "Let's go sit by the tracks. The train should be coming soon, and we can wave at our friends."

Soon Betty and Jean came and sat down beside us. "We figured we'd find you here," Betty said. "What're you doing?"

"Just moping about our haircuts," Joan said. "Bonnie keeps yanking on hers, hoping to make it longer."

"Well, at least we're all in the same boat," Jean teased. "Except for Bonnie—she has a smaller boat." She tickled me in the ribs, and in spite of our disappointment, we managed to giggle and crab about the Benders as we waited for the next train to come chugging down the tracks.

31

Our Secret Is Out

The new school year began with Jean, Joan, and me entering the seventh grade and Betty entering the sixth. And to our surprise and delight, we found that Daryl Williams was gone and we'd be having a lady teacher. But as the bell rang to start the day, I felt suddenly shy about my terrible haircut and ran to hide behind the school as the other kids rushed inside. Soon I was aware of an arm around my shoulder. I looked up and saw a lady with a pleasantly plump face and a slightly turned-up nose smiling down at me. She had soft blue eyes, and her hair was a mass of soft brown curls that rested on her shoulders. "Hello there," she said. "I'm Mrs. Lenhart, your new teacher, and you must be Bonnie. What a pretty name. Your sisters told me that you're ashamed of your haircut and afraid the other children will poke fun at you."

I nodded, and she went on, "Well, don't worry about that. If they tease you, I'll assign them extra homework. And besides, I think you have beautiful hair — even some nice red highlights. I'm so jealous. And before you can say *abracadabra,* your hair will be long again." She then took my hand, and I walked bravely into the school. She was right. No one poked fun at me.

We adored Mrs. Lenhart. Her kindness and understanding moved us to work extra hard at our studies, and our grades improved. I brought home sketchpads and books from the school library and spent my evenings reading and drawing pictures for our art class. I spent many hours reading *Les Miserables* – my first big book – and felt sad for Cosette, the little orphan girl who slept under the staircase. "She didn't have any parents either," I said as I relayed parts of the story to my sisters.

Mrs. Lenhart encouraged me in my love for art and writing, and I worked hard to please her. She often posted my pictures in the top corner of the display board that was reserved for "best of class" work or read my compositions to the students. I was finally beginning to feel good about myself.

Just before the Christmas break, as I was putting on my coat to go home, Mrs. Lenhart called to me. "Wait just a minute, Bonnie. I have a letter for your parents."

My throat tightened as I began to think over the day's events, wondering if I had done something wrong.

As she handed me the note, she saw the look of concern on my face, smiled, and laid her hand on my shoulder. "Don't worry, Bonnie, you didn't do anything wrong. It's a nice note."

I sighed with relief and hurried to catch up with my sisters.

"What's the note for?" Joan asked. "You're the teacher's pet, so you couldn't have done anything wrong."

"I'm not her pet! And I don't know what the note says. She just said it was a nice note."

"Well, there's no sun, so we can't look through it, but

there's a flashlight in the tool shed," Jean said. "Let's use it to read the note."

"No, I'm giving it right to Mrs. Bender. Maybe she'll tell me what it says."

"Ha," Betty chuckled, "fat chance of that."

As I entered the house, I handed Mrs. Bender the note and stood by as she read it.

"Well, what are you standing around for? Get to your room!"

I was antsy for days, worried about the contents of the note and wondering whether Mrs. Bender was going to reply, but no further mention was ever made of it.

The Children's Aid Report stated:
Mrs. Lenhart had suggested that Bonnie's artwork be seen by someone with a special knowledge of art to determine her artistic ability and that perhaps she should be enrolled in special art classes.

• • •

Christmas came and went much the same as usual, and the New Year arrived. Jean and Joan would turn fifteen and Betty and I thirteen. In the spring Mrs. Lenhart told us about the Norfolk County Annual Spelling Bee and picked some of the students to enter. I was one of those chosen, and my sisters were excited for me.

Mrs. Lenhart sent a request slip for Mrs. Bender to sign and give permission for me to attend.

"Do you think she'll sign it?" Jean asked as she read the note on the way home.

"I don't know. I'm so nervous about the whole thing. She said our whole school will be attending and there'll be hundreds of kids from all over. We have to go by bus, and I'm so afraid Mrs. Bender won't let me go."

I handed her the slip during supper and held my breath for her response. After reading it over, she laid it on the table, saying only that she would have to think it over.

I stewed all evening, unable to think about anything except the note. "Why couldn't she have let me know one way or the other?" I whined to Joan.

"Oh, you know what she's like—just wanting to keep you on pins and needles, the mean old so-and-so. Besides, she never did tell you what the last note said."

"I'll cry my eyes out if she doesn't let me go. Besides, I have a chance to win a prize if I'm lucky."

"We'd be so happy if you won. That would show her!" Betty boasted.

As I prepared to go out the door in the morning, Mrs. Bender handed me the signed note. I glanced twice at the signature before believing my eyes. I turned to look at her. "Thank you," I said as I skipped happily down the porch steps. "I can go! I can go!" I whooped at my sisters, waving the note in the air.

The big day arrived, and my sisters watched as I stood on the platform with the other students. Finally, after I had bitten my nails down to the quick, they were all eliminated except a girl named Virginia and me. I was given the word "chauffeur," but as I had never heard it before and didn't know what it meant, I had no idea how to spell it. Virginia spelled it correctly and got the first prize of ten dollars, and I got the second prize of five dollars. Overjoyed at being handed a crisp, five-dollar bill, I rushed over to my sisters to show them my winnings.

We all fondled the five-dollar bill, handing it back and forth before I hid it in the pages of my spelling book.

"Are you gonna tell Mrs. Bender?" Betty asked.

"No. She might think it's too much money for me to have and take it from me."

"Well, I'm gonna tell her you came in second," Joan said, wanting to brag for me.

As soon as we entered the house, Joan blurted out triumphantly, "Bonnie came in second place!"

"Oh, that's nice," Mrs. Bender said flatly, but made no further comment.

"Gee whiz," Joan said as we headed upstairs, "is that all she can say?"

"She could've at least given you a pat on the head," Jean kidded.

I smiled, happy Mrs. Bender hadn't asked me if I had won a prize and hoping she wouldn't find out about it.

• • •

After some heavy spring rains, Betty noticed the roof in our bedroom was leaking and told Mrs. Bender. That evening Mr. Bender brought up a bucket and put it on the floor to catch the water. "Keep your eye on this bucket and let me know if there are any more leaks."

After he was gone, we hurried over to watch the drops splatter noisily in the tin pail.

As we were walking home from school a few days later, Jean let out a loud groan. "Oh my God!" she said, burying her face in her hands, "they're fixing the roof!"

Wondering why she was so upset, we strained to look toward the house and saw the men on the roof, but what stopped us dead in our tracks was the sea of white covering the front lawn. We knew immediately it was our years of stored-up trash. After the roofers had removed the shingles, the wind sucked the paper out from the rafters, strewing it all over the yard.

"Oh no! We're really in for it this time," Joan groaned, covering her mouth with her hand.

Slowing our pace to a crawl, we wondered what to do. With thoughts of the last beating, we had no idea what was in store for us this time. We were panic stricken and on the verge of tears.

"Oh my gosh, what can we do?" Betty quavered, her face turning pale.

"I think we should run away," I said. "That's the only way out."

"Uh-uh," Jean said, "we're just gonna have to go home and face the music, but for sure we're gonna get the crap beat out of us this time."

"Bonnie's right. We should just run away," Joan groaned.

"Let's go hide in the woods," Betty choked out as tears welled up in her eyes. "Besides, my stomach hurts, and I'm not goin' any further!"

"Yes, you are," Jean said, grabbing her hand and tugging her along.

We were still arguing and debating about what to do or say when we neared the house. As we crossed the lawn, the roofers looked down and grinned at us. They knew we were in deep trouble.

Mrs. Bender was waiting for us at the door—her face pinched tight, her arms crossed firmly beneath her breasts. She was furious. "Get in here this minute!" she barked, smacking each of us on the back of the head as we passed by. "What is the meaning of this? I've never been so embarrassed in my whole life!"

We stood there, speechless and frightened, not knowing what to say.

"Jim will deal with you all later. Right now I want you to get some bran sacks and pick up every last piece of trash. And I don't care if it takes you all night!"

It was after six o'clock and the roofers had packed up and left by the time we finally got all the trash picked up.

Then Mr. Bender called us into the house, and we watched as he wrapped the buckled end of his belt around his hand. "You're getting almost too big for a whipping, but I swear to God I don't know what else to do with you!"

This was the first time he threatened to use his belt on us, so we huddled together in the corner, hands clenched to our chests, waiting for him to grab one of us.

After he finished giving us the belting, we stood aside, whimpering, not knowing what else was expected of us.

"Now, get the hell out of my sight," he commanded. "And don't expect any supper tonight!"

Jean, taking off ahead of us, hurried to check out her bedroom. "Well, the hole is still there," she said, eyeing the plasterboard as she rubbed her backside.

"There's one in my stomach, too," Joan groaned.

Late in the evening, Mrs. Bender opened the door. "Here's some food for you," she snapped, as she set the plates noisily on the steps. "And a bran sack for you to put your garbage in from now on."

I scurried to get the food from off the bottom step. It was nothing but bread and butter.

"Who cares? At least it'll fill the hole in my stomach," Joan said, trying to overcome her disappointment.

"Would you believe she's beginning to feel sorry for us?" Jean hissed angrily.

"Well, she should," I replied sarcastically. "After all, what did she think we were doing with our garbage all these years—eating it?"

• • •

One hot summer night I was awakened from a deep sleep by a lot of commotion downstairs. Noticing a red glow coming from my sisters' bedroom, I looked in to see what was happening. Panic gripped me as I saw their window glowing red. "Wake up! Wake up!" I screamed, tugging at their arms. "The house is on fire! We have to get out!"

They jumped up, dazed and scared; and we were fumbling our way toward the darkened stairs when our bedroom lights were switched on and Mr. Bender opened the door and yelled, "Hurry, you kids, and get down here! The barn's on fire and we gotta get the animals out!"

Wearing only our nightgowns, we ran through the house to the outside in time to see the whole top of the barn, which had recently been filled to the rafters with hay and straw, completely enveloped in flames. Hurrying into the smoky barn along with Doug, we quickly released the cows from their stanchions and opened the pigpen door. Mr. Bender ran to take care of the three horses and colt. We managed to clear the animals out just as the timbers above our heads caught fire.

"Get out! Get out!" we heard Doug screaming above the mooing and squeals of the animals that were as frightened as we were.

We had just run out into the yard when a large section of the ground floor exploded in flames. We then watched in horror as the three mares and the colt bolted back into the burning barn.

Jean and I made a move to rescue them, but Mr. Bender grabbed us. "It's too late to go back in. I latched the bottom half of the door, but they broke it open. I should've chased them outta the barnyard," he muttered, angry with himself.

We stood beside the apple tree and watched in horror as their wooden stalls burned down around them, the red-hot tongues of fire licking their bodies as their tortured screams pierced the midnight air and the smell of burning flesh drifted across the barnyard. Mr. Bender, not wanting us to see such a horrible sight, sent us back to our rooms. But it was too late. The sight and sound of the trapped horses, standing upright and burning to death, would haunt me for days.

Some people who wanted to help and others who were simply curious started arriving. On my way back to the house, I overheard one say to Mr. Bender, "My friends and I were sitting on the steps of the Williamston hotel when we saw a huge ball of lightning drop from the sky. We knew it hit something, but we didn't know what."

I told my sisters what I'd overheard. "Well," Jean snipped, "at least he can't say we set it on fire."

Too wound up to sleep, we sat at the bedroom window, watching as the barn burned to the ground. Then as we were creeping into our beds, we heard the Benders come into the house. I heard them latch our bedroom door and then they turned the lights out.

That was a night to remember, I thought, as I nestled down in bed.

The following day, the insurance adjusters poked around the embers, checking out the lightning rods and wiring, asking questions and taking notes. Within a week neighbors and friends began helping to build a new barn.

My sisters and I hauled bundles of shingles up the ladder as Mr. Bender finished the roofing just in time for the tobacco harvest.

32

A Fair Day

It was quite a surprise for us when the Benders planned to visit some friends one evening and take us with them. Since we'd never gone with them before, we were a bit on edge, not knowing why we had to go this time, especially since Betty was feeling sick to her stomach.

"Betty's still not feeling very good," I said to Mrs. Bender as we piled into the backseat of the car.

"Oh, I'm sure she'll be okay. It's probably just something she ate."

We arrived at the Kendrick home, and after giving us each a glass of orange pop, Mrs. Kendrick led us into the living room, gave us some magazines to look at, and told us to sit on the couch while they visited with the Benders.

"Thank you," we each said as we sat down side-by-side on the long couch.

"Now, behave yourselves in there and don't go nosing about," Mrs. Bender warned from the kitchen doorway.

Embarrassed by her cutting remark, I frowned as she left the room. *Does she think we're a bunch of snoops?* I felt put down.

As we looked through the magazines, we whispered among ourselves and listened as the noise and laughter from the kitchen grew louder. Leaning forward, I peered in and saw that they were drinking beer and playing cards.

An hour or so later, Mrs. Kendrick came into the living room while Mrs. Bender leaned against the door frame. Walking unsteadily toward us, Mrs. Kendrick stopped and wagged a finger at Betty. "You must be Betty — the one with the blonde hair? Stand up and let me take a look at you."

Betty gave us a puzzled sideways glance and stood up.

"Your mom tells me you're not feeling too good, a bit nauseated, she says. Here, let me feel your tummy," she slurred, while reaching forward and rubbing her hands over Betty's stomach. "Why, you poor little dear, I bet you're pregnant. Your mom thinks you're going to have a baby."

The color drained from Betty's face as she hurried behind the couch to get away from Mrs. Kendrick, but she staggered after her.

"Leave me alone," Betty pleaded. "I'm okay now."

"Oh, just let me check you," Mrs. Kendrick insisted. "I won't hurt you. I'm a nurse, you know."

"She's not pregnant, and she's not having a baby!" I said, raising my voice, upset at them for picking on Betty while snickering with each other.

Betty circled the couch and made it behind a chair, out of reach, as Mrs. Kendrick shook her head, turned back toward the kitchen, and said, "Well, I'm not sure what to think. Just keep an eye on her, Mary."

We sat stiffly on the couch, staring at our magazines, too bewildered to speak. I slipped my arm around Betty's waist and could feel her trembling. "Do you suppose that's why they dragged us along, just so she could feel your belly?"

"Probably," Jean answered for her. "Don't surprise me none."

We were happy when the nightmarish evening ended and we returned home. "I hope they never take us there again," Betty grumbled as she kicked off her shoes.

"They're all crazy. Besides, I don't even know what *pregnant* means, and I probably can't spell it either," I said, trying to make light of things.

"Guess it means you're gonna have a baby, but I haven't the slightest idea how you have a baby," Joan said. "Sure wish someone would tell us."

"Well, if I ever get a stomachache, I'll be damned if I tell anyone," Jean said, "even if I get it from eating too many green apples."

We chuckled as we recalled the day we ate several green apples, flavoring them with a piece of salt we had chipped off the cows' blue salt-lick block in the pasture. That day ended with all of us buckling over with terrible stomach cramps and a bad case of diarrhea.

• • •

It was the last day of the harvest, and I was standing around the washtub with the rest of the tobacco gang, scrubbing away at my hands to remove the stubborn tobacco tar. I was deep in thought and looking forward to entering my last year of public school when Mr. Bender began telling the group about a terrible accident involving a fourteen-year-old girl. "Yeah," I heard him say. "She was cutting tobacco stalks when the horses bolted, throwing her beneath the cutting machine."

"Was she killed?" one of the men asked.

"Yeah! For sure! From what I hear, her screams were heard from way back in the field as she was wrapped round and round the drum blades. Neighbors had to actually pick her body off in pieces," he continued.

I shuddered as I listened to the gruesome story and thought of Mr. Bender's big 500-pound stalk cutter—a big round drum with horizontal blades and a spring-steel seat at the top that had nothing to protect you if you slipped or fell.

"Well, that father should be more than just ashamed of himself," one of the men said. "A young girl like that shouldn't be cutting tobacco stalks. That's a man's job."

"From what I hear, she wanted to do it," Mr. Bender said.

"Just the same, it ain't no job for a little girl."

"I guess it was her stepfather who let her do it," Mr. Bender replied.

Stepfather, I thought. I had only heard that word once before. It was when the teacher asked me to stay outside with my best friend, Shirley Winter, who was feeling ill, until her stepfather came for her.

"That's a terrible tragedy," one of the women said. "Do you know the family?"

"Naw, it's some foreign name. I don't rightly know," Mr. Bender replied with a shrug. "He has a small tobacco farm about two miles south of town."

"There's a family by the name of Duba on that road," one of the men said. "They have a young daughter around that age. I worked for them last summer. Wonder if it could be them?"

"Could be," Mr. Bender said, flicking his cigarette butt into the tall weeds.

I entered the eighth grade that week, happy that Mrs. Lenhart was still the teacher. But my happiness died when I learned that the young girl who had met such a tragic death was my good friend Shirley Winter.

• • •

The town of Simcoe put on a fall fair every October, and even though Mr. Bender promised he'd take us if we worked hard, he never seemed to get around to it. One day Mrs. Lenhart told us that the next day was students' day at the fair. "Make sure you tell your parents that there's no school and that a bus will be taking you to the fair for the day." And so we hatched a scheme not to tell the Benders about the fair because we were fearful they wouldn't let us go. We would go without their knowledge.

On our way to school we stopped in at the Roberts' store and restaurant to pick up our school friend Gloria, who lived in the back half of the building.

"I have to get some money from my mom before we go," Gloria said as we settled into a booth. "Do you have money to buy your tickets?"

"Tickets?" we asked, looking at each other. Our hearts sank. We hadn't thought about having to buy tickets. We pooled our pennies and showed her what we had, and she laughed. "That's not enough money to get into the fair."

"Maybe we can sneak in," Jean suggested.

Seeing how disappointed we were, Gloria went to talk to her mother. Soon Mrs. Roberts came to talk to us. "Gloria tells me you don't have enough money for the fair. Is that right?"

We only nodded, ashamed that we had to admit being so poor.

"Didn't you tell your parents you were going to the fair?"

"We forgot," I said.

"You forgot? There's four of you and you all forgot? Hmm," she said, cupping her chin in her hand. "Wait outside. I'll be right out."

I knew she was on to us and said, "Wouldn't it be nice if she gave us some money to go to the fair?"

"That'll be the day," Joan said. "She's probably still mad at you and Betty for the time she caught you sneaking into her meat counter and stuffing your pockets full of wieners."

"Yeah, you're right, but she still gave us one to eat," I countered with a grin.

Soon Mrs. Roberts came out and told us that she had phoned Mr. Bender and that he would be picking us up at school.

Our spirits fell. We knew we were in trouble again but tried to put on a brave front as more kids joined in with us.

As we neared the school yard, my sisters and I darted off to hide from Mr. Bender behind a garage repair shop across from the school. We watched as his truck pulled into the school yard and noticed him talking to some of the kids. One pointed in our direction, and he started toward our hideout.

"He knows where we are," Betty whispered, ducking farther back behind the wall.

"We'd better show ourselves," Joan said, "or he's really gonna be mad."

As we sheepishly emerged from behind the garage, he demanded, "What the hell is going on? Why didn't you tell me you wanted to go to the fair?" Not giving us a chance to explain, he reached into his pocket. "Here's five bucks for each of you. Now get yourselves on the bus."

"Thanks!" we squealed, totally surprised by his actions. Quickly pocketing the money, we scampered off to the bus.

After having had a great day at the fair, we walked home exhausted and happy.

"Why do you think he was so nice this morning? I thought for sure he was coming to take us home," I said.

"He always promised to take us, so I guess we forced him into it," Jean said.

"Do you think we're gonna get it when we get home?" Betty asked. "We probably took all his beer money."

"Guess we'll have to wait and see," Joan said. "Anyway, it was worth it."

We entered the yard as Mrs. Bender was removing clothes from the clothesline, and she asked if we'd had a good time.

Feeling relieved at not getting a scolding, we told her we had the best time of our lives and ate way too much candy floss. We then chatted excitedly about our day at the fair as we pitched in to help her remove the clothes.

"Whew! That was a surprise!" Jean exclaimed after Mrs. Bender had lugged the clothes inside. "Why do you suppose she was so nice?"

"I don't know," I said. "I overheard Mr. Bender saying something about the buyers coming around. Maybe he got a good price for his tobacco."

"Could be," Joan agreed. "But they've been promising to take us to the fair for a long time, and it's about time they paid us back for all our hard work."

33

Dashed Dreams

The Benders were invited to spend Christmas Day with their son Chuck and his family. We were not invited but were told to stay in our rooms until they returned. So after grumbling amongst ourselves about not being able to go with them, we settled down to play games to keep ourselves occupied.

"I'm getting chilly," Jean said as she climbed out of bed to get her winter coat. She put her hand on the stovepipe. "No wonder it's cold. The fire is dying down. There's hardly any heat coming up."

Before long the fire died out, and we were shivering from the cold. After gobbling up the sandwiches Mrs. Bender had left for us, we huddled together in one bed to keep warm.

We were becoming pretty big girls now. Jean and Joan were almost sixteen and over five feet tall, and Betty and I were not far behind. For us all to fit in one bed, Jean suggested that Betty and I sleep with our heads at the top of the bed and she and Joan with their heads at the foot. This way we'd have more room. The arrangement was working out quite well until Joan complained to Betty that her toes were scratching her back.

Betty giggled and scratched some more.

"And your toes are up my nose," I said to Joan.

Soon our rambunctious behavior brought the bed down with a loud thud. One side of the mattress fell onto the floor, causing us to roll into a tangled mess on top of each other. Surprised, we untangled ourselves and crawled out onto the floor.

Looking over the wreckage, Betty observed, "I think we broke the bed. What are we gonna do now?"

"Let's pull off the sheets and mattress and take a look at it," Jean suggested, tossing the pillows onto the floor.

We managed to pull the mattress off the frame, exposing the bedsprings that had slid off one side of the angle-iron support rails.

"We're making a lot of noise up here," Joan said as she went over to look out the window, "so we'd better get this fixed before they get home."

We hoisted the bedsprings back onto the rails, banged and kicked it into place, and then replaced the mattress. Everything was back in order before the Benders returned.

I wondered if we should tell the Benders about the bed breaking down, but Jean told me that it should hold up okay now and that we should just keep mum about it or we might get into trouble.

• • •

We started back to school after Christmas, and I was happy to be finishing up the eighth grade. Jean, Joan, and I talked excitedly about going to high school in the fall and how we were looking forward to riding in the big yellow school bus that went by every day. I was really feeling grown up and said, "Just think, we'll be waving to the kids who'll be walking to school. I can hardly wait for grade eight to end."

"But we have to pass our entrance exams before we go anywhere," Joan said. "And that ain't gonna be easy. Not everyone passes, you know."

"There's no way I'm gonna fail," I boasted. "I'll study real hard. And I'm sure glad we still have Mrs. Lenhart."

Betty was depressed as she listened to our happy chatter about going to high school. We felt bad about leaving her behind and assured her that the year would fly by and in no time at all she'd be joining us.

I studied hard that year and, along with Jean and Joan, waited impatiently for Mrs. Lenhart to receive the final grades.

This year we were required to write many compositions, and I chose a green-covered scribbler to write my stories in. The last story I turned in for grading was about a chicken thief and how he got caught.

Mrs. Lenhart handed back my scribbler, and I took it quickly to check my grade.

"You got an A," she said with a smile. "And now I have a favor to ask. Would you mind leaving your composition book with me? I'd like to use it as a reference to show other students the proper way to write a good composition."

I'm sure she must have seen the sparkle in my eyes as I checked my grade, read her comments, and handed back the scribbler.

A few days later, as Mrs. Lenhart handed out the report cards, she informed us that we had passed our final examinations. We were so tickled about the good news, we used it as an excuse to stop in and see Grandma and Grandpa Tillman on our way home.

"Tell them about your composition book, too," Joan urged.

"I will," I said, bursting with pride.

"And will you tell the Benders?"

"Naw. She wasn't interested about the spelling bee, and so I'm not gonna bother. But do you think she'll be surprised that we passed our finals?"

"I don't know, but I surely was!"

Grandma and Grandpa congratulated us on our achievements. Grandma took her porcelain shoe from the china cabinet and counted out some pennies. "Well, I'm very proud of your accomplishments, and I think that warrants at least ten pennies each," she said as she counted the coins out onto the table.

"Careful there, Nellie, don't be giving away all my chewing tobacco money," Grandpa chuckled.

It was a happy and rewarding day for us. We waved good-bye to them and skipped down the front steps and out onto the road.

We arrived home and handed our report cards to Mrs. Bender. Glancing quickly at them, she remarked, "I'm happy you all passed. I'll be letting the Children's Aid know soon."

The Children's Aid sent Mrs. Bender the necessary records for our high school enrollment, and we were churning butter in the backyard when she came out to give us some news. "I've received your birth certificates, and it looks like Bonnie and Betty's birthday is on May fourth, not April fourth, as I had thought."

Betty and I were surprised, but as our birthdays came and went without any mention from the Benders, it didn't matter much to us. It was only because we were in school during these months and our teacher was in the habit of chalking the date on the blackboard that we were even aware of the occasion.

• • •

With the planting and hoeing season behind us again, we made our usual treks into the woods. Some days we picked wild raspberries or elderberries for Mrs. Bender to preserve, but one day as we were digging through the dumps hoping to find old jewelry or trinkets for high school, Jean squealed with delight when she uncovered some makeup. "Look, she called. "Come on and see what I found."

Leaving our digging spots, we hurried excitedly to her side.

"I found a compact and some lipstick. Do you think the high school girls wear lipstick?"

"Maybe," Joan said. "But remember, Mrs. Bender said that if she ever caught lipstick on us before we're eighteen, our heads would be on the chopping block."

"I'll just put it on in the bus and wipe it off on the way home. So there! She'll never be the wiser." Stuffing her treasures into her pocket, she remarked, "Now all I've got to do is sneak it upstairs and find a good place to hide it."

"You can smuggle it up in your new brassiere," Joan snickered, "and once you get into high school, you can leave it in your locker."

She made it to her room with her loot, and we waited patiently for Mr. Bender to switch on the radio, praying that he'd leave it on so we could listen to our favorite programs. With years of practice, we'd become good at softly tiptoeing around and listening down the stovepipe without banging our heads against it.

We had crept back into our beds and were just settled in when Jean and Joan's bed came crashing to the floor and we all screamed.

"What the hell's going on up there?" Mr. Bender yelled from the landing.

342 • Bonnie E. Virag

"Our bed fell down," Jean called back.

"I'll be damned! If it's not one thing, it's another!" he muttered as he looked over the broken bed. "I'll get a sledge hammer and be back to fix it. Pull the mattress off while I'm gone."

He returned with the hammer and banged away at the metal frame. "There," he said, bending the frame a bit. "That'll have to do you for a while longer."

"A while longer? I wonder what he means by that," Joan said after he left the room. "Do you think we'll be getting a new bed?"

"Maybe," Jean said. "I'd love to have a nice wooden one like I've seen in the catalogs."

"Me too," Joan chimed in wistfully.

"Maybe they'll get a new one for themselves and give you their old one," I said, still puzzling over what he'd meant by his remark.

• • •

Suckering the tobacco seemed more bearable this year, for we knew that within a month school would be starting. As we worked, we chatted away, full of anticipation about starting high school, our excitement growing with each passing day.

"Mrs. Bender hasn't mentioned anything about school or about getting us new clothes," I noted. "And school starts soon."

"Oh, she'll probably leave it until the last minute," Joan said. "And besides, we'll probably have to finish the harvest before we start high school. I doubt if we'll be able to start on time." We grimaced at that thought.

"I sure hope she buys us some new coats. My arms stick out of my sleeves by a foot," Jean complained. "I look like a scarecrow, and there's only one button left on it."

Joan was right. We were in the midst of harvesting the tobacco crops and still nothing had been said about starting school. As we gathered in our rooms one evening wondering what was in store for us, the stairway door opened and Mr. Bender shouted up to us: "Bonnie, come down here for a minute. Your mom wants a few words with you."

My stomach tightened as I slid off the bed and straightened my clothes. "What could she possibly want me for now?"

"Did you do or say something wrong?" Betty asked.

"I don't think so," I said, shaking my head and chewing my nails. "But we don't have to do anything wrong to get in trouble with them. They'll blame us for something anyway."

"If you need help, just holler," Jean said, trying to cheer me. "I'll come and take a round out of them."

"We're gonna eavesdrop down the stovepipe just in case," Joan said.

Leaning over the rail, they watched as I walked haltingly down the steps.

I was scheming to leave the door open a bit, but as I stepped out into the kitchen, Mrs. Bender said, "And you can close that door."

Everything looked like a setup, and I felt as if I were walking into a trap. Mr. Bender was sitting in his chair, a bottle of beer at his elbow and his belt coiled on top of the green plastic radio as if he wanted me to see it. What caught my attention next was the white pad of lined paper on the table with a pen lying across it and Mrs. Bender standing stiffly beside an empty chair, holding what looked like a letter in her hand. I checked their faces, looking for a clue of what they had planned for me. They looked somber, almost guilty. For a brief moment we faced each other, no one speaking.

"Get over here and sit down," Mrs. Bender commanded, her voice a bit strained as she adjusted the chair in front of the pad of paper.

"Did I do something wrong?" I asked, easing reluctantly into the chair.

"No," Mr. Bender said. "Your mom wants you to write a letter to the Children's Aid. She's already prepared it for you."

"Me?" I questioned, putting my hand on my chest and becoming more bewildered and frightened by the moment. "W . . . what about?"

Mrs. Bender laid the letter beside the pad and handed me the pen. "I want you to write a letter to the Children's Aid telling them you want to take grade eight over again so you can start high school with Betty."

I was stunned. My dreams came crashing down around me as I threw the pen back on the table and sat on my hands. They were ordering me to tell a lie. I shut my eyes, gritted my teeth, and rocked back and forth on the edge of the chair, unable to comprehend the unthinkable thing she wanted me to do. "No!" I blurted out. "That's a lie. I'm not gonna do it! I wanna go to high school! You can't make me do this!"

At that Mr. Bender leaned forward, shook his finger in my face, and snarled, "Don't get lippy, young lady. You'll do exactly as you're told if you know what's good for you. Now copy that letter there, just like she's written it!"

"Please don't make me go back to public school!" I pleaded, tightly hugging my shoulders. "I worked hard and passed my exams. And what about Jean and Joan?"

"Never mind them. This is about you. Now, get the damn letter written!" he commanded, his face growing red with anger.

I picked the letter up and read it over, tears streaming down my cheeks. "It's already written. Why do I have to rewrite it?" I blubbered, plunking the letter on the table.

"Because it has to be in your handwriting. Now, quit your sniffling and get started. We ain't got all day."

Glancing at the belt on the radio, I knew there was no way out. I had lost the fight. Slowly and painfully, word by word, I copied the letter.

"Quit crying, you're getting the paper wet," Mr. Bender commanded, whipping out his handkerchief to blot up a tear before handing the handkerchief to me. "Here, wipe your face off, for God's sake."

I shoved his hand away and pushed the pad toward him, but he pushed it back and snapped, "Now sign your name at the bottom!"

After signing my name, I tossed the pen onto the table and ran from the room, unable to control my emotions any longer. I ran upstairs, threw myself across my bed, and banged and bit my pillow. Then I buried my face in it, wrapping it around the sides of my head as I rolled back and forth in anguish. There was no escaping the pain ripping through me. *How can they be so cruel, and for what reason?* I couldn't understand anything. I felt like a puppet on strings, able to do only what they wished and nothing more.

I was vaguely aware of my sisters' presence as they bombarded me with questions. "Bonnie, Bonnie, what's wrong? What did they do to you? We couldn't hear much down the pipe. Are you okay?"

I could hear the sounds of their voices but was too deep in my own agony to understand what they were saying and continued to cry and pound my fists on the bed. Then as they climbed in bed beside me, I regained some composure and blurted out, "They forced me to write a letter to the Children's Aid telling them I wanted to take grade eight over again so I could start high school with Betty."

They looked at me in total disbelief. "Why would they do that? Why didn't they just rip your guts out?" Jean said, drawing me into her arms. "Just wait. She's gonna get hers someday!"

"That's really dirty of them. How can they do that?" Joan asked. "You're losing a whole year of school."

"And what about us?" Jean said. "Are they gonna let Joan and me go to high school? Maybe they'll keep us out to work."

"I don't know," I sobbed, shaking my head. "I just don't know anything anymore!"

We were still trying to make sense of what cruel plans the Benders might be hatching when the lights were turned out, leaving us in the dark, wondering what lay ahead for us.

Lying in bed that night, Betty blamed herself for my problem. "If only I hadn't fallen behind, none of this would've happened."

"It's not your fault," I said, laying my hand softly on her arm. "Don't blame yourself. Let's wait and see what happens. Pray the Children's Aid will come by or the school won't let me repeat the year."

Too upset to sleep, I lay awake, thinking about the past and the year that Betty fell behind a grade. I was angry about the past and depressed about the future. Eventually, my frustrations exhausted me, and I buried my head in my pillow and fell asleep.

The Children's Aid Report stated:
A letter arrived from Bonnie explaining that she wished to attend Public School another year in order to wait until Betty, her twin sister, is ready to come in to High School, so that they can come together.

f. W.

Sept 23/50

Dear Sir

I started back to public
school at the beginning of
September. And I would like
to get go to public school for
another year. As there is more
I would like to learn before I
start to high school. Then
next year My twin sister Betty
& I could go to High School
together. I hope that this will
be alright with you as I am
having started back to public
school and am getting along fine.
And like my teacher very
much.   Yours Truly
            Bonnie Mudford

34

Untold Grief

After sulking for days, I became resigned to the fact that my hopes for attending high school were dashed. But I was still angry with the Benders and found it difficult to even look at them. Jean and Joan, not wanting to upset me, seldom talked about school, even though Betty and I knew they were fretting about their new clothes.

Watching from our window in mid-September, we noticed Mr. Bender bringing in a large package from the truck. We looked at each other, full of anticipation. Within minutes, the door opened, and Mrs. Bender called Betty to the foot of the stairs. "Here, these new clothes are for you and Bonnie," she said offhandedly. "Your sisters' package should be arriving soon."

Jean and Joan, though disappointed their clothes hadn't arrived, joined in the excitement of opening our package, eager to see what she had ordered. "Well, at least she got you a decent-looking skirt," Jean said.

"But it's all wrinkled," I complained, holding it against my waist.

"Oh, quit complaining," Joan said. "Just dampen it a bit and press it against the warm stovepipe. That'll help. At least you got some new clothes."

Betty and I started back to school just before the end of harvest. Jean and Joan were left with a few more days of work. After they were through handing leaves, they walked down the road to meet us as we trudged home from school.

"Well, I still have my favorite teacher, Mrs. Lenhart," I told them as they met up with us. "And she told me that the Superintendent of Schools wasn't too happy about letting me repeat the year when I had already successfully passed my entrance examinations. But things must have gotten ironed out okay."

"Well, we can only guess what lies the Benders told them," Jean said.

"But I miss Marie's breaded chicken now that she's gone," Betty complained.

"Did you get your new clothes yet?" I asked, trying not to think about the breaded chicken. I was already hungry enough.

"No, and Mrs. Bender hasn't mentioned a word about high school, either," Joan said. "I watch the high school bus go by every day and wonder why we aren't on it."

"Well, I've almost worked up enough nerve to ask Mrs. Bender if she doesn't say something soon," Jean said crossly. "I wanna know what's in store for us."

A few days later, Betty and I were on our way home and looked eagerly down the road for our sisters. "I wonder why they aren't coming to meet us," I said. "That's not like them."

"I don't know. They didn't have to fill a kiln today, so maybe Mrs. Bender finally took them to get new clothes."

"I hope so. Guess we'll know soon," I muttered as we turned into the driveway.

We couldn't find them anywhere in the backyard, so we went inside. Mrs. Bender was sitting at the kitchen table sipping tea, apparently waiting for us.

"Where are Jean and Joan?" I blurted out. "They didn't come to meet us."

She looked a bit uncomfortable as she set the cup down. She then looked up and said flatly, "The Children's Aid removed them today."

"Removed them?" My mouth dropped open as panic gripped me. "Why? What did they do wrong?"

She shifted uneasily in her chair and said, "It was time for them to go. That's all."

That's all? Just like that? Like chalk erased from a blackboard? I was totally confused, unable to grasp what she was telling us. "What do you mean? Will they ever come back?"

"No, I'm afraid not. The Children's Aid has found new homes for them."

"But we didn't even get a chance to say good-bye!" Betty whimpered.

Tears welled up in my eyes as we held hands and stood numbly beside the door. "Why didn't someone tell us they were going?"

"I thought it would be best this way," she replied flatly.

"Will we ever see them again?" I sputtered.

"I gave them our address and told them they could write to you. Now go to your rooms and I'll make some macaroni and cheese for your supper."

"Macaroni and cheese? Does she think that'll make us feel better?" Betty sobbed as we trudged upstairs. "I don't even feel like eating without them, and I ain't even hungry now."

Unable to fathom everything, we hurried into our sisters' room, desperately hoping they might still be there. But it was empty and freshly swept. Nothing was left but the old linoleum in the middle of the floor. "Look," I said, "they've taken away their old bed! That's why Mr. Bender said that it would have to do for a while longer, and that's why their new clothes never arrived. They were planning this all along." We had it figured out now.

We scoured their room, looking for something they might have left behind—anything to hold on to—but there was nothing. Not even a bobby pin. We then checked under the linoleum hoping to find a note they may have hidden for us—but found nothing. Our spirits broken we returned to our rooms, threw ourselves across our bed, and wept bitterly. Nothing could have prepared us for this horrible turn of events, and nothing could have equaled the pain we felt by having our sisters torn away from us once more, leaving us wondering whether we'd ever hear from or see them again. My anger had grown toward the Benders because they had made me repeat the eighth grade, and it now turned to hatred because they had sent our sisters away. We felt lonely at dinner that night, the table seeming twice as big without them.

Noticing our sulkiness as we picked at our food, Mrs. Bender set her lips in a tight line and dug in her handbag for some loose change. "You'd better find time to take these girls to the movies today, Jim. Why, I swear, I've never seen such sour pusses in all my life!"

We enjoyed the movies, but nothing cheered us up for the loss of our sisters and all the things we had enjoyed together. We would never listen down the stovepipe again. Instead, we waited impatiently every day for some news from them.

"Do you think they'll write us," Betty asked, "or do you think she was lying about giving them our address just to make us feel better?"

"I don't know, and I wouldn't believe anything she says. We'll have to wait and see."

As winter came and the days grew cold and gray, we helped Mr. Bender dismantle our bed and move it into Jean and Joan's room. "This room with the stovepipe will be warmer for you during the winter," he remarked as he left the room.

"Warmer? I'd like him to sleep up here and see how warm it is," I crabbed. "There's no heat at all in this stupid pipe when the fire goes out."

• • •

It was almost Christmas when Mrs. Bender handed us an envelope, saying that it was from Jean, and it was evident that she had already opened it. It contained a Christmas card with a letter inside.

Sitting side by side on our bed with our backs against the wall, we read it over and over, laughing at her funny remarks as she described her new home:

We even have an inside bathroom here with a flushing toilet to boot. Yesterday I had a bubble bath in a real tub with real taps where hot or cold water comes out. Why, I swear to you, I've never been so clean in all my life. I even got the map of the world off the back of my neck.

"Wow," Betty exclaimed, "she even gets to take a bath! Wouldn't it be nice if Mrs. Bender would let us have a bath?"

"What do you mean? I've never seen a bathroom." I furrowed my brow. "How do you know she even has one?"

"It's just off the laundry room, hidden behind a curtain. She left the door open one day, and I snuck in and took a peek."

"Why didn't you tell me?"

I thought you knew. Did you ever see her use the outhouse?"

"No."

"Well, that's why."

I was puzzled over this news and wondered why Mrs. Bender never let us have a bath.

Jean went on to tell us that she lived with an older couple; that Joan lived with a family a few miles away; and that on Sundays they'd walk to meet each other halfway and visit. They were both happy, but Joan had four young children to help care for and was quite busy.

I help out around the house and am learning how to cook and clean. I even get to eat with the family. Come spring, I might be looking for work in town. Joan and I won't be attending high school; didn't much like school anyway.

My heart sank as I read the last part. The very thought of not going to high school was almost more than I could bear. "I'll throw myself across the railroad tracks if they don't let us go!"

"Maybe the Children's Aid will take us away too," Betty mused.

"Who knows? But it sure would be nice to get away from here."

After brooding over our future for a few moments, I put Jean's card over our headboard as we settled down to reply to her letter. "We have to be careful what we say because she's probably gonna read it."

At breakfast Betty handed the letter to Mrs. Bender for her to mail.

"I bet she won't even mail it," I grumbled as we hurried out of the house. "She'll probably use it to start the fire."

We waited eagerly each day for another letter from Jean or perhaps one from Joan, but nothing arrived, and we never heard from them.

• • •

Christmas Day came, and we were hoping for some extra privileges now that there were just the two of us. Perhaps we'd be allowed to eat Christmas dinner with the family, we thought, but it didn't happen. We were called down for our usual bag of nuts and fruit, and May gave us each a chocolate bar. Minutes later we returned to our room and waited impatiently for our supper plates to be put on the bottom step.

Near the end of January, the social worker stopped by for a visit, and for the first time ever, Mrs. Bender let us sit on the sofa in her living room. She had already primed us as to how we should answer any questions, so we felt very awkward and uncomfortable as we sat on the edge of the seat and tried to answer the questions the lady asked. When the ordeal was over, we returned at once to our room.

The Children's Aid Report stated:
We saw the girls and find it difficult to discuss their ideas as they appear too painfully shy and unable to express themselves, but sit stiffly, glancing at the foster mother and often merely smiling in answer to a question. We are not sure what is the cause of this subdued manner.
There is a certain furtiveness in Mrs. Bender's manner that is disturbing, though this may be her natural way.

35

The End of the Row

Betty and I had to work harder during the tobacco-planting season to fill the void left by our sisters. On a few occasions, Mr. Bender helped out by filling the water tank while we were at school. Doug and Jack, who had both married the previous summer, had steady jobs; but Marge and May often came on the weekends to help us with the hoeing and then again in midsummer to help with the suckering.

Betty and I didn't feel safe enough this summer to wander too far away without our sisters, so we spent our idle time playing close to the barn. Still wondering whether we'd be attending high school in the fall, we waited anxiously for Mrs. Bender to tell us something.

One day, as we were working in the fields along with Mrs. Bender and Marge and May, I overheard Marge ask her mother, "So when are the girls leaving?"

"Jim wants to get most of the tobacco off first, so it will probably be around the end of August."

"Too bad they can't stay until it's finished," May said.

"Well, the Children's Aid wants to get them settled in their new home at least a week before school starts. I'm counting on you two and a couple of others to help finish up."

"What'll Dad and you do when they're gone?"

"Your dad wants to put the farm up for sale next spring."

As I glanced their way, I noticed Marge and May whispering and snickering behind their hands and wondered what they were up to. *Marge probably wants to play another prank on us before we leave*, I thought.

And sure enough, as Betty went to get a drink of water, they wrestled her to the ground.

She kicked and thrashed about, crying and struggling to get away. But they just continued on. "Oh, we just want to see how you're developing—check you over and see if everything's in the right place."

I ran to help her and watched in disbelief as Marge held her feet while May ripped off her shirt. And then May held her arms while Marge started yanking off her shorts and underpants. "Let her go! Let her go!" I screamed at them, tugging at Marge's waist to make her stop. I looked helplessly at Mrs. Bender and pleaded with her to make them stop. But she ignored my cries as they continued their fun.

Betty, who was now stark naked, embarrassed and sobbing, tried desperately to hide her nakedness with her arms.

"Well, she looks like she's sprouting nicely," May said to her mother.

"Yep, everything seems to be in the right place, don't you think, Mom?" Marge announced with a triumphant laugh.

"Leave her be now. Quit fooling around and get back to work," Mrs. Bender said with a nonchalant wave of her hand.

Humiliated and ashamed, Betty ran naked through the fields to find a place to hide. Grabbing her clothes, I ran after her and found her cowering under the leaves of two large plants. "Here," I said, getting down on my knees, "let me help you get your clothes back on."

"I hate them both!" she sobbed, as she jerked her shirt over her head.

"Me too! That was a horrible thing they did, and Mrs. Bender didn't even try to stop them. I'm disgusted with the whole bunch of them! But I overheard them talking and found out that we're leaving at the end of August. I think they'll keep us together, and we might be going to high school after all."

"I can't wait to get away," she said, trying to smile through her tears as I pulled her to her feet. And then she pointed to two of the plants and cried, "Oh look, I broke a few of the big leaves! Mrs. Bender will be angry!"

"Who cares!" I squeezed her hand. "Let's go down and start at the far end of the row, away from them. And I don't give a toot if Mrs. Bender likes it or not. If she says anything, I'll spit in her eye."

• • •

"You'd better start sorting out your stuff, for you'll be leaving for a new place in a day or two," Mrs. Bender said one day as we were finishing our work. On the day of our departure, Mrs. Bender came up to our room and checked our dresser drawers to make sure we'd packed all our belongings. "What's all this garbage?" she asked as she looked at the pile of artwork and school papers I had readied for packing.

"That's some of my best art work and compositions. I want to keep them."

"You can't be taking all this junk with you—just your clothes," she snapped as she grabbed my work off the corner of the dresser. "The lady from the shelter will be here soon, so get a move on."

As she turned to go downstairs with my schoolwork, I stuck my tongue out at her. I was so crushed that I had a sudden urge to push her fat, ugly body down the stairs. "She's gonna burn all my stuff," I fumed. "I just know it."

"That was mean of her," Betty said. "She could've at least let you ask the lady about it. Come on, let's go sit at the window and wait for her."

We had just settled ourselves at the window when we saw a small black car pull into the driveway. "Here she is," Betty said excitedly.

We watched as she stopped at the front porch and Mrs. Bender welcomed her inside. Soon Mrs. Bender opened our door and called sweetly, "Grab your bags and come down, girls. The lady's here."

We were greeted by a tall, lovely looking, well-dressed social worker. "Hello, girls. My name is Mrs. Sanders, and I'll be taking you to your new home."

She took our bags and put them in the front seat as Betty and I climbed into the back. Then before getting into the car, she turned and waved to Mrs. Bender.

"It's still early in the day, girls," she said as we drove away, "so we'll be going into town to shop for some new school clothes. How does that sound?"

We clapped our hands and bounced around on the seat as she watched our reaction in the rearview mirror. "Well, that sounds like a positive yes," she said, turning to smile at us.

We never turned to look back at the house we'd lived in for the past five years. We were happy to be leaving but concerned and worried about our next home.

Having never been shopping in a big department store, we ran from one counter to another, looking with wide-eyed wonderment at all the things to buy. We were thrilled as the social worker helped us select some beautiful skirts and blouses. "My, you girls are showing an awful lot of excitement," the social worker said as she put the dress I had chosen over her arm. "I just can't settle you down." She led us toward the shoe section and added, "I know you'll need some shoes."

"Can we get some girls' shoes?" I pleaded, looking down at my scuffed-up boys' shoes with their broken and knotted laces.

"You most certainly can." She looked down at our shoes, shaking her head in dismay. "We'll get the prettiest ones they have."

The Children's Aid Report stated:
We called for Bonnie and Betty at the Benders, and the girls left this home without much emotion for having been with this family for over eight years.
We shopped for clothes in Simcoe, and were surprised at the girls' animation in this situation.

36

Out of the Darkness

"Well, I don't know about you girls, but I'm getting a bit hungry," Mrs. Sanders said as we left the store with our shopping bags. "I think we should stop at a restaurant and get a bite to eat before we continue our journey."

Betty and I nodded, excited at having our first meal in a restaurant.

During lunch, Mrs. Sanders prepared us for our meeting with our new foster parents. "They're an elderly couple, very proper and well bred with a fine standing in the community, having lived there for many years. They were fine foster parents some years back, so I'm sure you'll be quite happy with them. They have a comfortable home in the town of Waterford, and the high school is only about ten blocks away."

We smiled, happy to learn we would be in a small town again, away from a farm and the long days of hard, demanding work.

Mrs. Lawson answered immediately when Mrs. Sanders rang the doorbell, and Betty and I smiled in amazement as we heard the chimes. Then when we entered the house, Mr. Lawson rose from his high-back chair to greet us, and I noticed right away that they both looked much older than I had expected. Mrs. Lawson had tinted bluish-gray hair that was loosely permed, and she wore squarish glasses. Her mouth turned down at the edges, giving her a sour look, but she seemed pleasant. Mr. Lawson was a distinguished-looking man with thinning gray hair and wore half-glasses. He was of medium build, slightly stooped, and nicely dressed in a tweed suit jacket and solid-color trousers. In the days following, we learned that he was a semiretired businessman who sold farm equipment parts to local farmers. He had a small office in the house and an implement shed in the backyard.

Betty and I felt as if we were coming out of the darkness as we settled into the Lawson home. We no longer felt like outcasts, but it would take many days for us to adjust and feel comfortable with our newfound freedom — a freedom far removed from the invisible wall of fear that held us captive for so many long years with the Benders.

Mrs. Lawson showed us to our bedroom, a nicely decorated room with a large-mirrored vanity and a chest of drawers for our clothes. We giggled as we stared at ourselves in the mirror. "I've never seen so much of myself all at once," I remarked. "It's gonna take some getting used to." I laughed, thinking about the small shard of mirror we hid under the linoleum before we left the Benders' house.

Mrs. Lawson then showed us the bathroom. And as we followed her inside, my eyes swept the room. There was a four-legged bathtub and white porcelain sink with colorful towels hanging nearby — and even a flushing toilet!

"I expect you to take a warm bath every weekend, and there's a large bottle of bubble bath liquid. You just need a capful."

Thinking of Jean's letter, I smiled and nudged Betty.

Betty and I were thrilled with our new surroundings and happy that we wouldn't have to empty an old paint can every day or freeze our backsides in a cold outhouse. And we looked forward with great enthusiasm to the weekend when we could have our first bubble bath.

That evening Mrs. Lawson asked us to set the table for dinner, and we just looked at each other before I admitted shamefully, "Uuuh, we've never set a table before."

"You're fifteen and you've never set a table?"

"No. All our work was outside in the tobacco fields, and we had barn chores to do."

"Well, I'll show you the proper way," she sighed, as she handed Betty four dishes from the cupboard.

"Do we eat with you, too?" Betty asked, examining the four plates. Then seeing her puzzled look, she added, "We never ate with the Bender family. We were called down to eat after they finished their meals. That was the only time we were allowed downstairs."

"Well, while you're in this house, you'll be having your meals with us," she replied, shaking her head in disbelief as she fished in the drawer for the cutlery.

After showing us the proper placement of the silverware, Mrs. Lawson handed Betty four cloth napkins. "Do you know what these are?" she asked.

As we shook our heads, she said, "These are called ser-viettes, and it looks like you have a lot to learn." She then went into the living room where Mr. Lawson was sitting. "Would you believe how little these girls know?"

Betty and I smiled helplessly at each other, shrugging our shoulders. "I'm not sure she believes us," Betty whispered as she put a serviette beside each plate.

"She thinks we're lying. And she said she'll be teaching us how to clean house and polish the furniture tomorrow and that every Monday is wash day."

"Well, at least we know how to hang clothes on the line. It doesn't seem like there's going to be much work for us to do, and I'm beginning to like it here already."

Our first dinner with this new family proved to be a learning experience for us. Having forgotten almost everything Mrs. Miller had taught us so many years ago about good manners and common courtesies, we felt awkward and uneasy as we watched and copied the Lawsons' every move.

"Surely you said grace before your meals?" Mrs. Lawson asked.

We shook our heads.

"Well, we say it here," she said, "so please bow your heads."

When I finished my dinner, I pushed my chair back and prepared to leave the table. But Mr. Lawson gently took hold of my hand and said, "When you leave the table, you say 'Excuse me, please.'"

I nodded. Mrs. Lawson was right. We would have much to learn.

In the evening we all sat out on the front veranda that had large steps leading downward almost to the edge of the sidewalk. Across the street was a row of small stores and a restaurant. Betty and I enjoyed watching the people going about their business. Since word had gotten around about our arrival, many friends and neighbors stopped by the porch to meet Betty and me or to question the Lawsons as to why they were taking on such a responsibility. Elderly ladies visited at some length with Mrs. Lawson in order to catch up on all the local gossip.

As dusk fell, we retired to the living room, and Betty and I tried our hand at preparing a pot of tea and serving it in pretty floral cups along with some shortbread cookies. Mrs.

Lawson invited us to join them and to pour ourselves a cup as well.

Although Mr. Lawson was very down-to-earth, Mrs. Lawson liked to put on airs and was a bit uppity. Still feeling shy and uncomfortable with all the formality, we fidgeted nervously as we sat on the sofa near them. Mr. Lawson turned on the large floor-model radio and listened to a few of the same comedy programs that Mr. Bender enjoyed. Hearing the familiar broadcast brought back thoughts of the stovepipe and of our big sisters whom we longed to see again.

Mrs. Lawson left the room and returned with two plastic bags filled with a white, lard-looking substance. Handing one to each of us, she remarked, "Here, you can do me a favor while you're enjoying the programs. Have you seen these before?"

We shook our heads.

"This is a new product called margarine. It's a butter sub-stitute, and if you look closely, you'll see what looks like a red cherry in the middle. All you do is pop this little cherry and then knead the juice throughout the contents until it's completely yellow and looks like butter."

"We use to churn the butter," Betty said.

"I understand, but this is what we use here, and we'll need it for our toast in the morning," Mrs. Lawson replied.

Betty and I enjoyed kneading our plastic pillows, watching the red streaks move around inside until we had worked it into a buttery yellow. It settled us down, keeping me from biting my nails and Betty from chewing on her hair, for which we'd already been reprimanded.

The rooms in the house were all comfortably warm and cozy with small radiators against the walls. The one in our bedroom fascinated us. "No stovepipe in here," Betty said.

"I know. That's because the stove in the kitchen is gas heated. Everything is so different and so nice."

We folded our clothes, put them neatly away in the drawers, and then opened the closet, surprised to find hangers instead of nails.

That evening as we sat on the edge of our bed enjoying the comforts of our new home, there was a knock at our door. "Are you girls decent? May I come in?" Mrs. Lawson asked.

Betty and I looked at each other, surprised that anyone would ask permission to come into our room. "Should we let her in?" Betty asked, nudging me playfully.

"Yes, you may," I replied, tipping my nose in the air as though I had made a most profound decision.

Mrs. Lawson removed two tall, narrow boxes from a paper sack. "These are some personal items that Mrs. Sanders left for you." She set the boxes on our dresser. I picked one up, looked quizzically at it, and began reading the instructions.

"Kotex pads? What are these for?" I asked, although I had sort of figured it out.

"Surely you must know that they're for a lady's time of the month," she said. "What did you do before?"

"We made our own out of old flannel sheets," Betty said. We've never had any store-bought ones."

"I don't believe it. One would think you lived in the Dark Ages," she said, shaking her head as she turned to leave the room. "I'm sure you'll find these much more appropriate."

I quickly dug into a box and pulled out one of the pads to examine it. "It even smells nice, sis," I said, holding it to my nose and then playfully shoving it under hers.

She giggled and pushed it away. "We're really coming up in the world—shopping, restaurants, and now this. I can hardly wait to get my period," she said, rolling her eyes.

Laughing and giddy, we shoved the boxes onto the top shelf of our closet.

• • •

We were enjoying the last two weeks in August as we waited eagerly for the start of our high school. Though they were quite elderly, the Lawsons treated us like family, taking us most everywhere with them. Church was a weekly must, and Sunday was often spent with Mrs. Lawson's many nieces and nephews and their families. On Saturdays we were allowed to walk downtown and visit the stores. Mr. Lawson often gave us enough money to get an ice-cream soda at the restaurant or attend a movie matinee. Each day seemed to bring about a new adventure for us.

Once the school year began, we looked forward to each new day, walking back and forth with many of the town kids and making new friends. It seemed like the whole world was opening up for us, and our fragmented and cloistered lives were slowly beginning to change as we emerged from our shells. We were no longer fearful of asking even the simplest questions, and our basic needs of warmth and hunger were met. We were now enjoying and participating in adult activities and conversations instead of being isolated and repressed, and with our natural development no longer subdued, we began to mature normally. No longer were we intimidated by or subjected to severe reprimands and beatings, nor were we belittled or made to feel less than we were. Instead, we were encouraged to make our way in the world and were praised for our accomplishments. We were slowly becoming our own persons, gaining confidence and poise each day.

• • •

During this first high school year, Betty really blossomed, turning from a timid young girl into a beautiful, lithe, and vivacious teenager. She was popular with the boys and girls and had many boyfriends on the string. "You change boy-friends as often as we change the fly stickers on the back porch," I kidded her.

Many nights when she went out on a date, I would sit at the kitchen table, working on my school lessons long after the Lawsons had retired, worrying about her, watching the clock, and hoping she'd get home by curfew. Overly concerned and exasperated with her tardiness, I would go to our room and pace the floor. The side-door entrance was right below our window, and with the porch light on, I could hear and see her when she came to the door with her boyfriend. When I heard their voices from below, I would get up and peer down at them from the window. Feeling pangs of jealousy, I would watch them hugging and kissing, wondering when I would also have a boy-friend.

As soon as I heard her coming up the stairs, I would jump into bed, cover up my head, and pretend to be asleep.

"Are you asleep?" she would ask, jiggling me.

"No, I was worried about you. You were out past your curfew again. Besides, I'm afraid to go to sleep. I keep having this same crazy dream, night after night."

"What's it about?"

"Nothing much; it's just strange. It's as though I'm looking out across a barren desert toward the horizon when suddenly these strange, sandy shapes start forming, all in a row, like people under a blanket. And they keep coming from the horizon toward me. As soon as they're real close, they recede into the horizon, sink into the desert sand, and the whole thing starts all over again. It just goes on and on and on. They frighten me. I feel like they're gonna drive me crazy. Do you think it means something? Grandma Tillman always said that dreams often mean something."

"Maybe you should talk to Mrs. Lawson about it."

"Naw, she'll probably think I'm nuts."

"Well, if you get sand in our bed, I'm gonna tell her," she giggled, as she snuggled in beside me. And after I had been in our new home for a while, the dreams finally stopped.

We were always first downstairs in the mornings to get the table set and sometimes make Cream of Wheat for breakfast. A beautiful carpeted staircase with carved posts led from upstairs to the front door, and a smaller, enclosed one led to the kitchen. It was these stairs that were used most of the time. As soon as Mr. Lawson heard us prattling about in the kitchen, he would come down, leaving Mrs. Lawson to sleep for a while longer.

We'd been there only a few weeks before Mr. Lawson got the urge to feel our breasts. Sneaking up softly behind us while we were stirring food on the stove or setting the table, he would slip his hand under our arms and try to touch them. We were forever dodging him, scooting behind the kitchen table out of his reach, and flashing him angry looks. Mrs. Lawson came down unexpectedly one day and sensed that something was wrong. I was about to tell her about Mr. Lawson's annoying behavior until Betty kicked me under the table. Realizing he'd almost got caught, he never tried it again.

Once as Betty and I were sunning ourselves on the back steps, Mr. Lawson came by on the way to his implement shed and asked us to go with him, saying he needed to discuss things with us and teach us the facts of life.

Puzzled and skeptical about what he had in mind, we didn't follow him. "What are the facts of life, anyway?" I asked Betty.

"I don't know," she said with a chuckle. "It probably has something to do with the birds and bees."

"You go out with guys, so does it have to do with dating, kissing, and all that stuff?"

"Yeah, kinda," she said. "I can tell you a few things."

Realizing we were not following him, he turned, and saw us still sitting on the steps.

"Come on, girls," he shouted, gesturing with his arm.

When we shook our heads, he threw his hands up and went on with his work.

• • •

The first school dance of the year was fast approaching, and Mrs. Lawson promised to take us shopping for new dresses if we did well in our studies. Hoping that she'd take us to the big department store in Simcoe, we were disappointed when we ended up shopping in a small shop in Waterford. "The choices here are terrible," I said to Betty. "I can't find anything I like."

"Me neither. They look like old ladies' clothes."

"Here, girls, I found some dresses for you. Go and try them on," Mrs. Lawson said, handing us two identically styled dresses. "The green one's for you, Betty, and the burgundy one's for Bonnie."

The dresses were made of a crepe material with three-quarter length sleeves, a simple round neck, a matching covered belt, and flapped pockets on the skirt. We wrinkled our noses as we headed for the fitting rooms. "I can't believe she chose these old-lady dresses for us," I grumbled. "We'll be the only girls at the Christmas dance with crepe dresses. I'm not too keen on going now."

"I look like an old 'granny grunt,'" Betty said, eyeing herself in the mirror as I zipped up the back of her dress.

The purchases were made, and I felt down in the dumps as we carried our packages home.

At the Christmas dance, Betty, who was more popular with the boys, seemed to be enjoying herself as she danced around the gym floor. I sat in the farthest corner like a wallflower, hoping that no one would ask me to dance because I was too embarrassed about my dress. Luckily, no one did.

Our first Christmas at the Lawsons was a joyous occasion. Mrs. Lawson dug through boxes in the closet and brought out some old decorations so that we could trim the inside of the house. "Why, I haven't used these old decorations in decades, not having any young people around and all." Seeming pleased as she dusted them off, she looked fondly at them as if recalling memories of the past.

We pranced around the house, trying to find the best place to show off the old Victorian Christmas ornaments and where to hang the streamers and garland. We were enjoying ourselves and were happy when Mrs. Lawson approved the final result. Mr. Lawson, whom we'd grown quite fond of despite his earlier quirkiness, lugged in a small fir tree for us and set it up on a small table. "We simply must have a place for Santa Claus to put all his gifts," he said, winking at us, knowing full well we had outgrown that stage.

On Christmas we traveled out into the country to spend the day with Mrs. Lawson's married niece, their three daughters, and other relatives. They were a wealthy family and owned a large cattle ranch near the little town of Jarvis. After a wonderful Christmas dinner, the men went out to the barn to look over the prize-winning Angus cows, while we girls scurried around, petting all the animals.

Later in the day, their daughters, who were all proficient on the piano, played Christmas carols. But still finding it difficult to adjust to our new surroundings, we sat timidly on the sofa. "Come on, girls, join the sing-along," the girls said, tugging our hands to coax us over to the piano. They gave us a song sheet, and we shyly joined in with the group.

"It looks like you girls had a lot of fun," Mr. Lawson said when we got home.

"It was a great Christmas," I said

"The best Christmas ever!" Betty added, as she set her gifts on the table.

"And did you ever see such lovely, well-mannered young ladies — and sooo gifted," Mrs. Lawson added, referring to her niece's daughters.

I felt a twinge of resentment ripple through me. *Is she comparing them with us?* I wondered.

On Christmas night Mrs. Lawson handed each of us a gift from the Children's Aid, and Mr. Lawson gave Mrs. Lawson her present. Betty and I were happy to receive some jewelry and a silk scarf, but Mrs. Lawson's gift stole the show. She opened a large package and was overcome to find a full-length, black, Persian lamb fur coat.

"Oh, my goodness," she said, fanning herself with her hand as if feeling faint and acting a bit theatrical, "what have we here?" She pulled the coat out of the box and carefully slipped it on. She then waltzed over to the floor-length mirror and twirled about back and front for a full inspection. "My goodness, Harold, you've really outdone yourself," she purred, hurrying over to embrace him. "When we go to church this Sunday, let's be the last to enter. We'll let the girls go ahead of us, and then I can make a grand entrance and show off my new coat. Why, I'll be the talk of the town!"

"Now, Violet, don't get carried away," he said, as he took a long draw on his pipe.

"Well, I've made up my mind. That's precisely what we're going to do."

Betty and I snickered behind our hands. "I'm gonna wear my new stuff, too," she whispered, sticking her nose snootily in the air.

• • •

I was enjoying the rest of the school year, but Betty was having a difficult time, preferring to socialize rather than buckle down and work. She was becoming a bit wayward and a real challenge to Mrs. Lawson, who scolded her often for her rebellious behavior.

"Come on, Betty, you have to knuckle down and do your homework," I warned her, "or you're going to fail."

"Why don't you let me copy yours," she asked with a mischievous smile. "Besides, my head aches again."

Disgusted with her excuses I shoved my work toward her. "Here, then, copy it. Just don't copy it word for word. You know, Mrs. Lawson told me that you're getting almost too much for her to handle, and I hope they don't decide to split us up."

"Oh God, I never even thought of that. That would be terrible!" she groaned with a wounded look.

Mrs. Lawson, hearing Betty complaining of headaches once too often, discussed the problem with Mrs. Sanders at her next visit. Mrs. Sanders picked Betty up from school the following day and took her to an optometrist who determined her need for glasses. The glasses seemed to help her with her studies, and as the school year progressed, Betty settled down, and we were both promoted to grade ten. Happy with the results of our school year, we celebrated over a soda pop at the restaurant.

The Children's Aid Report stated:
This situation seems a much more normal life for these

girls, and they are generally given the advantage of
family. The change in these girls is remarkable.

• • •

During the summer vacation, Betty and I found it difficult to keep ourselves occupied and out of Mrs. Lawson's
hair. We wandered around town, stopping in the stores and
asking for job opportunities, but nothing was available. A
few of our friends had found jobs on the local tobacco farms,
but we'd had enough of that. It suited Mrs. Lawson, for she
didn't have a high opinion of farm laborers.

Arriving home after job searching, we were surprised to
find Mrs. Sanders visiting with Mrs. Lawson. After some
small talk, Mrs. Lawson turned to Betty and said, "I have
some chores in the kitchen I want you to help me with while
Mrs. Sanders takes Bonnie over to the restaurant. She has
some things she wants to discuss with her."

We looked quizzically at Mrs. Sanders and then at each
other, sensing that our lives were about to change again.

I could feel my stomach tightening as I walked silently
across the street with Mrs. Sanders. Then, sliding into the
booth across from her, I watched as she graciously draped the
serviette across her lap, often using it throughout the course
of our lunch to dab gingerly at her mouth. Impressed by her
elegance, I tried to appear well mannered and followed her
lead.

We talked about my schoolwork and my love of art. Although I knew she was holding something back, it wasn't
until we were nearly finished eating when she broke the
news to me. "I'm afraid I have some rather unsettling news
to share with you," she said, reaching across the table to lay
her hand on mine.

They're splitting us up, I thought, and my insides began to
churn as I waited for the news.

Seeing the look on my face, she patted my hand. "Mrs. Lawson has been telling me for some time that it's too much of a challenge for her to handle two big girls. She suggested that we find a new home for you and that she'll keep Betty."

"Betty?" I choked out. *Why her?* I wondered. *I was the obedient one. I never gave Mrs. Lawson any cause for concern.*

"Yes. She feels you're more settled and mature and would be able to fit more readily into new surroundings. She feels Betty is a bit giddy and very contrary and she would like to work more with her."

"But I don't want to leave my sister. I just don't want to. We'll be lost without each other. Please don't take me away!"

"There, there, I know how you must feel," she said. "But it might please you to know that we've found a home for you in the country, and you'll still be attending the same school as Betty. You'll see each other every day during the school year. Perhaps you can even telephone each other." She smiled and gave my hand a little squeeze before we got up to leave.

Feeling defeated, I walked silently back to the house with my head bowed. The thought of life without Betty was too much to accept. I had looked after her most of my life. *Who'll care for her now?* I wondered.

"Everything will work out for the best," Mrs. Sanders said as we entered the house.

Mrs. Lawson gathered us all into the living room to discuss the situation, and after some light conversation as we sipped tea that Betty had prepared, Mrs. Sanders broached the news to her. Crushed, she dashed off to our bedroom in tears.

"I'll go and get her," I said.

But Mrs. Lawson held up her hand to stop me. "No, let her settle down on her own. She needs time to think things through."

"I understand how disturbing this news must be to both of you," Mrs. Sanders said as she slipped her manicured hands into her white gloves. "I must go now, but I'll be back next Saturday morning to take Bonnie to meet her new foster family."

Foster family! I now hated that expression and all the pain that came with it.

The week flew by for us as we tried to have as much fun as possible in order to forget about the impending weekend. In the evenings we hugged our pillows and snuggled close to console each other.

37

A Long Good-bye

On the day of our departure Mrs. Sanders chatted in the living room with Mrs. Lawson, allowing Betty and me some time alone in the kitchen to say good-bye. We hadn't slept much on our last night together. Instead, we had sat up talking about the fateful days that lay ahead and hoping the morning would be slow to come. "I'll never manage here without you, Bonnie," Betty said. "I just know I won't. Besides, Mrs. Lawson isn't too fond of me, and it's two months before school begins and we see each other again."

"We'll just have to be strong," I said. "I don't know what's in store for me. Suppose I don't like this family? Or worse yet, what if they don't like me? I'm so nervous that I've nearly bitten my nails all off."

"Oh, don't worry. They'll like you! You're the queen of hearts, and I'm a wild card."

We smiled as we breathed deeply and made our way into the living room.

"I guess I'm ready to go," I said to Mrs. Sanders.

"I hope you like your new home, my dear," Mrs. Lawson said, laying a comforting arm on my shoulder. I squirmed out from under it, still stinging over her decision to split us up, feeling she was keeping Betty because she was prettier than me. Without looking back, I hurried out to the waiting car and climbed into the front seat. Then as we pulled out onto the road, I looked back and saw Betty waving to me from the driveway. I closed my eyes and swallowed hard to choke back my tears. It was our first separation, and the pain was unbearable. *Who'll care for her now? Who'll she turn to when she's in trouble?* We'd been there for each other all these years, and now it was ending. It seemed like only yesterday that they took Joan and Jean away . . . and now this. Clasping my hands together, I stared solemnly down at my lap as we drove through the little town of Waterford.

Mrs. Sanders reached over and touched my knee. "You're awfully pensive, Bonnie. Do you care to talk about it?"

"I don't want to leave Betty, and I'm nervous about this new home."

"Well, let me brief you a little more about your new family. Maybe that will help calm your collywobbles," she said, thinking the word would tickle me.

It did — at least a little — and I smiled.

"Today we'll be meeting with Mrs. Klinchuk, and maybe her daughter Elinor. Mrs. Klinchuk has a disability in her arms that leaves them almost completely paralyzed, and her arms hang limply at her side. Mr. Klinchuk is a semiretired farmer. I'm sure you'll enjoy Elinor's company. She's about twenty-two and has cared for her mother since she was six years old — the time her mother contracted her affliction. There are two older sons — Stewart, who works in Hamilton, and Gerald, who's married with two young children and runs a small grocery store in a nearby village. They're an ambitious family and respected in the community. Elinor has charge of some youth groups, so I'm sure she'll get you involved. I believe the family is of Ukrainian background."

I gasped. *Oh my God, I'm going to live with foreigners. I wonder if they eat blood pudding. Will I even understand them?* Numerous thoughts flashed through my mind. I was beginning to feel uptight, wishing she'd turn the car around and take me back to Waterford. "Do they speak foreign? Will I be able to understand them?"

"No, I don't think you'll have any problems. The children were all Canadian born, and I'm sure English is spoken in the home."

I was apprehensive as we pulled into the farmyard. The thought of living on a farm again and with a foreign family and a crippled lady frightened me, and I was missing Betty. It was the first time I had to face a new situation without her, and I was petrified.

Mrs. Klinchuk and Elinor were at home when we arrived. The table was set for tea with an assortment of pastries in the center, and the smell of the freshly baked goods still lingered in the kitchen.

As I was introduced to Mrs. Klinchuk, I reached out to shake her hand and immediately realized my mistake. But Elinor reached out for my hand. "There are some things you'll get used to," she said, giving me a quick wink.

They were tall, formidable women, towering eight or nine inches above my five- feet-two. I found it unsettling.

After Mrs. Sanders left, Elinor showed me to my bedroom. It was the smallest of three upstairs bedrooms and had one twin bed, a small closet, and a small dresser. The other rooms were for Elinor and her brother who came home on the weekends.

"When you're finished unpacking, come back down. Mom and I want to have a discussion with you," Elinor said as she turned to leave.

I nodded and thanked her as she left the room. Then, feeling lost and lonely, I sat on the bed to collect my thoughts and get a feel for my new surroundings. I looked around and saw a small, gray hot-water radiator, similar to the one at the Lawsons, and walked over to touch it. It was cold and dusty. Directly above it was a window that offered a view of the side yard and the driveway. This pleased me, for I'd be able to see who was coming and going. Farther down among the trees were an old red barn, a corncrib, and a chicken coop with a fenced-in yard. A few red rock hens were scratching for their food. *Familiar sights,* I thought, but the idea of living on a farm again didn't make me happy.

When I returned downstairs, Mrs. Klinchuk gave me a brief tour of the rest of the house—the living room, their bedroom, the large dining room, and finally the bathroom that was just off the kitchen. "There's only one bathroom, but if it's tied up, there's always the outhouse in the back. I know you're familiar with them, for Mrs. Sanders told me that you lived on a farm for quite some time."

"Yes," I replied. "It was a tobacco farm."

We returned to the kitchen table, and Elinor and Mrs. Klinchuk questioned me about my general background, my schoolwork, and my skills at housework. "Can you bake, cook, can, or sew—anything about housework?" Elinor asked.

I cooked some at the Lawsons the year I was with them. I don't know much about sewing, but I want to learn. I want to take a home economics class when school starts again. When I was on the farm, I worked out in the fields or in the barn doing chores."

"Well, it seems you have a lot to learn," Elinor said. "Tomorrow we'll be picking vegetables in the garden and will start canning them for the winter months. During the week, my dad gathers up eggs from the local farmers; and they have to be washed, candled, and graded in preparation for delivery. I'll be teaching you how to do that. Early on Friday and Saturday mornings, we leave for our egg route in Hamilton where we deliver them to our customers. During these days when I'm gone, you'll be looking after my mom."

"Oh, I don't require much looking after," Mrs. Klinchuk interjected, noticing my puzzled look. "I'm much more self-sufficient than I look."

It was clearly apparent that I wouldn't have the leisurely life I had enjoyed at the Lawsons.

•••

Only a couple of weeks had passed when Betty phoned to let me know that Mr. Lawson had died suddenly from a heart attack. I felt sad for her, knowing she was much fonder of him than of Mrs. Lawson. Several days later she called again, terribly upset. "Mrs. Lawson's becoming very demanding and miserable to live with. She's getting quite frail and expects me to prepare all her meals and wash and bathe her each morning. I can't do this, Bonnie," she wailed. "I don't want to bathe her. I can't handle this. I really don't know what to do."

"Try to hold on until school starts and we can discuss it some more," I urged her. "But I can't talk too much now."

"Why? Is someone there?"

"Yes. I'll see you in school, if not before," I added, trying to give her some hope. I wanted to tell her more about my situation, but it was not a good time. She already had enough on her mind.

•••

I felt ill at ease during the early months and found it difficult to fit into this family. Because she'd cared for her mother for so many years, Elinor was a wiz at whatever she did. She was an outstanding cook and all-around homemaker. She was an accomplished seamstress who made special clothes for her mother, who—because of her illness—had unusually long arms. With her speed and ability at tackling all the household chores, she had little patience with a novice like me. Working with her took some getting used to. Her sharp-tongued criticism of almost everything I did brought many quick trips to my outhouse retreat where I wallowed in self-pity until I could regain my composure. The pain of missing Betty and adapting to this new foreign family was proving difficult.

Whenever the family wanted to discuss things they felt were none of my concern, they reverted to speaking Ukrainian. This always hurt me, for I was certain they were talking about me. Lacking the nerve to discuss the problem and afraid of being ridiculed, I bottled my feelings inside.

One evening as Elinor was hurrying off to one of her many speaking engagements, she asked me to feed her mother. Elinor and her mother shared one plate and the same cutlery, but I insisted on my own plate and my own cutlery. I also had my own way of eating, keeping the different foods on my plate separated, not letting them touch. I ate my food in a certain order, and the thought of messing up my plate with gravy, which I hated, was unthinkable. My plate was the exact opposite of the one shared by Elinor and her mom.

"Do you think you're too good to eat off the same fork and share the same dish as my mother?" Elinor asked sarcastically. "If she doesn't mind, why should you?"

"No, I . . . I . . . ju . . . just prefer this way," I stammered, feeling belittled.

"It's all right with me, Elinor; just leave her alone. As long as I get fed, that's the main thing," Mrs. Klinchuk said, making light of the matter.

"Humph," Elinor muttered as she kissed her mother good-bye and cast me a scornful look.

I felt terrible. I wanted to oblige and feed her the way Elinor did, but sharing my utensils was something I couldn't bring myself to do.

"I'm sorry," I apologized to Mrs. Klinchuk as soon as Elinor closed the door.

"That's okay, I understand. But you do have a strange way of eating. I hope it's just a phase you're going through."

"It probably is," I replied.

• • •

Unlike the English families with whom I had lived, this family was very ambitious and hardworking. They all pitched in and did their share of the workload. They met every challenge head-on, and every minute of the day was precious and not to be wasted on sports, television, reading a book, or lying around. During the weekdays idle hands were not tolerated. Free time was allowed only in the evenings and on Sundays. Plans were made at the dinner table for what chores had to be attended to the following day. Mrs. Klinchuk, a habitual clock-watcher, estimated the time it should take me to complete each assigned chore. Perhaps it had something to do with her illness, for she was always drilling into my head the value of each minute and how time should never be frittered away. She felt a person should learn or accomplish one new thing every day.

Life was overwhelming at times. I felt as if I were buried under a snowdrift and trying to keep it from smothering me as I struggled for the acceptance of this strong and aggressive family. I often felt sorry for myself and the burden that was placed on me, but the fact that I had the use of my arms and Mrs. Klinchuk did not, helped me keep things in perspective. I was amazed at the many things she was able to do just by sheer determination. After I would remove the dust mop from its handle and place the mop head on the floor, she could step on it and dust the floors. Or if I put a polishing cloth on the dining room table, she could heft her arm onto the cloth and drag it around the table. In the morning as she sat on the edge of the bathtub, I'd put some toothpaste on her brush and put the handle between her knees so that she could brush her teeth. A phone stand was jury-rigged so if the phone rang she could grab the phone cord with her teeth and mount the receiver into the stand and then replace it back onto the cradle when she was finished talking. I smiled every time she turned the light switches on and off with her chin, and when she scolded me for forgetting to turn off a light, I would return to the switch and use my chin. "I want a dimple in my chin, too," I teased. We shared many laughs. Helping her was never a bother. Elinor was the one who rattled and intimidated me.

Mrs. Klinchuk often looked over my shoulder as I was baking a cake or cooking something, offering advice or suggesting a more efficient and time-saving way of doing it. "You're making me nervous," I said one day while I was trying to follow a cake recipe.

"I'm sorry," she replied, "I don't mean to make you nervous. I'm just trying to help. Sometimes when I'm watching, it makes me feel as if I'm doing it."

I thought that through, imagined myself in her shoes, and understood how she felt. And so whenever I was making something I felt experienced at or comfortable doing, I didn't mind her standing nearby.

Mrs. Sanders visited just before I was to start back to school. I complained to her that Elinor and I were not getting along too well and that when the family spoke in their foreign language, I felt uncomfortable. She told me that Elinor's older brother, Gerald, had lectured her on her mistreatment of me and that things should be a lot better. She asked me not to be offended by their lapses into their native language, that it's sometimes much easier for older people to converse in their old language rather than in an entirely new one. She assured me that the family was very fond of me, and she promised to check back before Christmas to see if things had improved. Her visit helped lessen some of my uneasiness, but it still upset me some whenever they talked in Ukrainian.

These first summer months were hectic, for I was learning many new things. The kitchen was the center of activity with so much baking, cooking, and canning that I was sometimes overwhelmed by it all.

There were breads, rolls, cakes, and pies to make and bake as well as time-consuming European dishes that I'd never heard of. Food took on a whole new meaning to me now. It was interesting to make and delicious to eat. And so I soon began to put on more than a few pounds.

A beautiful, sunny Sunday in the summer would bring many family friends from Hamilton out to the farm for a country drive and a farm-fresh dinner. These proved to be busy times for Elinor and me, as we often prepared for sixteen or more table settings.

My first order of the day was to go to the chicken coop to snare at least three plump chickens. After scattering around some ground corn, I removed a long wire hook from the wall, and while the chickens were eating, I hooked their legs and pulled one at a time from the flock. After bagging them, I took them over to the old stump chopping block. One by one I laid their heads across the stump and chopped them off with one fell swoop of the hatchet. I then tossed them toward the wire fence and watched until they were through running erratically around and dropped before I picked them up.

This was one job I didn't enjoy, and it always left me feeling a bit queasy. Elinor would then come with some old newspapers and a large kettle of boiling water that she poured into a bucket and would ask me how I was doing.

"I'm doing okay, but I hate chopping their heads off," I said one day, as I shivered my shoulders and winced. "I always want to close my eyes."

"Well, there are times in life that we have to do things that we don't particularly like to do, but it is all in a day's work and you'll get used to it," she assured me. "We do have to eat, you know."

I dunked the chickens into the boiling water, then pulled them out and quickly plucked off their feathers. After crumpling up the newspaper and setting it on fire, I held the chicken by the neck and legs to singe off the fine downy feathers. I then took them into the kitchen, laid them on the table, and gutted them. Then Elinor and I prepared them for dinner while Mrs. Klinchuk paced the floor, worrying that we wouldn't have things ready before company started arriving. "We'll need to get out the good china and set the table for about sixteen," she said. "Oh, we'll also need the big tablecloth—and serviettes, too. Let's see, we'll also need the silver tea set. I do hope it's polished." On and on she'd go with her orders.

"Mom, you're making us all nervous. She knows what to do without your telling her."

"I know," she'd say with a laugh. "I just get carried away." We laughed with her. At last, everything was ready for company.

Stewart, home for the weekend, was at the table along with Gerald, Gerald's wife, Pauline, and their two-year-old son. I was very fond of Pauline and Gerald, for they were always understanding and friendly. Elinor received many compliments for the exceptional dinner, but Pauline — knowing that I helped with much of the preparations — put in a word of praise for my efforts. She made me feel important and recognized. After dinner she'd pitch in and help me clean up the kitchen mess while Elinor entertained and visited with their guests. She was like a big sister to me and always listened to my problems, having encountered many of the same herself by marrying into a foreign family.

• • •

Knowing that I wanted new clothes for school and some spending money, Elinor said she knew a tobacco farmer who had a large farm west of Waterford and was in need of two more leaf handlers to make up a team of ten 'table-gang' workers. She asked me if I knew how to hand leaves. I reminded her that I had lived on a tobacco farm and had handed leaves for many years. "That's great," she said. "It pays good money and you'll be able to open your own bank account."

It sounded too good to be true. "Can I keep all the money I make?"

"Of course. So shall we try it?"

"Sure. I hate the job, but the money's too good to turn down, and it's one thing I already know how to do."

Elinor phoned him on the weekend and was told to show up for work at 6:00 a.m. the following Monday.

We soon discovered that we would be working in the harvest every day; weather permitting. It was a grueling long six weeks before the harvest was completed. We were happy when the work was finished, and our lives returned to normal.

After the harvest was finished, Elinor and I decided to take a trip into Simcoe to shop for new clothes and dress fabric.

On the way into town, she told me that she was president of the 4-H Club and the Junior Farmers and wanted to get me involved. "Our fall project will be making a dress, so you'll be learning to sew both at school and at home."

"It's always been a dream of mine to make my own clothes, so I know I'll enjoy it," I told her.

"Once school starts for you, I'll be involved in conventions, seminars, workshops, and speaking engagements. I will be traveling a lot, and so you'll be chief cook and bottle washer. Before you catch the school bus, you'll have to fix Mom a sandwich with some cookies and a glass of water. Dad will be in and out during the day. He does some barn and field chores and collects eggs from local farmers, so Mom won't be alone for long."

38

A Whole New Setting

I was thrilled when school started and I would see Betty again. Two months had passed, but I still felt the pain of our separation. We were sixteen and going into the tenth grade.

It was a mile walk down the gravel road to the main road where the school bus stopped. After a hectic morning of tending to Mrs. Klinchuk's needs, I was running short on time and hustled to catch the bus. I thought back to the days at the Lawsons where life seemed to move in slow motion and Betty and I enjoyed leisurely walks to school. Life with this new family was always in high gear, but in a short time I had learned so much, grown so much, and knew more about life.

Betty and I were overjoyed to see each other again, and we signed up for most of the same classes so we'd be together. It was not long, however, before our lives again took different paths. Betty, ever popular and fun loving, would have her own set of friends, and her carefree ways eventually took a toll on her studies. On the other hand, I had only a couple of close friends and worked hard on my homework. Many times it would be late in the evening before my household chores were done and I was able to sit down and do my homework. I often studied until the wee hours of the morning before Mrs. Klinchuk would shoo me off to bed.

I scolded Betty when her grades slipped, but she just shrugged everything off with, "Oh, you'll help me out when it comes to writing the finals."

One day we were told to write a composition that would take five minutes to read, and Betty showed up the next day with a mere two pages. "That's not going to take five minutes to read," I said. "Look, I've written twelve pages."

"Well, I couldn't think of anything else to say," she said, nonchalantly tossing her blonde curls.

She was called first to read her composition, and it took barely more than a minute. Glancing at the wall clock, she announced to the teacher, "I know I haven't taken up my five minutes, but my sister will probably make up for it."

The students snickered as she took her seat, but I shook my head at her boldness. True to her statement, I ran over on my time, and the teacher, acknowledging her remark, gave us both full credit.

By the end of the year, Betty had lost all interest in school, and no amount of coaxing or pleading could change her mind about quitting. She had found employment at the drugstore downtown and wanted to earn her own spending money. Except for an occasional double date, our lives were going in different directions.

• • •

My first Christmas with the Klinchuks was an exciting and hectic event. A few days before Christmas, Mr. Klinchuk brought in a tree from the woods, and Elinor and I spent an evening trimming it, wrapping presents, and hanging garland and decorations around the house. After the decorating was completed, we capped off the evening with some mulled cider as we chatted and relaxed around the tree. Mrs. Klinchuk, never one to let her mind idle, was already formulating plans for the Christmas Eve dinner.

Christmas Eve is the most beloved of all Ukrainian festivities. Its main feature is the evening meal, called Holy Supper, and according to custom, all family members must be in attendance. Twelve Lenten, meatless dishes — symbolic of the twelve apostles who gathered at the Last Supper — had to be prepared.

Under the watchful eye of Mrs. Klinchuk, Elinor and I spent the whole day in the kitchen, preparing all the special dishes and making all sorts of holiday breads and fancy pastries.

"Come here," Mrs. Klinchuk said. "I have a chore for you. See that large pan there?" she pointed with her chin. "Take it out to the barn and fill it to the brim with wheat from the granary."

"What on earth am I ever gonna do with wheat?" I furrowed my brow, puzzled at all the strange dishes that had to be readied.

"I'm going to teach you how to prepare the main dish called *kutya*."

After I brought the wheat in, she told me to put it into a large heavy pot, add some water, and set it on the stove to cook. I stirred the wheat off and on the whole day long as it simmered and thickened. From time to time she asked for a sampling to check for doneness. Just before serving time, she had me add some honey, ground poppy seeds, and chopped nuts. Then she asked for one more sampling.

I scooped out a heaping tablespoonful and put it to her

mouth. After savoring it slowly, she remarked, "Very good. We'll make a Ukrainian out of you yet."

While I was making *kutya*, Elinor prepared the cabbage soup called *borscht*.

Just before the dinner hour, the finest embroidered Ukrainian tablecloth was spread and the table set with fine china. A special loaf of home-baked bread with a braided top, called *kolach*, adorned the center of the table—a symbol of health and prosperity. Dishes of pickled herrings, mushrooms, stuffed fish, cabbage rolls with rice, perogies, and fruit compote—along with the *kutya*, *borscht*, and holiday pastries—filled the table.

On Christmas morning the gifts were opened, and another big dinner was prepared. The merriment went on throughout the week with guests constantly coming and going, exchanging gifts and holiday treats. Wines, whiskies, and liqueurs were always on the table along with an assortment of cheeses and holiday pastries. Christmas was now a special time to remember—a far cry from our days of listening down the stovepipe and having our dinner dishes set on the bottom step of the staircase.

• • •

Life was really beginning to change for me. I was becoming more confident and developing more self-esteem. Elinor and I finally reached a better understanding as I became more accomplished around the house. Her high-priority job as the first woman president of the 4-H Club and Norfolk Junior Farmers put her in touch with many important people, and there were always parties and weddings to attend. Many times we went with our friends to a popular dance hall where big-name bands played.

During the summer months I picked strawberries, worked on tobacco farms, and often babysat for Gerald and Pauline's small children to earn my spending money. This summer when I was seventeen, my good friend Eva, who was four years older than me, boarded at a tobacco farm during the harvest. With our earnings, she suggested that we take a train trip to Buffalo, New York, to see the sights and do some shopping. I was so excited about her idea and begged the Klinchuks to let me go. They were reluctant, but since Eva was older and had been raised in the city of Hamilton, they gave in to my pleas and entrusted me to her care.

Once we arrived in Buffalo, we took a cab to our hotel. The driver was a middle-aged, pleasant man, and upon learning that we were a couple of Canadian farm girls, he seemed genuinely concerned about our safety. "I'm going to turn off my meter," he said, "and I'll take you on a tour of the city and show you some of the sights. After that we'll stop at a popular lounge for a bite to eat. How does that sound?"

We agreed that it was nice of him to do that for us.

After touring around for a few hours, we stopped at a bar and grill for lunch. It was then that he lectured us on how to take care of ourselves and warned us not to stay out on the streets at night. He insisted on buying our lunch and then took us to our hotel.

After unpacking, we went out to do some shopping. Eva proposed going to the hotel dining room for dinner. She suggested that we order martinis with our meals. And trying to act sophisticated without knowing what a martini was, I went along. The strong drink went right to my head, and I didn't enjoy the tipsy feeling one bit.

After dinner we returned to our room to try on our new dresses. Then we went down to the café for an evening snack, but I refused to have any more martinis, sticking to a glass of ginger ale instead.

Two young men in the booth across from us caught our attention and struck up a conversation. I was uneasy chatting with them and toyed nervously with my fork. But Eva seemed relaxed and talked amicably with them. Soon they pulled me into the conversation.

I chatted a bit, but still feeling edgy, I nudged Eva and suggested that we return to our room. As we were sitting on our bed discussing our plans for the next day's shopping trip, there was a knock on the door. "Who in the world could that be? Should we answer it?" I asked.

"Oh, it's probably just the maid," she said, as she hurried to open the door. As she swung it open, we were both surprised to see one of the men from the hotel café. Before Eva could say anything, he pushed his way into our room, kicking the door closed after him. Frightened, I ran toward the closed door, but he lunged at me and grabbed my sleeve, partially tearing it off my dress. Because I was a strong girl, I was able to fight him off. He then turned away and grabbed Eva, shoving her onto the bed. Without a moment's hesitation, I ran to the door, opened it, and screamed for help.

Letting Eva go, he shoved me aside and ran out the door. We hurriedly locked it. Then, shaking with fright, we returned to sit on the bed. "That was a very silly thing we did," I said. "We shouldn't have carried on a conversation with them."

"I know. It never dawned on me that they'd try to pull anything like this."

"We can thank our lucky stars the other guy didn't show up, or we would have had our hands full. Who knows what might have happened."

It was a bitter and scary lesson we learned that night, and we vowed never to mention our stupid behavior to anyone.

The rest of our weekend was fun and exciting as Eva took me around to all the big city stores. It was a whole new adventure for me and I was wide-eyed with wonderment as we traipsed into one beautiful store after another. I was amazed at Eva's shopping knowledge as she checked out the name-brand clothes for me to try on.

Arriving home exhausted, I was still able to summon up enough energy to try on my new clothes and show them off to Elinor and Mrs. Klinchuk.

"Well, it looks like you've made some nice choices," Elinor said, and her mother agreed.

I felt proud of myself and looked forward to the new school year as I hung my clothes in the closet and prepared for bed.

39

A Surprise Reunion

Toward the end of summer and several days before the start of my eleventh grade year, my sister Joan learned of my whereabouts and phoned to say that she was coming to visit. Excited about seeing her again, I sat in a lawn chair near the driveway to wait for her. A silver pickup stopped several feet from my chair, and without acknowledging me, a thin, blond-haired man stepped out and hurried around to help Joan out. Happy to see each other again, we hugged and giggled like little children.

"Well, I see you still have all your freckles," I said, "and you've grown some."

"And you're still as brown as a bear, and chubby too."

"I know. The food is so good here that I eat too much, and I got a good tan working in the tobacco harvest."

Joan screwed up her nose, and so I added, "But this time I got paid for it!"

"It's about time," she said as she turned to take the young man's hand and pull him next to her. "I want you to meet Mike, my boyfriend. We're engaged to be married." She held out her hand to show me her ring.

"It's beautiful, and I'm so happy for both of you," I said, offering Mike my hand.

He seemed shy and smiled slightly as he shook my hand.

"We're getting married in October," Joan continued, "and I came to ask you to be one of my bridesmaids. I've already asked Jean and Betty, so there'll be the three of you."

I was pleased with the news and excited about being in the wedding party. "Where will you be living? Not too far away, I hope."

"Mike has a small farm several miles from here, and we'll live there."

Mike nodded, smiled proudly, and slipped his arm around her waist. "She's gonna be a farmer's wife."

Joan and I sat at the picnic table while Mike—realizing we wanted to talk privately—strolled down to look around the barnyard. Eager to know how her life had been since we were separated, I asked, "Betty told me she heard you had left the Burroughs' home and were living in Vittoria with a family by the name of Danson. Is this true? What happened? Didn't you like it at the Burroughs' place?"

"I had a lot of problems there. Whenever I was alone in the house with Mr. Burroughs, he would try to get at me. I think you know what I mean. I finally had enough and told his wife. It caused a big argument, so the next morning I packed my bags and phoned the Children's Aid. Mrs. Sanders came at once to get me."

"So how is your new place?"

"It's one of the best homes I've been in. They really treat me nice, and they're fond of Mike."

Mike returned, and we chatted for the better part of an hour as Joan filled me in on her wedding plans. "Once we're married, I want you to come and visit us often. You'll always be welcome. It'll be your home away from home."

Gently reminding Joan that he had barn chores, Mike rose to leave. "I'll be back in touch with you regarding the gowns, rehearsals, and such," she said as Mike helped her into the truck.

Waving to me as they pulled away, Joan slid over on the seat to be close to Mike. I smiled as I watched the truck disappear from view. Reflecting on our past as I walked back to the house, I felt happy for her and glad that at last she would have a home to call her own.

Though I was overjoyed about the upcoming wedding, I was concerned about the rumors about Betty's behavior during the summer. She had also worked in the tobacco harvest and had fallen in with a fast crowd. Some of her friends were in my high school, and I knew I had to talk to her about straightening out her life. Fortunately, Mrs. Sanders had arranged another meeting with me at the restaurant to discuss my school plans and to give me permission to sign up for a weekly evening art class at the high school to pursue my art interests. During lunch I was surprised when Betty dropped in to visit. Lively and animated as usual, she excitedly told us about her new boyfriend who was of strong Baptist religion and had convinced her to join his church. As she wiggled into the seat beside me, she immediately withdrew some pictures of him from her wallet. "His name's Carl, and even Mrs. Lawson approves of him."

Mrs. Sanders and I were happy that she'd found a nice young man, and I hoped this news would squash the ugly rumors about her wild behavior. We tried to convince her to return to high school with me, but she would have none of it. "I've got a full-time job at a factory in town. Carl and I are planning for our future together, and I want to start saving my money."

"I'm sure you girls have lots of news to catch up on," Mrs. Sanders said as she slipped on her white gloves, "so I'll go across the street for a visit with Mrs. Lawson and leave you to chat for a while."

I followed her every move as she walked out the door. "She's such a pretty lady, isn't she? She's always so smartly dressed and never has a hair out of place. I hope we'll be able to afford to dress like that someday."

"She's very pleasant, too, and she checks on me often to see if I have any problems," Betty said.

"She comes to see me a few times a year, too," I said. "Remember when we lived at the Benders' and the social workers rarely checked on us?"

"Yes. And when they did we were always too frightened to say anything. I'm so glad things are different now."

"Are you having any problems with old Mrs. Lawson?"

"Oh, yes," she moaned. "We're not getting along well. I don't like her, and she doesn't care two bits for me. She said she should've kept you because you were easier to control and more obedient. Now, that should make you happy."

A friendly dig, I thought, as she went on, "How are you making out at the Klinchuks'?"

"Not too bad, but I still don't feel completely comfortable with them. Their foreign language still bothers me, and there's always so much work to do. But at least I'm finally learning how to cook and sew and wash eggs. A couple of evenings a week I go into the basement and get dozens of eggs ready for their egg route."

"Egg route? What's an egg route?"

"Every Friday and Saturday Elinor and Mr. Klinchuk deliver them to customers in Hamilton. They've already told me that I'll have to fill in for Mr. Klinchuk this coming Saturday, and I'm a bit nervous about it."

"What do you have to do to get the eggs ready?"

"I wash them in warm soapy water, dry them, and then candle them."

"Candle? What does that mean?"

"I hold them up to a light shining through a small hole in a black box and look through them. If there are any blood spots or specks, they're rejected. Then I weigh and grade them for size—small, medium, and large—and put them in cardboard trays for delivery. Kind of like sorting apples when we were kids, remember?"

"Do you mind doing that?"

"No, except when the chickens lay poopy eggs—and they often do. But I get to listen to Mr. Klinchuk's radio while I'm down there, and that I enjoy. It's almost identical to the one that Mr. Bender had."

"Well, it doesn't sound like something I'd care to do."

"I know. But we've done a lot of things we didn't like, like filling that damn water tank at the Benders'. But I'll be so glad when I'm through school and can get a job."

Just then Mrs. Sanders returned to the restaurant, and Betty and I rose to leave.

"Hope everything goes all right with your new job and your new boyfriend," I said as we hugged good-bye. "I'll try to keep in touch."

Elinor came into my bedroom early Saturday morning and tugged at the blankets wrapped tightly around my body and covering my head. "Bonnie, wake up! We have to deliver the eggs, and we're already running late."

Excited and eager about going on my first trip to Hamilton, I threw the blankets off my head and saw Elinor staring at me with a puzzled expression. "What's the matter? Is something wrong?"

"Do you always sleep like that?" she asked.

"Like what?"

"With your head all covered up. For goodness' sake, how can you breathe?"

I shrugged. "I've always slept this way."

I wasn't exactly truthful. I was seven at the time this started and was afraid Doug would come into our room and hurt me as he had hurt Betty. Covering my head made me feel safer. I shuddered as I reflected on the horrible event and scrambled downstairs in time to hear Elinor telling her mother that I slept with my head covered up. "She wraps the blankets around her body and completely covers her head. Not even her nose is sticking out. I'm surprised she doesn't suffocate."

Why are they making a big to-do about it, I wondered as I entered the kitchen.

"Why do you sleep with your head covered up?" Mrs. Klinchuk asked, furrowing her brow and looking bewildered.

"I've always slept like that," I replied nonchalantly, hoping they wouldn't press me about it. They then began to talk in their Ukrainian language, and I could tell by their gestures and glances that it was about my sleeping habit. I was getting annoyed and was relieved when they dropped the subject and settled down to breakfast.

40

A Pivotal Moment

My first four months of eleventh grade were proving to be difficult. Although I was doing well in most of my classes, algebra and geometry were a real challenge, taking me into the wee hours of the morning to finish my homework. The excitement of Joan's wedding and the sadness I felt about Betty not returning to school didn't help the situation, and my interest in school was waning.

The brightest spot of my week was my Tuesday evening art classes when I stayed in town overnight with Gerald and Pauline. They had purchased a small hotel and restaurant and were busy getting it under way and negotiating for a liquor license—a first for the small, dry town of Waterford. Churchgoers were campaigning fiercely against it and causing much dissension. Although it was a crucial and hectic time for them, Pauline always had time to listen to my personal "young girl" problems and offered me advice and guidance. In appreciation for her kindness and support, I helped out in the kitchen and spent time with her two young children.

• • •

It was an exciting first for us to dress up in our bridesmaid gowns and participate in Joan and Mike's large Ukrainian-style wedding. And it was wonderful to be with Jean and Joan after our long separation from the Bender home. Throughout the evening we tried to catch up on some of the events of those missing years.

Soon after the wedding, my Christmas exams rolled around and another busy holiday season was upon us. The days were going by too fast; my extra activities were taking time away from my schoolwork, and I was falling behind in my chores at home.

Elinor's many speaking engagements meant more traveling for her, and this left me to care for her mother.

Upon learning that I had done poorly on my exams, Mrs. Sanders stopped by the school in early January, and we sat in her car to discuss my problems.

"How are you getting along with the Klinchuk family?"

"I'm not very happy there. There's so much to do, and I can't do everything Mrs. Klinchuk expects of me. I can be washing the floor when she notices cobwebs in the corners or dust on the stovepipe. She just sees so much that has to be done. I understand, but I can't do it all when I have things of my own to do. It's overwhelming and frustrating. I feel they aren't too happy with me and want someone younger who doesn't have so many interests. Could you find me another home?" I sat stiffly with my hands together, pinching them between my knees as I waited for her response.

After hearing my complaint, she reached over and patted my knee. "There, there," she said softly. "Putting myself in your shoes, I understand how difficult it must be."

Oh, if only she could, I thought.

"I've talked to the Klinchuk family. While they agree that a younger girl with fewer interests might better fulfill their needs, they're very fond of you and want you to stay at least until the end of this school year. You'll be eighteen in May and technically out of the foster care system, but you can stay in until you complete your schooling and find employment."

My ears perked up. "I'm no longer a *foster* child when I'm eighteen? I'm just plain old me?"

"Right," she said, smiling at my exuberance. "But I don't know about the 'plain old me.' You've grown up to be a lovely and very accomplished young lady. You have much to be proud of, and don't you forget it! So let's try to hold down the fort at the Klinchuks' until the end of the school year. Do the best you can. Keep a happy outlook, and don't let things get you down. We've come this far, and before you know it, you'll be through school and out into the world."

Out of the foster care system? The words buzzed around in my head. My eighteenth birthday was only a few months away, and the thought filled me with euphoria as I lay in bed that night. It was as if I were being released from a jail sentence — my shackles finally removed. *"Wow,"* I whispered to myself as I huddled down in bed, "I'll be free at last!" Free from what, I really didn't know, but I could now look at my life differently and set my sights on goals I wanted to accomplish. I awoke in the morning with renewed vigor, eager to settle down and do better in my schoolwork.

• • •

My life for the following months was a whirlwind of activity both at school and at home. There seemed to be many weddings and showers to attend for friends of the

Klinchuks. A new dance hall had opened in Waterford, and my weekends were filled with dates and dances. I was beginning to enjoy life—finding new friends and breaking out of the shell that had imprisoned me for so long. The stigma of having to explain away my foster childhood no longer existed. I was finally becoming my own person— free to be me, alone and standing on my own two feet.

In May, Elinor gave me my first birthday party and invited many friends and family to celebrate the end of my eighteenth year. It was a thrilling time for me and endeared them more to me.

With the experience I had gained through the Junior Farmers organization and my sewing classes, I was becoming a pretty good seamstress—this to the point that Mrs. Klinchuk now let me make a few items for her.

"Come here," she said one day. "Elinor will be away for a week, and there's some material she had intended to use to make me a long-sleeve blouse. Shall we surprise her and have it finished before she gets back? I'll work with you and show you how to lengthen the sleeves and make any other alterations. Shall we tackle it?"

"Sure, I think I can do it, but I'll probably need lots of help. Did you sew when you were young?"

"Yes, my mother taught me when I was growing up in Romania. When I was a young wife, I made most of the clothes for the family until my arms went bad on me."

She then told about the slow deterioration of her arms and that her husband had taken her first to Oral Roberts, a faith healer in Tulsa, Oklahoma, and then to Lourdes in France. "But despite my strong faith, nothing seemed to work for me," she admitted with a shrug. "In desperation I even tried an old European wives' remedy of soaking my arms in fresh spring cow manure, but all to no avail. But I don't usually tell anyone about this nonsense."

"Well, I won't tell a soul," I laughed, picturing the episode in my mind. "I probably would've tried the same thing."

She asked me to put her glasses on and then watched as I laid the fabric on the dining room table and smoothed it out with my hand. She stopped me as I was pinning the pattern to the fabric and came to the sleeve piece. Marking imaginary lines on the hardwood floor with her toe, she showed me how to cut and make the sleeve adjustment.

As I worked away on the blouse, she stopped me periodically to explain how to pin the darts or set the sleeve into the bodice. It took us the better part of the week to finish, but we were proud of our efforts.

"Maybe someday I'll be a fashion designer. Oooh, wouldn't that be a nice career?" I cooed as I helped her try on the blouse for a final fitting.

"Well, it doesn't hurt to dream so long as you don't get too carried away."

"If anyone asks me how I learned to sew, I could tell them that a woman who was unable to use her arms taught me how to sew with her feet. Wouldn't that make a good story?"

"And also with my head," she added with a broad smile. "And yes, that would make a good story."

Sewing was becoming a passion, and I spent much time and money on fabric and patterns. It brought Elinor and me closer together, and we spent many weekends behind the sewing machine stitching up a storm.

After having buckled down at school, I passed my year satisfactorily and enrolled in the Business Commercial class for the fall of my final year to prepare for work as a secretary.

The Children's Aid Report stated:
Bonnie has made a good adjustment in this home. She accepted Mrs. Klinchuk's handicap easily and is most thoughtful and helpful.

• • •

I spent my last summer of school vacation picking straw-berries and working in tobacco to earn money for my school wardrobe and entertainment. Betty and I were beginning to see less of each other now, since her life was revolving around Carl and his circle of friends and most of my friends were out in the country. We phoned each other only when something important or exciting was happening.

It was one of these eventful days when she phoned with the news of her upcoming baptism into the Baptist church. "I'm being baptized this Sunday, and I want you to come and be with me. It's a big day in my life, and I'm a little nervous. Please say you'll come," she pleaded. "We'll pick you up."

Never having seen a baptism, I was curious and happy to oblige her. "What're they gonna do to you—dunk you in the river?"

"No," she replied curtly. "It's a very serious ceremony. There's a place near the altar where the service is performed. You step down into a small pool, and the minister immerses you into the water."

I agreed to attend the ceremony and reconfirmed the time they would pick me up.

That Sunday as I watched Betty walk across the stage, I couldn't help but notice how thin and frail she looked. After the ceremony was over, I spent some time visiting with her and was surprised when she told me that she'd left the Lawson home and moved in with a family recommended by her boyfriend. "I just couldn't put up with the old biddy and all the personal things she expected me to do. I was tired of being her nursemaid. I wish they hadn't taken you away. Ev-erything seemed to go to pieces after that, and I just couldn't cope with life anymore."

"You're looking pale and thin. Are you still a picky eater?"

"I just don't seem to have much appetite anymore. Nothing appeals to me."

"The last time I visited with Mrs. Sanders, she told me that you were having fainting spells. She seemed concerned and said that you're under a doctor's care. Is this true?"

"Yes. I'm seeing old Dr. Anderson. Remember him?"

"Yes. He's a nice doctor. Does he know what your problem is?"

"Sometimes thoughts get cluttered up in my head or some past memory gets triggered, and I just black out. The doctor said I was anemic and gave me pills for it, but they aren't helping much."

"Did you tell him that you once fell out of a car, that you got hit by a car, and that you fell off a moving truck? That might account for something." I smiled.

I told her that she could always meet me at school during my lunch hour if she wanted to talk over any problems. We then hugged and walked to Carl's car for my ride home.

• • •

I enjoyed my last year of school. It was my third year at the Klinchuk home, and I was finally fitting in and learning some of the Ukrainian language and many foreign dances. On weekends Elinor and I got together with our friends for dancing and drinking at the German, Polish, or Hungarian halls in the small town of Delhi. There we met lots of young men and had fun dancing late into the night to polkas, waltzes, and intricate foreign dances.

Early in December Mrs. Sanders dropped by to visit and bring me a Christmas present. Fixing a beautiful tea tray, I sat down with her and Mrs. Klinchuk to discuss my plans for the future. I told her that I was doing well in all my classes and that as soon as I graduated, Elinor would take me into Hamilton to apply for a secretarial position. I then asked about Betty's health, for I hadn't heard from her for some time.

"She isn't well, and we've taken her to the Toronto Children's Hospital for testing. We've also found a new home for her with Mr. and Mrs. Mason, who live directly across the street from your high school. You may visit her there when she comes home."

"I'm worried about her. Do you think she'll be okay in this new home?"

"We're doing everything we can to make it pleasant for her. The Masons know her friend Carl through the church and are fond of both of them. I think this more stable environment will be better for her overall health."

Relieved that Mrs. Sanders seemed to be taking a personal interest in Betty, I was able to concentrate on my Christmas exams and help prepare for the busy Christmas holidays.

One day during the holidays, Elinor had to go into town and dropped me off to visit with Mike and Joan. I was only there a short while before Mike answered a knock at the door. "Are you expecting company?" I asked Joan.

"No. Not company. An insurance salesman is here to try to get Mike to buy an insurance policy. We'll stay in the kitchen while they discuss it."

As we sipped coffee, I couldn't help sneaking a peek at the insurance salesman and whispered to Joan, "He's really handsome."

"He sure is. Bet you wouldn't mind polishing his shoes! He's been here before. Would you like to meet him?"

"No! I'm too shy and wouldn't know what to say. Besides, I probably look a mess."

After the young man had left, Joan told Mike about my fascination with him, and he had fun teasing me. "You should've come out to meet him. You'll never find yourself a husband if you always hide behind a door."

A few months into the New Year, Elinor and I attended a dinner and dance sponsored by the Lions Club, and that handsome young man was there. Her brother Gerald was president of the organization, and the young man was a member.

As the evening was winding down, one of Elinor's friends came along with him to talk, and she introduced us. His name was Tony. And after we'd talked a while, they invited us to go for a ride.

It was apparent that the two guys were more interested in Elinor than me, but Tony agreed to pair with me as we climbed into the backseat of the car. As we talked, I said that I had seen him at my sister's house, and he was amused to learn that I had been peeking at him from the kitchen. We enjoyed each other's company, and before we parted, he asked for a date for the following Saturday.

Later I was walking on cloud nine as I prattled on to Elinor about my upcoming date and quizzed her about Tony. "How do you know him?"

"I dated him a few years back. He's really a nice guy and lots of fun, but he's a little too short for me—but he is a great kisser! His family owns a large dairy farm, and I'm certainly not interested in ever becoming a farmer's wife."

"He told me about their farm and said he sells insurance during the winter months when work on the farm slows down. How old do you think he is?"

"About the same as me—twenty-four or so, I guess.

We said good night, and I tiptoed softly into my room, trying not to arouse Mr. and Mrs. Klinchuk, whose room was directly below. I didn't sleep well and worried all week that

Tony would change his mind and cancel our date. But he phoned on Friday, confirming the time and suggesting we go to a movie. We enjoyed each other's company and began dating regularly.

One night Tony asked about my relationship with the Klinchuk family. At first I was embarrassed and ashamed to tell him about my life in the foster care system, thinking he would think less of me as so many of my other dates had. But instead, he was very understanding and accepting.

• • •

My class was interrupted one spring day when an announcement came over the school speaker summoning me to the principal's office. I feared the worst as I hurried up to the secretary's desk. She told me that Mr. Mason had called the school to tell me that Betty was very sick and was asking for me. It was raining heavily, and seeing that I had no protection, the secretary offered me her umbrella.

My heart was pounding as I dashed through the rain. Mr. Mason was waiting for me on the porch, and Mrs. Sanders's car was in the driveway. "What's the matter with Betty?" I blurted out as soon as I entered the kitchen.

"She seems to be having a bout of amnesia," Mrs. Sanders said. "She doesn't seem to recognize any of us and keeps crying out for you. She's hysterical and behaving irrationally. Maybe you can calm her down."

Frightened and not knowing how to help, I followed Mrs. Mason into Betty's bedroom and found her sitting on the side of her bed, weeping bitterly into her hands and rocking back and forth. She looked up at me as I sat down beside her and put my arms around her shoulders. I was surprised and frightened when it became apparent she didn't recognize me either.

"I want to go outside. I want to go for a walk!" she wailed.

"We can't," I said, pointing toward the window. "It's pouring down rain."

"I don't care. I can't stand being cooped up in here. I can't breathe. I want to go for a walk," she pleaded, as she tried to squirm away from my arms.

It took some time before I was able to quiet her and coax her into lying down to rest. At long last she drifted off to sleep, and I remained near her bed to watch over her.

More than an hour passed before she awoke from her sleep, gazed around the room, and stared blankly at the three of us hovering around the bed.

Quickly grabbing a picture of Carl from her bed stand, I asked, "Do you know who this is?"

"It's Carl, *silly*," she replied, looking bewildered. "And why are you all looking at me like that?"

I was so thrilled that she recognized us that I threw my arms around her. "You had a bout of amnesia, and you didn't know who we were," I said, breathing a big sigh of relief. "You scared the living daylights out of us!"

"Amnesia?" she questioned. "That's strange. That has never happened to me before."

"And I hope it never happens again," Mrs. Mason said. "We were all worried about you."

Mrs. Sanders took over from there, and I returned to school. Within the month Betty would return to the Toronto Western Hospital for neurological evaluation, and I would be finishing up my school year.

Having done well in my Easter examinations, I was exempted from writing final exams and was able to start looking for work in Hamilton.

Mrs. Sanders stopped to visit me one more time before my move to Hamilton and to update me on Betty's health.

"The doctor tells me that your sister's problems are mostly due to emotional stress and hysteria. However, Mrs. Mason says her condition has stabilized. Betty is beginning to settle down now and is making plans for the future with her friend Carl."

I was happy to hear of the good news and could now concentrate on my job-seeking efforts with peace of mind.

41

My Cup Runneth Over

Adversity will either make you bitter or better

It was the month of May, 1955, and I had barely turned nineteen when I accepted my first secretarial position with an insurance firm in Hamilton. I moved into a small upper flat with my two best friends, Eva and Betty, and took a bus every day to work. I enjoyed my newfound freedom with my friends but was unhappy about being so far away from Tony. Since neither my friends nor I had cars, we occasionally managed a ride home with Stewart Klinchuk when he was going to visit his folks. Even though I was now out of the jurisdiction of the Children's Aid, the Klinchuk farm was still my home base, and they expected me to come on some weekends to help with the farm work.

It was on a Friday evening in early June after an exhausting day of hard work that Tony began to feel the strain of the long drive back and forth to see me, and he proposed marriage. I accepted, and the next day we went into town to select our rings and go out for a celebratory dinner. He told me that his parents wished to meet me and that his mother was preparing a nice Sunday dinner. I tensed up. "Do you think they'll approve of me?"

I was holding my breath as he teased, "Well, they're Hungarian, and they already had a nice little Hungarian girl picked out for me, but that was so they could have someone who spoke their language. But they'll probably like you. My brother, John, got away with marrying a Ukrainian girl, and they are certainly pleased with her."

He said this with a smile, but still I was edgy about meeting his parents as I readied myself for bed that evening. I wondered how much he'd told them about me and whether they would bombard me with questions. He had asked very little about my background, and what little I had told him didn't seem to bother him at all. But would they feel the same? "Well, I'll say my prayers and hope for the best," I muttered aloud as I turned down the covers.

• • •

It was a glorious summer day the Sunday Tony sped down the gravel road past his parents' fields of freshly cultivated corn, turned into their long driveway, and pulled up beside the large, two-story brick home.

"It's such a huge house," I remarked as he helped me from the car and swooshed away Bundy and Curly, their two nosy farm dogs.

"Well, it's actually a duplex—two homes in one. The house—as you'll see when we get inside—is divided into two living quarters." Pointing to the far right windows, he went on, "My brother, John, lives on that side with his wife, Mildred, and their young son."

As we entered the kitchen, I was surprised to see that his mother already had the table set for Sunday dinner, and after a brief introduction, we settled into our chairs to eat.

It was evident that Hungarian was the main language spoken here, and Tony often interrupted the conversation to let me know what was being said. His mother, concerned that I was being left out, reached over to pat my hand. "Vas I sorry you no understand Hungarian. Maybe my Tony teach you." I smiled and nodded. "Vas my Tony tell me that you have no mother and father. Vas how come?"

I tried to explain to her the best I could by mimicking her broken English. "My mother had very big family and no could feed us all, so the Children's Aid Society come one day and take some of us away."

"You no see your momma again?"

I shook my head, and Tony explained a few more details in Hungarian that seemed to satisfy their curiosity. His mom reached over again to pat my hand. "Vas I sorry you never see your momma and dad."

I smiled and shrugged, happy the conversation had ended.

After dinner we went for a walk out to the barn and met John and Mildred, who were doing some cleanup work around the barn. Then we took a leisurely stroll around the 270-acre farm, discussing our plans for the future and the family's offer to help us build a small home there.

I was happy that the day turned out well and Tony let me know that his family liked me and were pleased with his choice. "They suggested that I try to teach you Hungarian, but I told them that it was better you didn't know. My father can use some rather colorful language at times."

We had a nice drive back to the city, and I hurried excitedly up to our apartment to spill the news to my friends.

"My gosh!" they exclaimed almost in unison. "You no sooner get a new job and a place to live than you get a husband!"

"Now all I have to hear is that you're getting married tomorrow," Eva teased.

"No, we're getting married in July," I chuckled.

"Are you planning on a big wedding at the Hungarian hall in Delhi?" Betty asked.

"No. We've already discussed this. His folks wanted to give us a large wedding, but since I don't have a family to help with the expenses and the work, we've settled on eloping or having just a small church ceremony in Waterford, then leaving for our honeymoon."

"What do you know about marriage?" Eva went on. "You know, the birds and bees and all that stuff?"

"Not much, but I guess I'll learn. I'm a good cook, though, and I know how to sew, too," I announced proudly.

"Well, there's more to marriage than that," she remarked as she started rummaging around in the bottom of the clothes closet. "Here," she said as she dusted off a book with her sleeve and gave it to me. "Read this."

"*Love and Marriage*?" I remarked as I read the title. Smiling, I took the book and curled up on the bed to read. And after a few chapters, it became obvious that my good friend knew a lot more about life than I did, so I had to stop every now and then to question her about things. Some parts caused me to blush and exclaim, "Oh my goodness!" That never failed to get a giggle out of her.

The next day I headed to the nice city shops to look for a wedding dress. As Tony and I were planning on a simple, civil ceremony, I didn't feel it necessary to buy an expensive, fussy dress, but rather one that would do double duty and could be worn again. Besides, having gotten only a little over a month's pay, I was being thrifty. And so I was excited when I finally found the perfect dress and couldn't wait to show it to my friends, hoping for their approval.

Opening the shopping bag, I pulled out the simple, white-linen A-line dress with a Peter Pan collar and cuffed short sleeves and held it against my body. "Well, what do you think of it?" I asked, waiting for them both to ooh and aah.

"That's your wedding dress? It looks more like a nurse's uniform," Eva quipped.

"You don't like it?" I asked, feeling a bit crushed.

"Oh, I like it—just not for a wedding. You need something more glamorous, something in silk or satin that'll take Tony's breath away." She winked as she glanced at Betty. "Don't you agree?"

Betty nodded, and Eva continued, "Why don't I go with you tomorrow and see if we can find something more suitable?"

"Okay," I said halfheartedly, "that'll be fine."

Eva helped me pick out a beautiful, white shantung dress with a scooped neck, short capped sleeves, tucked bodice, and gathered skirt. It was a beautiful dress, and I was happy to have such a good friend to steer me in the right direction.

• • •

It was during this happy time that I visited Joan to tell her of my wedding plans and let her know that Gerald and Pauline Klinchuk were planning an informal wedding party for us at their hotel following the ceremony. As she poured us each a cup of coffee, I told her that Betty's health was improving, that she would be my only bridesmaid, and that Tony's brother, John, would be the best man. After inviting her and Mike, I asked her if she could contact Jean to see if she would be able to attend. "My wedding day won't be perfect without the three of you there to help me celebrate," I said.

"Unfortunately, Jean won't be able to attend."

The tone in her voice caused my stomach to tighten, and before I could ask why, she said, "She's expecting a baby."

"A *baby*?" I exclaimed.

"Yes. The Children's Aid is helping her get through this and have placed her in a home for unwed mothers. I think the baby's due sometime in August."

"Why did she ever let something like that happen?"

"I don't know. We were always kept in ignorance about everything, and as you know, she's always been a little on the wild side."

"Will she keep the baby or will the Children's Aid take it from her?"

"I think she wants to keep it. I suggested to Mike that perhaps we could help her out until she can get back on her feet."

"That's kind of you," I said, giving her a hug as we left the house to join Tony and Mike on the porch. "I feel so sad and worried about her. Give her my love when you see her again."

As we drove down the long gravel lane and turned out onto the main road, my thoughts flashed back again to Jean, and feelings of melancholy swept over me as I inched closer to Tony and told him the story.

• • •

The sun beat down mercilessly on the twenty-third of July—the day we'd chosen for our wedding. I'm sure it was the hottest day of the year. I was happy that it cooled a bit by evening as we exchanged our vows in a beautiful candlelight service. I was nervous and excited. My knees trembled, and I was relieved and grateful when the minister asked us to kneel, for I was certain they were about to give way.

After the wedding reception had ended, Tony and I were off on our honeymoon. It was to be only four days, for it was a busy time on the farm and Tony would be needed.

"We'll have an extended honeymoon after the harvest is completed," he promised.

After visiting Niagara Falls and Buffalo, we returned to the family farm and settled in with his folks until work on our own home could get started. This posed a new and different challenge for me, one much different from growing up in those foster homes.

At this point in my life, I was more capable of handling adjustments and adversities. And with my husband's help, the understanding nature of his family, and the experience I had gained living with a Ukrainian family, I finally felt at ease, and at home.

My father-in-law was a little on the gruff side, and it took me some time to warm up to him. However, my mother-in-law was a kind and pleasant woman, and before long she was teaching me Hungarian cooking and I was becoming more adept at talking to her in broken English. Soon we were sharing laughter and lengthy conversations.

"I think Mom's quite happy with you," Tony said. "She tells me that you're a jokey little girl, that you make her laugh too much, and that you're a good cook."

I smiled, thinking I had probably made the grade.

• • •

John and Mildred were a positive force in my new life. They were a happy, easygoing couple, and Mildred and I had much in common. We would go out to the barn in the mornings and evenings to help with the milking chores. After the men had finished milking the cows with the milking machines, it was our job to hand-strip the cows of the last bit of milk. I was nervous about milking the more rambunctious and skittish ones, but Mildred was kind enough to take care of them and let me milk the gentler ones.

As the weeks passed, I began to realize what it was like to live without any imposed restraints on my freedom. I had finally found the acceptance, recognition, and independence I had longed for and a family that was not critical or demanding of me but cooperative and encouraging—a family I could work alongside without feeling demeaned in any way. I was now in charge of my own time and could pursue my dreams knowing that I had their support.

During the slow months of winter, I was able to continue my art interests and did oil paintings to decorate the walls. In summer I enjoyed playing softball on a team of young married farm girls, something I had always wanted to do but was never permitted. And I was never chastised for wasting time.

I enjoyed much happiness with my family and especially liked the early evenings, when after a hard day's work we all gathered around the table to share some drinks and lively conversation or watch a favorite television program before bedtime.

One night after saying good night to the family, Tony and I retired to our bedroom. There, cuddling up in his firm embrace, I knew I had at long last found the peace of mind and security that had eluded me for so long. It was this new found protection and his friendly cajoling that finally got me to peek my head out from beneath the covers.

"Don't worry," he joked, "I won't let the bogeyman get you."

I smiled and cuddled closer as he turned off the light.

The Children Aid's Report stated:
It is gratifying to find that Bonnie has resolved her future so pleasantly. This case may be closed.

Epilogue

"If our American way of life fails the child, it fails us all."
— Pearl S. Buck

A soft breeze, like a gentle hand from heaven, brushed across the golden fields of wheat. They gently bowed their heavy heads as if in silent prayer. Deep in thought, I listened to the stones pelting the bottom of our car as it bumped along the country road. A yapping dog startled me as it sprang from the ditch and raced beside us. Unable to keep up, it gave a final bark and then slunk back into the tall weeds. Being heavy with child, I adjusted myself to a more comfortable position. It was the fall of 1960, and my husband and I were leaving the family farm and moving to the city of Waterloo, Ontario, where he could pursue a graduate degree in engineering at the University of Waterloo. Excited as we were about our move, the thought of leaving the secure and happy life on the family farm left us each with a myriad of emotions.

We had just settled into a small upper-story flat in late October, and Tony had hardly opened his newly purchased textbooks when our son was born. And when we brought him home to show off to the family, his Hungarian grandpa begged us, "Vas name some simplee name. Vas no give me troublee to say." So we named him Mark. But he called him "Makos," which is Hungarian for poppy seeds. With a sigh and a shake of his head, Tony said, "We just can't win."

Later in the day, as I eased my son into his crib, I brushed a strand of hair off his tiny brow, kissed the plump round of his cheek, and whispered, "Don't worry, little one, Mommy will never let anyone take you away from me." After admiring him for a few more minutes, I pulled down the shade and tiptoed softly out of the room.

Four years later we moved to Detroit where jobs were plentiful and my husband could finish his graduate studies in the evening while working during the day. It was during this time that I jumped at the chance to enroll in evening classes at the Academy Nvart to pursue my longtime dream of becoming a fashion designer. Two years later, after receiving my certification, I began designing clothes for a select clientele. This experience lead me to more challenging work in the window fashions industry and I eventually opened a home-based business in designing and fabricating window treatments. Years later, failed surgery on my right hand made it necessary to close my business.

One day, while using my old typewriter for hand and finger therapy, the idea struck me that perhaps I should give some thought to writing my autobiography. As I took some time out to read, I stumbled across a quote from a well-known television talk-show hostess that read: "Follow your instincts. That's where true wisdom manifests itself." With this thought in mind, I made the decision to write the story of my life as a ward of the Norfolk County Children's Aid Society in Canada. Surely this was a case of divine intervention, and by the grace of God I did just that.

It was a great challenge to write a personal story, especially one so rife with fear, heartbreak, upheaval, and grief. However, if the story of my experiences and those of my siblings can save other children from falling through the 'cracks' of the foster care system, and if that system will recognize its shortcomings and failures to take action to address them, then it will have been worth all the time and effort of producing this book. Then the story will have accomplished a good measure of success.

While I was writing this story my husband and I took a brief vacation that took us through the beautiful countryside of Kentucky, where there are a number of old, dilapidated gray barns standing alone in open fields. They seemed to be in the middle of nowhere, and seeing them conjured up terrible memories of a time long ago when Betty and I were just seven years old.

Over the years my sister and I never discussed the rape incident, and I would often wonder why no mention of it was made in her Children's Aid report. Upon my return— with this event fresh in my memory, I visited my sister and broached this subject with her. I suggested that perhaps she might wish to share her feelings in my book. She agreed to give it some thought and to let me know her decision. Days later I received the following letter and could tell by the shaky handwriting that she had great difficulty putting her thoughts into words:

Dear Bonnie,

On that terrible day Doug grabbed me by my arm and pulled me into the barn, telling you to go and get the cows. You were yelling at him as he shoved you aside, slammed the door, and bolted it. He picked me up and lifted me over a low partition made of two boards with a large one on top. This partition separated the part of the barn where the hay and straw was kept, but because the barn was not used, there were still some scattered remnants of straw and hay. He was clutching me so tight I thought he would break my arm; I was so skinny and frail.

As he climbed over the top board, he threw me down on the ground. I said, "What are you going to do to me?" He just yelled, "Shut up!" I started to cry because I knew how mean he could be. He threw up my dress and pulled my panties down, leaving them on the bottom of one leg, covering my shoe. He took his pants down and turned away from me. Crying, I asked, "What are you doing?" He told me that if I made a sound he would kill me. Still crying, I said, "I want Bonnie. I want Bonnie!"

I could hear you banging on the barn boards outside but knew you couldn't get to me. I was terrified because I knew in my heart I was going to die and you had no way of helping me.

He came to me, and kneeling down, spread my legs so far apart I thought they were going to break. He lay down on top of me. The weight of his body was so crushing I could hardly breathe. He told me again that if I hollered or made any noise, he would kill me, and I really believed him. I tried so hard to be quiet, but then all of a sudden I felt a terrible ripping pain shoot through my whole body and I let out a loud scream. He immediately clamped his hand over my nose and mouth, and I was unable to breathe. Things started to go black, and all I could scream in my mind was, "Bonnie! Bonnie!"

I don't remember when it was over. I vaguely recall him ripping off a piece of his shirt and stuffing it inside me, and seeing the blood, I must have passed out again.

I don't remember walking home. I faintly recall Mrs. Bender removing my bloody panties and pulling the piece of shirt out of me and the blood in the white basin. Then she put some clean panties on me, tucking a piece of cloth inside.

Mr. Bender drove us to the doctor, leaving Doug at home. The doctor took Mrs. Bender and me right in. She told the doctor the story Doug had told her about the fence.

The doctor asked her to wait in the waiting room while he examined me. He examined me very gently and helped me to get dressed. He then lifted me back on the table and asked me to tell him how this happened, and he didn't want to hear the "barb-wire fence" story. I started to cry, but he held me and said he wanted the truth. I knew it was bad to tell a lie, so I told him what I remembered.

After lifting me off the table, he sat down in a chair and held me in his arms. He told me that this would never happen to me again and I don't need to be afraid that it will. If it does, he said there will be a lot of trouble for Doug. He promised that he wouldn't tell them that I had told him the truth, but really I think he had a talk with Mrs. Bender because Doug never tried it again. Thank God.

As I approach the later years of my life, I can't help but think that overall life has been very good to me. If, as the saying goes, "Adversity will either make you bitter or better," then I'm thankful that it worked in my favor—having made me a better and stronger person with love for those I hold dear and empathy for those who are not so fortunate. I feel very blessed. But one can never erase the memories and sorrows of a lost childhood.

After Thoughts

*"Loneliness and the feeling of being unwanted
is the most terrible poverty."*

— Mother Teresa

My mother: I saw my mother only once after the time at the tobacco farm mentioned in the story. She had remarried; was in her early eighties, and suffering with bowel cancer. She wanted to see Betty and me before she died. I never saw her again. She lived several more years after our visit and died in 1988 at age 89.

My father: I met my father quite by surprise at a Christmas party given by my sister Joan. I was about thirty years old at the time. It was an emotionally disturbing experience, and I never saw him again and do not know the date of his death.

My twin sister Betty: Having outlived three of her husbands, Betty has recently married again. She is happy and lives in Ontario, Canada. We keep in touch and visit often.

My sisters Jean and Joan: Jean and Joan live near each other in Ontario but are not in good health. They are both widowed. I visit them often. My sisters and I are very close.

My brother Bobby: I had been married for two years when Bobby learned where we lived and came with his wife and their three-year-old twin daughters to visit us at our farm. I did not see him again but learned later that one of the twin girls had died of pneumonia during the winter following their visit. He died on June 2, 1988, at age 57.

My older sister Margaret Rose: I saw Muggs, my beloved older sister, in the summer of 1957 while she was visiting with my sister Joan and Joan's husband Mike. Sadly, I did not see her again and years later learned of her death on May 13, 1988, at age 64.

My younger brother Peter: Peter was born about eighteen months after Betty and me but I have no recollection of him living at home with the rest of the family, and can only assume that he was cared for by our grandparents. He was not put into foster care. In 2005 Betty and I flew to Vancouver to meet him for the first time after our separation. Unfortunately, he died of cancer in 2007 before we could visit him again. He was 70 years old.

My younger brother Jack: Jack was born after we were taken away from our home. I met him in 2009 while visiting Joan. We plan to keep in touch with him and his wife.

My older brothers Jim and Hank: They were still living at home but were probably at school when we were taken away. At that time, Jim was 14 years old and Hank was 11. I did not see them again and later learned that Jim passed away on March 28, 1993, in his 66th year and Hank passed away on January 5, 1998, at age 68.

My older brother Albert: Albert was born on May 18, 1923, and was 13 years older than I. I vaguely remember him. In 1975, when I was 39 years old, I waited while my husband, Tony, went into a liquor store in the small town of Burford, Ontario. Before returning to our car, he helped another man with his supplies. For some reason the man looked oddly familiar — something about his eyes, perhaps. And as I watched, I got the strange feeling that he might be a brother of mine. So I urged Tony to ask him his name, and we were all surprised to learn that he was indeed my brother Albert. We had a short but happy visit in the parking lot. I would not have the good fortune of seeing him again and do not know the date of his death.

My other siblings: I have seven other siblings whom I have never met and do not know their whereabouts, or even if they are still living.

Our foster families: Except for a few children and grand-children, the foster families with whom we lived have all passed away.